1/22/08

P.O!

To all Montgomery
Bd., I appreciated
hearing you was working on
the group was working on
the Edie & Tom Case... "It is
This is what leaders do...
think outside the box, trust in
the positive rather than the
negative assumptions or mindset
I wish you well on this added to
your enduring money problems.

Best wishes & God bless.

Jim Moss

Prov. 3:5-6

Leadership is a Covenant

*Leading People and Living
Life More Effectively*

by

Leonard J. Moisan, Ph. D.

Bloomington, IN   Milton Keynes, UK

AuthorHouse™
1663 Liberty Drive, Suite 200
Bloomington, IN 47403
www.authorhouse.com
Phone: 1-800-839-8640

AuthorHouse™ UK Ltd.
500 Avebury Boulevard
Central Milton Keynes, MK9 2BE
www.authorhouse.co.uk
Phone: 08001974150

First published by AuthorHouse 8/15/2007

ISBN: 978-1-4343-1076-7 (sc)

Library of Congress Control Number: 2007903329

Printed in the United States of America
Bloomington, Indiana

This book is printed on acid-free paper.

Dedication

First, I want to thank my father, my brothers and sisters, the Mercy nuns at St. Gabriel Parish, the brothers at Leo High School and the people of my Canaryville neighborhood in Chicago. You gave me a strong foundation, taught me how to use my mind, made me think on my feet and introduced me to hard work early in life. Dorothy and Lou, in particular, thanks for all of your help and love. Louie, as my nephew you're a great guy, but you still can't shoot.

Second, I give thanks to my lifelong friends Dan and Therese Keenan and the Byrne family. You befriended me, believed in and celebrated me and included me in your families at a time when I really needed it…Kevin, don't ever forget who taught you how to drive so well. David, Molly and Danny, your Dad would be proud of the people you have become.

Third, I want to thank my spiritual family and friends from church and in particular, the people of the Emmaus class. You keep me grounded in the important things in life, and you honor me by allowing me to teach you each week.

Fourth, I thank my in-laws, George and Barbara Rogers. You have demonstrated to me what it means to be a family, taught me by example what a covenant commitment in marriage is, modeled exceptional parenthood to me, pointed me to God and loved me unconditionally. I am and will continue to be eternally grateful to you.

Fifth, I give thanks to my children Dan, Sarah, David and now Brian and Joshua David. You bring smiles to my face, happiness to my heart and love to my life. You are the joys of my life. I am amazed at your talent, kindness, spiritual depth and humility. You make the world a better place to live and you make me very proud.

Finally, I give thanks to my wife Gigi, my best friend, partner and constant encourager. I am a much better person as a result of having you in my life. Your friendship, unconditional love, faithfulness and kindness both warm and humble me...your spiritual commitment challenges me...your beauty rocks my world. Clearly, I married above myself. You are a gift from God and the love of my life. Thanks for being so good to me.

Table of Contents

Introduction

At any upscale bookstore these days, it's fairly easy to find a wide variety of well-marketed, attractively packaged books on leadership—leadership laws, leadership habits, leadership secrets and more. In one store alone, I counted twenty different titles with the word "Leadership" in them and dozens more on subjects related to leadership.

With so much literature available on the topic, one might assume that we have a pretty good grasp on the essence of leadership. But, even a cursory view of the nightly news demonstrates that in reality, quite the opposite is true. Almost daily we are confronted with stories of people entrusted as "leaders," who violate that trust with breaches of integrity. A business fails because of illegal accounting practices ... a CEO is implicated ... a senator cheats ... a spiritual advisor and civil rights leader breaks his wedding vows and has a child out of wedlock ... soldiers are convicted of prisoner abuse ... they are all haunting reminders of people who were entrusted as leaders but failed. Why is it that we see record numbers of books about leadership on our shelves at the same time we see record numbers of leaders failing on our television screens? Is this type of inconsistency truly that pervasive, or is there another explanation?

I believe that we hear and read so much about leadership because we are in the midst of a leadership crisis. This crisis is not limited to business or political realms. It is evident in our homes, our colleges, our communities and even our places of worship. Simply stated, people are deeply interested in leadership because they long for it but rarely see it. And when they do experience leadership at its best, it inspires them to follow. Yet, if leadership is really that rare, then what do we call the many organizational heads we normally refer to as leaders? Some, like James MacGregor Burns, call them power wielders. Others, such as Peter Drucker, refer to them as managers and in some cases even misleaders. The point is, whatever we call them; there is a big difference between being the head of an organization and being a leader.

Ultimately, true leaders are known not only by what they accomplish, but also by how they accomplish it and how they influence people in the process. In fact, leadership is far more about relationships, influence and methods than it is about achievement. Certainly achievement is a by-product of leadership, but a resume is a poor tool to use if you want to capture the true essence of leadership. It simply cannot be found in the results of a performance contract, increases in profit margins or growth in share price. Rather, it resides in the dynamics of relationships between leaders and followers. It is found when leaders and followers relate to each other in ways that go beyond basic contractual obligations. Certainly contracts help facilitate achievement by defining the legal parameters, performance expectations and working conditions of a given relationship. But contracts cannot motivate or inspire followers, nor can they facilitate their growth. Those are the responsibilities of a leader, responsibilities that extend well beyond the basic requirements of a contract.

In just about any field imaginable relationships are the key to success. The best teachers forge strong relationships with their students; the best singers and actors connect emotionally with their audiences; the best coaches bond with their players; the best sales people relate well with their customers and the best leaders identify with and engage their followers. More than one expert has pointed out that during the Kennedy-Nixon debates, John F. Kennedy may have actually lost the debates on substance. Yet, President Kennedy was an overwhelming success and actually went on to win the election because he was able to connect with the American people. This president certainly was not without his flaws, and history has revealed that his tenure in the White House clearly had its problems. But as a leader, President

Kennedy identified with his followers, and they identified with him and, as a result, they were willing to follow him.

Like President Kennedy, effective leaders are able to connect with and engage followers emotionally in relationships. Through those relationships, they pursue common purposes and achieve common goals that are larger than those of any one individual. In so doing, leaders are also able to provide meaning and hope for followers in ways that create high levels of synergy, productivity and fulfillment. At its core then, leadership is a relationship in which leaders and followers are connected and emotionally engaged in pursuit of common purposes. It is much more complex than a simple contract. Instead, leadership is a covenant between leaders and followers and the organizations they serve. That covenant binds them together in a common quest and enables them to achieve far more than they ever would on their own.

So why does all this matter or, more to the point, why study leadership? The simple answer is to help us get better at it and thereby help our organizations prosper. That certainly is my intention in writing this book. However, my belief in the importance and power of leadership is not just based on anecdotal evidence. There is a growing body of empirical data suggesting that leadership really does make a difference, and relationships do matter in the bottom line success of any enterprise. For example, in *Good to Great*, Jim Collins showed how companies with certain kinds of leaders outperformed the general stock market by an average of 6.9 times. In *The Loyalty Effect*, Frederick Reichheld demonstrated how improving loyalty in customer and employee relationships can add 25 percent to as much as 100 percent to a company's bottom line profitability. And these represent just a small sampling of the growing body of work that points to the efficacy of leadership and the bottom line profitability of strong relationships.

Beyond the formal process, my study of leadership has also been a personal journey of growth. It is a journey that began in a very ethnic neighborhood on Chicago's south side. Called Canaryville, this mostly Irish and Italian enclave was home to many 1st generation immigrants who came to America to build a better life. There were Caseys, Kellys, O'Donnells, Gormans, Murphys and Flynns, but there were also DeMarcos, Cariottis, Dilabertos, Moraleses, Garcias, Jackabowskis, Feldmans and more. The neighborhood was truly a melting pot of diversity, but the people were bound together less by their ethnicity and more by their common struggle of trying to create a better life for their families.

They worked mostly in blue collar jobs in the trades, the steel mills, the stock yards or in one of the more coveted positions as a police officer, fireman or city worker. It was a tough, densely populated neighborhood where people lived in framed single family or two flat homes that were in close proximity to each other. As a result of all this closeness the people got to know each other and they clearly looked after their own. When I was growing up as a kid and engaging in occasional mischief that I thought was undetected; on more than one occasion, by the time I got home my grandmother, father and the rest of the family would know all about my misdeeds. No doubt, their knowledge of my actions came as a result of several phone calls they had received from what I considered to be "nosy neighbors." Though it was annoying at the time, these people were assuming responsibility for teaching us how to grow into responsible adults.

The closer I got to adulthood the more benefits seemed to come my way. Of course, the primary benefit was knowing and being known by quite a few people. Though I took it for granted and even disliked it at times, I believe those interpersonal relationships helped strengthen both my sense of identity and my security. Beyond that there were summer jobs, special deals, scholarships and other opportunities that I enjoyed, all as a result of the relationships that I or members of my family had developed. At a young age I understood that the more relationships I had, or as people used to say in Chicago, the better "connected" I was; the more benefits that would accrue to me. Yet, I also knew that "being connected" was a two way, reciprocal street. In other words, I couldn't expect to enjoy the benefits of those relationships long term, unless I was also willing to give and serve the people of those relationships. To that point, my father would frequently remind me of my responsibility to the people and the organizations of the neighborhood. As he used to tell me, I had to "save my favors" and not be greedy. Also, in the process of relationship building, I learned that I couldn't be disingenuous or insincere because it was contrary to our values to try and use or manipulate people. Relationship building with a sense of integrity and genuine regard for others had to come first. The benefits were byproducts of building relationships and not the primary motivator for doing so. The primary motivator was a set of values that defined what it meant to be a good Christian, a good citizen and a good friend. In his own way, my father was both giving me a civics lesson and teaching me the value of establishing and maintaining covenants. It is a learning process that continues to this day.

Essentially, what has facilitated that learning process is the fact that throughout my life and career, I have had the good fortune of meeting and interacting with a wide variety of people. Those interactions have helped me grow both professionally as a teacher, coach, administrator and consultant, and personally as a student, athlete, friend, husband, father, volunteer, church member and more. They have also taught me a great deal about relationships and particularly about leadership, and hopefully they've helped me improve in both areas. While many of my lessons have come as a result of mistakes I have made, each of my roles has helped me to learn something important about leading people and living life more effectively.

Clearly, in some cases I had a natural inclination to learn more about how to deal with certain personality types and how to lead various kinds of people. For example, as a coach I wanted to learn about motivating, encouraging and leading a diverse group of players to higher levels of achievement. My job was to develop the talent in the players entrusted to me and then help them bring that talent to the forefront in ways that contributed to team success. It required knowing how to motivate players and then how to position them in the right roles, roles that would accommodate both personal and team growth and achievement.

It did not take me long to realize that I had similar desires in my relationships with students, clients, employees and even my own children. This desire to learn is really what was instrumental in leading me to pursue a more in-depth study of the dynamics of leadership in the first place. Now, after more than 20 years of study and many more years of experience, I have learned some of the specifics of what makes a true leader and why leaders can and do make a difference in the success of just about any kind and size of organization. Whether it's parents in a family, executives in nonprofits, pastors in churches or CEOs in corporations; the degree to which leaders operate within the context and apply the principles of a covenant will be the degree to which their people and their organizations are successful. To accommodate a bit more explanation about how I came to this conclusion, let me back up briefly.

My notion of leadership started to change somewhat in the early 1990s when I began studying both the concept and the power of close, dynamic and highly productive relationships called "covenants." Like most people, I understood the concept of covenant in the context of marriage, but I was fascinated to find examples of covenants existing in business, politics, sports, communities and just about every kind of organization I examined. Though the evidence of covenants existing in organizations is less obvious than in marriage, I found that in organizations where the principles of covenant were applied in relationships, the results were highly beneficial for everyone involved. That really is when I began realizing both that covenants are the result of leadership and that leadership itself is a covenant. The more I investigated and discussed these concepts, the more they seemed to resonate with people. Granted, it's important for readers to understand that while the presence of covenants between leaders and followers or among stakeholders of an organization does promise to maximize potential, in business or in any other kind of organization; covenants cannot by themselves guarantee success. True, covenants can greatly enhance the likelihood and the degree of success, but they are not a remedy for deficiencies such as poor products, obsolete services, ineffective planning, a lack of training, limited resources or other shortcomings that threaten the life of organizations. That point aside, I have also found it to be true that where covenants flourish in organizations, deficiencies are likely to be fewer.

In the course of my research, I have had several hundred separate discussions about covenants. Many of those discussions have been in the form of interviews with individuals from all walks of life including business executives, politicians, ministers, police officers, a fire chief, distinguished educators, sports figures, authors, line workers and just about anyone who would talk about the concept with me. Unfortunately, one book simply could not contain all of the wonderful insights they shared with me, so as difficult as it was, I had to do a lot of cutting.

My first actual writing about covenant was in the form of an article published in the *Indiana University Journal of Business Disciplines.* After I published the article, I started thinking and writing more about the idea of leadership as a covenant. The pages that follow are an extension of that original work. Essentially, there are two primary sections in the book that include **Defining Leadership as a Covenant,** and **Understanding and Leading by the Principles of Covenant.** The first section makes the case that leadership is a relationship and not a position and, at their best, leader-follower relationships are covenants and not contracts. After illustrating the dynamics of the leader-follower relationship and then providing a conceptual framework and examples for understanding the concept of covenant, the second section moves to a more in-depth discussion of ten principles that are central both to building and maintaining covenants . Finally, the book concludes with a brief, four-part process for developing covenants. Each of the 12 chapters is broken down into subsections, and most subsections are supported by research, anecdotal examples and/or interview excerpts that illustrate the points that are made. Through this work I am endeavoring to describe more fully the characteristics and dynamics of a covenant and demonstrate how this relationship captures the essence of what it means to be a leader.

PART ONE

I. Defining Leadership as a Covenant

Chapter 1

A Covenant – Not a Contract

Throughout history and in just about every culture known to man, people have committed themselves to each other in relationships called covenants. Most of us are at least somewhat familiar with the marriage covenant; but the concept also applies in community life, sports, business, religion and just about any kind of organization one could imagine. In many cases people have also established and participated in rituals that communicate their covenant commitments publicly. Again, the marriage ceremony is the most common form of this, but throughout history there have been many other forms. For example, Karat berît was an ancient near eastern ritual, consummated when individuals seeking to unite for a common purpose walked through two columns of blood and gore. Though primitive and somewhat graphic, the pieces of the slain animals to the right and to the left signified the gravity of the commitment. In essence the participants would be saying, "*May the fate of this animal be my lot if I do not fulfill my oath.*" Literally translated, "*To cut a Covenant*", karat berît was both an irrevocable pledge and a joint proclamation of mutual commitment between two parties.[1]

Although the cultural expressions of this ritual have evolved into less graphic forms, the fundamental underpinnings of the concept of covenant still exist today. However, that begs an important question. Are the covenants we see merely the faint residue of what some may consider to be an antiquated and barbaric tradition, or are they still relevant and vital to society today?

I am convinced that covenants are not only relevant today, they are vital to the success of our marriages, our communities, our businesses and more. In essence, a covenant is a reciprocal relationship based on mutual trust, respect, values and commitment in which two or more people are willingly bound together by a common and ethical purpose. That purpose is bigger and more important than any one individual's interests, and it provides meaning and hope for everyone involved. Interestingly, that definition of covenant also describes the results of effective leadership. Hence the title of this book emerged naturally from my studies of both the dynamics of leadership and the principles of covenant. But in order to understand leadership as a covenant, we will first examine a few examples of covenants that exist in society today and then we will look at an example of what covenants are not: namely contracts.

Covenant: A Model in Marriage - In its ideal form, marriage is a long-term, reciprocal commitment between two people who are willingly bound together by common purpose in a monogamous relationship. True, pundits often speak of "the marriage contract," but by definition, marriage is intended to be a covenant and not a contract. Covenants require a deeper level of commitment than contracts do, and to make them work it takes respect, trust, shared values and a willingness of each partner to give to as well as receive from the relationship. Though the marriage covenant is demanding, when spouses do commit to each other and to the marriage in this manner, it creates synergy, strengthens and transforms the partners in positive ways and makes the relationship highly beneficial for everyone involved.

Of course, not all marriages are covenants nor do they all survive. That's why marriage is also not without its critics. For example, beginning in the 1960s allegations about marriage started to emerge from a number of sociologists, psychologists and social activists. Popular among them was the notion that the marriage covenant was a bad deal for women and that divorce was the better alternative for children if their parents would be unhappy staying together. Over a period of several decades there have been studies of the effects of divorce on men, women, children and society in general, and many of those studies were used both to criticize marriage and to argue that marriage is a private choice and not a public institution. The courts and the public bought into those arguments and divorce rates in the U.S. more than doubled; increasing from 2.2 per thousand people in 1960 to 5.0 in 1985. [2]

Despite the existence of a voluminous amount of research on divorce, during that same period very few people, if any, studied the long-term benefits of marriage. Then in 2000, syndicated columnist, Maggie Gallagher, and University of Chicago sociologist, Linda Waite, wrote *The Case for Marriage*. The results are based on original research by Dr. Waite, as well as her synthesis of hundreds of large cross-disciplinary studies in sociology, economics, medicine, psychology, sexology and law. The book also carries excerpts from research interviews conducted by Maggie Gallagher and funded by Lilly Endowment. The authors found both empirical and anecdotal data that were quite contrary to the popular myths about the negative effects of marriage. Their work provides overwhelming evidence that the marriage covenant is better physically, materially and spiritually than being single or divorced. In short, their findings demonstrate that married people (individuals living together in a covenant) live longer, enjoy better health, earn more money, accumulate more wealth, are more fulfilled, have more satisfying sex lives, are at less risk of being victims of violence and raise happier, more successful children than people who are single, divorced or cohabiting.[3]

According to Waite and Gallagher, marriage is a type of "partnership" with benefits that accrue to partners in much the same way as economists see that they do in business partnerships. They explain that the mechanisms working in business to provide payoffs for partners *"are some of the same mechanisms that we believe underlie the impressive advantage married people demonstrate in just about every realm of life social scientists can measure, including but not limited to benefits."*[4] The authors observe further that because the marriage covenant holds the promise of permanence and is intended to be long-term, it *"encourages husbands and wives to make decisions jointly and function as part of a team. Each spouse expects to be able to count on the other to be there and to fulfill his or her responsibilities."*[5]

The truth of Waite's and Gallagher's findings was clearly illustrated to me one year during the Christmas season. I enjoy these holidays because they provide opportunities to slow down, take time from our busy schedules and visit with family and friends. Such was the case on a recent Christmas Eve, when a large contingent of relatives gathered at our home. Over the course of the evening I had the opportunity to observe and interact with four generations of family members. At one point several of us sat around our dining room table, and I was fascinated to hear the conversations of four of the great grandparents. At the time, both couples had been married nearly 60 years and had been friends with each other for more than 50 years. Now into their 80s, they shared family stories about their parents, their childhoods, their struggles, their child rearing years, their spiritual lives, their successes, their careers and much more. As I reflected upon what they said, I realized that their covenant commitments had not only enriched their own lives, but they had also established a legacy of health, prosperity, love and stability that enriched the lives of the three generations of family members who came after them. For me, it represents a living example of what Waite and Gallagher found in their research.

Essentially, what these authors observed about the marriage covenant is that each partner brings value to and receives value from the relationship, and together they add value to the marriage and the family as organizations. As a result of the covenant they share, the partners are able to achieve more and create more value than they ever could on their own. Empirical data supports that this same concept, when applied in a business environment, works in much the same way. For example, in trying to discover what made some companies in the same industry more profitable than others, Frederick Reichheld of Bain & Company found the companies that had the highest customer and employee retention rates were the most profitable ones. He explains that the time spent building strong relationships with employees and customers by serving their interests is crucial to their retention. By allowing employees to participate in creating value, it not only adds directly to the customer and thereby enhances retention, it also, *"... increases employees' loyalty by giving them pride and satisfaction in their work."*[6]

Reichheld notes further that "loyalty leaders" certainly focus on creating customer value and they hold employees accountable for doing the same, but they also treat employees more like partners: *"Whether they use independent employee teams or their logical extension, vendor partnerships, the same principles of partnership apply. The key is to compensate (or add value to) partner-employees by sharing the value they help to create for customers."[7]*

Again this is quite similar to the partners in a marriage covenant sharing in and benefiting from the value they help create for each other. Certainly there remain critics of marriage who would not agree. Yet, despite their sometimes vigorous insistence on the negative effects of marriage, the preponderance of research indicates that the critics are wrong. As Waite and Gallagher and others have proven empirically, when a husband and wife commit to each other in a covenant, they prosper much more abundantly than they would on their own. But this is not just a book about the benefits of the marriage covenant; I believe the principles of covenant can be applied in most relationships in ways that help make them more productive and more fulfilling. That really is the point that the research of these authors supports. Whether they exist in marriage, business or any other kind of organization, covenants both create value for and add value to partners that can be measured in real, life-enriching, bottom-line results.

Covenant: An Example in Civics - While marriage is the most intimate of covenants, it is not the only place the model of covenant applies. In the 1830's, French social philosopher, Alexis de Tocqueville decided to visit the U.S. and make observations on American society. During the trip he observed that the strength of America was found in reciprocal relationships he called "covenants" that existed between and among its people. Tocqueville saw that within these covenants Americans cooperated, helped and supported one another in ways that created functional communities.[8] In his most famous work, *Democracy in America*, he noted, *"A similar covenant exists in fact between all citizens of a democracy: they feel themselves subject to the same weaknesses and the same dangers; and their interest, as well as*

7

their sympathy, makes it a rule with them to lend each other mutual assistance when required."⁹

This tradition of benevolence is both guided and driven by the voluntary covenant that American citizens continue to share with one another, a covenant that upholds the promise of life, liberty and the pursuit of happiness for everyone. Evidence of commitment to this covenant abounds in the millions of volunteer man hours and the billions of dollars (more than $260 billion in 2005) Americans donate each year to assist their fellow countrymen. It helps explain why they donated an estimated $2.2 billion in the wake of the 9/11 attacks and then more than $7 billion in 2005 for disaster relief for victims of the 2004 Tsunami and the 2005 Hurricanes Rita and Katrina. Then in the wake of these hurricanes, private citizens stepped up again and voluntarily acted on this covenant commitment when they opened their homes, their communities and volunteered their time to help the survivors get back on their feet.

The effort by Americans to come to the aid of their fellow citizens is embedded deeply in the American culture. In New York, Louisiana, Mississippi or anywhere else people are in need, help comes because citizens recognize both the common purpose and the common bond they share with one another. True, the Federal government also plays a role, but much of the comfort and healing and encouragement for people to go on and rebuild comes from private citizens who take the initiative to assist their fellow Americans in many different ways. Why did California businessman David Perez spend $200,000 of his own money to charter a 737 and take 86 Hurricane Katrina survivors back to the Golden State to care for them? Why did young 18-year-old Jabbar Gibson go get a yellow school bus, pick up Katrina survivors, get them to pool their money and drive them to Houston, Texas out of harm's way? Why were church groups and missions and communities all over America opening their arms to welcome these survivors? Essentially, it is because they were compelled to take the initiative and act, and as private American citizens they knew they could and should act. And because they acted on the shared covenant in exemplary and even heroic ways, those individuals and communities are recognized and celebrated as models of how we are supposed to live.

That really is the essence of living, working and relating within the context of a covenant. Whether the relationship exists in a family, a community, a business or anywhere else; a covenant involves individuals giving (sometimes sacrificially) to achieve the purposes and the ideals they share with their covenant partners.

Covenant: An Example in Athletics - If you wanted to test management strategies by simulating a business environment, there would be no better laboratory than big-time sports. Granted, professional sports franchises are businesses in their own right. But they are also followed daily in the press, providing unique opportunities not only to measure the quantifiable outputs (such as a win/loss record and individual statistics), but also to observe the relational dynamics which drive the results. Accordingly, beyond win/loss records, topics such as player-coach relationships, team dynamics, conflict, and loyalty all matter. It is not surprising that in the competitive world of athletics, we see some of the best and worst examples of leadership in the player-coach relationship. By analyzing some of these examples, we can glean valuable insights. For instance, witness the rapid decline of the 2005 Philadelphia Eagles, due in a large part to the distracting contract dispute and eventual interpersonal conflict between Coach Andy Reid and all-pro tight end Terrell Owens. Each man was arguably among the best at his respective position. Yet, consider the words of Terrell Owens about the *"business side"* of football and his dysfunctional relationship with his coach:

"I just feel like I've learned a lot as far as the business side of football. It really hit home how dirty and cruel of a business that this is. Everybody always says that this is a fun game (and) that it is. But behind the scenes, it's a real dirty game. I mean, in my situation, I think there are a lot of people who can vouch for me when I say that, 'Yeah, I deserve the money that I was asking for.' I've seen guys come in one week and they (get) cut the next. Or come in here for a couple of days and (they're) cut the next. So, it's a cutthroat business. I had to really not fool myself into

thinking that there is loyalty with the franchises of these teams. ... I'm very reluctant to trust people now when they say things. And you just have to take a business approach to things."[10]

What is interesting about Owens' comments regarding a lack of trust is that he and his agent had just negotiated a 7 year contract reported to be worth $49 million, including a substantial signing bonus. In the spring of 2005, Owens hired a new agent and announced that he would seek a renegotiation of his contract for more money. [11] The point is that trust must work both ways in relationships. Although Terrell Owens and Andy Reid are both highly talented professionals, their relationship lacked trust, loyalty, and a common purpose. As a result of this "business approach", their interactions deteriorated, and conversations shifted from "What can we do for the team" to "What can you do for me?" Accordingly, it became evident that despite their winning record, the situation was not sustainable. Shortly thereafter, Terrell was suspended for the remainder of the season and the Eagles dropped from NFC champs and Super Bowl contenders in 2005 to last place in the NFC East conference the following season. True, there were other problems that also contributed to the Eagles' demise, but this very public conflict between player and coach was a major factor.

At its best coaching is a covenant between leaders and followers, where the coach as leader invests his or her time and energy toward the development of players. The most effective coaches endeavor to develop their athletes comprehensively, not just so they perform better in their respective sports. True, performance is important to these coaches. Yet, even more important is the need for coaches to teach players and develop them so they can operate effectively within the context of a team and rules and other players. If it is done well, the coach will have equipped players not only for a successful season but also for a successful life. For example, one of the very best college coaches ever was former UCLA basketball coach John Wooden. I had the opportunity to talk with the coach and he explained that his commitment to and relationships with players went well beyond the winning and losing of college basketball. As he was describing it, I realized that what this Hall of Fame coach had created was a close "family" culture based on covenantal rather than contractual principles. At the core of these relationships were high levels of commitment, trust and caring between the coach and his players. He explained, *"I often told my players that, next to my own flesh and blood, they were closest to me. They were my children. I got wrapped up in them, their lives and their problems."*[12]

Through the covenant that Coach Wooden shared with his players, he was able to create a culture where those players could develop individually but they could still come together as part of a larger unit. Essentially, the team could achieve incredible success, but at the same time, the individual players could grow in ways that would benefit them both in the immediate and the future. Coach Wooden further described the covenant noting that he,

> *"... wanted them to be considerate of each other. For example, to my wife and me, our players were an extension of our own family. I've had players often refer to my wife at times as just kind of like their mother. And I wanted them to feel that. I wanted them close with each other and I wanted them to know that I was concerned about them as I would be my own children and their future – not just as basketball players. They wouldn't know this when they first came to UCLA, but I hoped that they would perceive it as time went by."*[13]

The coach clearly demonstrated his leadership not only by his win/loss record but also by his lasting influence on players and peers alike. That influence is captured in the words of former UCLA star and NBA great, Bill Walton: *"John Wooden gave us the necessary tools to overcome the adversity and obstacles that he knew from the beginning would always be in our way. It wasn't until we left UCLA and ran into the adversity that he told us would be there, that it started to dawn on me just how special we had it. I thank John Wooden everyday for all his selfless gifts, his lessons, his time, his vision and especially his patience."*[14]

Covenant: An Example in Business - Discussions about leaders typically involve more about their strategies, wins and immediate results than they do about their long-term legacy. Yet, leaders who embrace the principles of covenant create a long-term legacy of prosperity in the lives of both the people and the organizations they serve.

Consider, for example, the leadership of the founders of the Mayo Clinic, arguably one of the finest healthcare organizations in the world. As surgeons and scientists, William and Charles Mayo, were virtually unparalleled in their day. Together they published over 1,000 of their professional papers and received worldwide acclaim for their surgical skills and advances in medicine. But it wasn't their superior knowledge and skills alone that made them leaders. Instead, their leadership was manifest in how they used their knowledge and skills and how they related to the people they served. It was this very attitude of service that compelled the Mayo brothers along with their father, Dr. William Mayo, Sr., to establish a work that would become known worldwide as the Mayo Clinic. Their work introduced many innovations that changed the practice of medicine including such concepts as recording a patient's medical history and creating a single file that followed the patient; creating medical specialties; integrating medical research and education with practice; and bringing all medical specialties, laboratories and services under one roof.[15]

The Mayos were also businessmen, but first and foremost they were compassionate people, dedicated to providing relief for human suffering. They had a vision for all people to be able to receive quality care, regardless of their ability to pay. That vision helped establish an incredible legacy that endures today because the Mayo brothers were committed strongly to making it a reality. As a result of their leadership and vision, clinic facilities still provide service for people who do not have the capacity to pay. Unlike the agency theory business model, which says that as an agent of the firm it is your fiduciary responsibility to maximize profits, the Mayos' business model put people ahead of profits. They shared a covenant relationship with the people they served, and were willing to sacrifice their margins to do what they considered to be right. But an interesting point is that serving people and putting them ahead of profits did not seem to hurt their business because the clinic became highly profitable.

The brothers further demonstrated their commitment to the covenant and the common purpose when they made a decision, early in their career together, to pay themselves only what they considered to be a reasonable wage for their services. The remainder of their income they chose to put into a fund that would carry on their work indefinitely. In 1915 they donated, in affiliation with the University of Minnesota, $1.5 million to support the Mayo Foundation for Medical Education and Research. Then in 1919 they dissolved their partnership and turned over the clinic's name and assets, including most of their life savings, to the foundation. In other words, the Mayo brothers could have been wealthy and still served mankind, but they decided to forego the wealth and give themselves totally and completely to the cause. As a result, they have created something enduring that has become much larger and more meaningful than their short-term self interest of profit and wealth. As leaders, they have transformed the lives of their fellow healthcare workers and the thousands of patients their vision has served over many decades. The Mayo brothers and many others who have been attracted to their vision have added to their original gift. Today the Foundation generates revenues of some $300 million annually in support of the work at the Mayo Clinic.[16]

The Mayo brothers were pioneers and leaders in providing high quality healthcare because they were driven not by their self-interest but by a desire to help and transform the lives of others. As a result of their covenantal leadership, their organization became one of the very best in the world, and they became two of the most admired and beloved people of their time. They established a spirit of excellence that was driven by a desire to serve humanity and the common good. It is a lasting legacy that continues serving people and prospering society today.

The power of covenants that we observe in the benevolent lives of the Mayos, the humane coaching of John Wooden, the civic duty of Americans, and the loving commitment of marriage partners all share a common thread which can be harnessed in any kind of organization. In fact, our company assists organizations and businesses in applying the principles of covenant to help them become more functional, both operationally and relationally. Our primary objective is to help people achieve higher levels of productivity and fulfillment both in their personal lives and in their work. We have seen relationships and organizations transformed by the power of covenants. Accordingly, one might assume that a concept like covenant, which is so powerful and has been so prevalent in the history of our country, might also be quite common in every day life in America. Yet, what we have found in our research and our work is something quite different. My experience convinces me that, while many of us truly desire the benefits of a covenant in our homes and our businesses, we don't always know how to achieve them and therefore we fail. I believe at least part of that failure is due to the fact that we often impose contractual expectations and a contractual framework on relationships that are intended to be covenants.

Covenant: It's Not a Contract - Webster's New World College Dictionary notes that a contract is *"an agreement between two or more people to do something...one formally set forth in writing and enforceable by law...a formal agreement... a document containing terms."* [17] Beyond that, legal experts tell us that contracts involve an offer, acceptance of that offer, a promise to perform, a promise to pay for that performance in some way (or what the experts call consideration) and a time period or event by which performance must be completed. The terms and conditions of a contract dictate the details of both performance and consideration. What I find interesting is that the same dictionary defines a covenant as being quite similar to and even a form of a contract. According to Webster's it is, *"a binding and solemn agreement to do or keep from doing a specified thing...a compact...agreement... a formal, sealed contract...."* [18]

I believe the definitions are similar because to some extent we have lost the language of covenant in our society. There are lots of reasons for this, but suffice it to say that a covenant is quite different from a contract. It is a far more complex agreement that demands more interpersonal commitment and promises more benefits than a contract does.

By illustrating some of the differences between covenants and contracts, I am not trying to suggest that contracts are inherently bad. On the contrary, contracts are an integral part of business as well as the legal system. However, considering the frequency with which we use contracts, it is important to understand their limitations. First, they encourage people to negotiate the terms based on their own self-interest. Consequently, as the contract is fulfilled, each of the parties tends to evaluate the value of the relationship based primarily on the performance of the other party. Second, if one of the parties believes his or her self interest is not being served through this contractual relationship, then that constitutes justification for either breaking or renegotiating the contract. Finally, a relationship defined solely by contractual interaction can and often does breed mistrust and commitment only to self. And as we have seen in the case of Terrell Owens, when trust is missing in relationships, contracts quickly deteriorate. In fact, most lawyers with whom I have discussed the subject, freely admit that for a contract to work for an extended period of time, it has to be supported by an underlying basis of "good faith." That "good faith" is one of the basic elements necessary for moving beyond a contract into a covenant.

In contrast to a heavily contractual environment that tends to commodify and mistrust people, covenants assume good faith on the part of everyone involved in the relationship. This is not to suggest that leaders need to be naïve in their relationships. Certainly, at times there will be individuals that leaders encounter who will not operate in good faith, and it will be necessary for them to deal with those "bad faith" people appropriately. That said, it's important to note also that just because a few people deal in bad faith, it does not justify being guarded with everyone. But dealing in good faith requires a certain amount of trust. While trust is often initiated by leaders, it is necessary on the part of everyone if the relationship is going to work. There simply can be no good faith and therefore no covenant if there is no trust. Consider the results of a marriage in which the partners don't trust each other. It is bound to set up anger, frustration, jealousy and eventually a breakup. While we understand both the importance of trust and the results of mistrust in marriage, many people lack that same understanding in the contract laden environment of business.

Thus, while contracts are binding *legal agreements*, covenants are binding and committed *relationships*. The former is bound by the law and the latter is bound by the character, values, and mutual goals of the people involved. I believe that the failure of our society to differentiate between the two concepts contributes heavily to our leadership crisis. As we have discussed earlier, both the dynamics and characteristics of a covenant are different than those of a contract. True, in some ways a covenant can be a far more demanding relationship than a contract, but it is also far more flexible and powerful than a contract.

So how then, should we regard contracts? Contractual expectations are clearly common in the business setting, so we can't really shun the entire concept and operate solely with informal agreements in a paperless society. Yet, it is important for us to realize that an overemphasis on contracts can sometimes detract from the good faith and spirit of trust that are central to building healthy relationships. When the interpretation of contracts becomes overly legalistic, trust and cooperation can quickly evaporate as can a sense of common purpose. I saw a firsthand example of this when a nonprofit client of ours recently went through a national search for a senior officer of their organization. After several rounds of interviews with staff and Board members, one candidate emerged as their choice. Both the candidate and the Board members were excited about the prospect of the relationship, as each of the parties assumed the best intentions of the other. They simply had to work out the details of the agreement.

After lengthy discussions that produced several versions of a work agreement, the contract was just about finalized. The candidate then chose to give the agreement to his lawyer for further review and good faith and goodwill began to fade. He came back with several additional demands that extended the negotiations and required more conversations and concessions by the organization. Even though he had clearly been the most qualified candidate, as the negotiations dragged on, the Board and staff began to question whether or not they could trust this candidate and decided to reopen the search. Eventually, they found another candidate who was almost as qualified but was also less demanding and they hired her. Unfortunately, the first candidate missed the opportunity to work with a great group of people because his demands demonstrated that he could not bring himself to trust them. As a result, he lost credibility with the group because they suspected the candidate was greedy and interested only in himself. On both sides, trust and good will diminished in ways that caused irreparable damage. In chapter five, there will be a more in-depth discussion of the importance of trust, but suffice it to say that without trust there can be no covenant.

In short, the dynamics, characteristics and results of covenants are quite different than those of contracts. The matrix that follows summarizes some of those differences. It is important to note, however, that since contracts are so pervasive in our culture, leadership is required for covenants and contracts to coexist productively in organizations. Understanding the tendencies and differences of both forms helps leaders enhance productivity and make informed decisions about how to establish relationships and where and how to lead. Too often would be leaders want to achieve many of the benefits that covenants produce, but they try to do so with a purely contractual framework and contractual expectations and thereby they fail. This matrix then is intended not only to illustrate the differences between each concept, but also to equip leaders to accommodate both of them.

Tend To	Covenants	Contracts
Build	Community & Mutual Responsibility	Clearly Defined Territories & Individual Rights
Promote	Common Good, Win/Win	Self-interest, Win/Lose
Foster	Relationships, Mutual Prosperity	Terms, Individual Prosperity
Be Driven By	Mission / Values	Transactions
Be Bound By	Spirit / Integrity	Law or Legal Interpretation
Encourage	Free Exchange / Vulnerability	Conditional Exchange / Protection
Be Oriented Toward	Service & Development of Individuals	Performance & Evaluation
Imply	Trust / Positive Assumptions	Mistrust / Negative Assumptions
Focus On	Giving and Sharing	Receiving
Support	Principles & Liberty	Rules & Restrictions
Define	Accommodation	Contingencies
Promise	Long-term Commitment	Short-term Execution
Lead To	Loyalty and Motivation	Shopping Around / Detachment
Favor	Recognition of Others	Recognition of Self
Create	Synergy / Emotional Attachment / Increased Social Capital	Limits / Emotional Distance / Diminished Social Capital

[1]Hillers, Delbert R. *Covenant: The History of a Biblical Idea.* (The John Hopkins University Press, London & Baltimore;1969). p. 31

[2]Friedberg, Leora. *"Did Unilateral Divorce Raise Divorce Rates?"* Economic Review, Vol. 88, No. 3 (June 1998). P. 608-627.

[3]Gallagher, Maggie, and Dr. Linda Waite; *The Case for Marriage* (Doubleday; New York, NY; 2000).

[4]Ibid., p. 24.

[5]Ibid., p. 25.

[6]Reichheld, Frederick; *The Loyalty Effect;* (Harvard Business School Press; Boston, Massachusetts; 1996) p. 21.

[7]Ibid., p. 23.

[8]Tocqueville, Alexis de. *Democracy in America*. J.P. Mayer and Max Lerner, eds. (New York: Harper & Row, 1966).

[9]Ibid, pp. 481-482.

[10]Bensinger, Graham. "Terrell Owens Unplugged". Website: http://sports.espn.go.com/espn/page2/story?page=to/unplugged/video/new

[11] Associated Press article "NFL PA Files Grievance on Owen's Behalf," 12/6/05 on asp.usatoday.com/community/tags/topic.aspx? req=tag&pg=78tag=phi. Also in Wikipedia Encyclopedia; "Terrell Owens", August 2006, www.en.wikipedia.org/wiki/Terrell-Owens.

[12]Wooden, John; *"They Call Me Coach"* (Waco; Word, Inc.; 1985) p. 62.

[13]Wooden, John; Interview with Leonard J. Moisan; September 6, 1995.

[14]Walton, Bill; in "Bill's Tribute to Coach Wooden." at www.billwalton.com.

[15]The Mayo Clinic; *"About Mayo Clinic"* (History) www.mayoclinic.org/about/history.html.

[16]*The National Cyclopaedia of American Biography*. (New York: James T. White & Company, 1943) p. 1-3.

[17]*Webster's New World Dictionary, Third College Edition*. Edited by Victoria Neufeldt (New York: Simon & Schuster, 1988) p. 302.

[18]Ibid, p. 320.

Chapter 1
Leadership Evaluation and Action Discovery (LEAD)

Evaluate the kind of relationship dynamics that exist in your organization by answering the following questions:

	A. Using the covenant/contract matrix, please explain whether the following relationships of your organization or team tend to be covenants or contracts. Also, please use other information in Chapter 1 to support your answers:
1	Management / employee relationships
2	Employee /employee relationships
3	Organization / customer relationships

	B. Research demonstrates that consistently "Creating or Adding Value" strengthens relationships, enhances management, employee and customer retention and improves profitability. In what ways does your organization or team now or might you in the future create or "add value" to the following stakeholder relationships?
1	Managers / leaders
2	Employees
3	Customers

Chapter 2

A Relationship – Not a Position or Commodity

Two recent Google web searches I ran on "Leadership" and "Leadership Shortage" resulted in 280,900,000 titles, demonstrating both a broad interest in the topic of leadership and a liberal use of the term. In fact, the word "leader" was used to describe everything from winners of races to top selling consumer brands to heads of multinational corporations.

Often when we think of leaders, images flash through our minds of the charismatic CEO, expounding a vision for the future to industry analysts. Or perhaps it's the cunning power-wielder we see, using political capital and tactical maneuvering to manipulate outcomes and sway results to their favor. Maybe we think of a politician or an elected official. Or maybe it's an inspirational coach that comes to mind, giving a Knute Rockne speech that turns a halftime deficit into a victory. Given the diversity of opinions reflected in the Google search, it's no wonder that there is confusion surrounding the concept of leadership. Nevertheless, regardless of how the term is applied, the consensus opinion appears to be that leadership is not only about "what" is accomplished, but also about "how" it is accomplished.

In the previous chapter we introduced the concept of covenantal relationships and discussed their dynamics, their benefits, and how they differ from contractual relationships. The following chapter will expand on this framework and look at some of the tendencies of leader-follower relationships within the context of a covenant. We will also explore how leadership as a covenant differs from the commodification of people and the contractual framework of power wielding and positional authority that it implies.

Influential and Dynamic More Than Positional and Controlling - As I read a large number of the titles from my Google search on leadership and a few selected articles, I wondered, *"Why is leadership becoming so obscure?"* Upon further reflection, I came to the conclusion that, in part, it's because people tend to confuse leadership with headship or with certain job titles or responsibilities. True leadership is much more than winning a race or establishing a brand, and its dynamics are far more complex than presiding at the top of an organization or getting things done through other people. Many heads of organizations (including Saddam Hussein in Iraq and Hitler in Nazi Germany) have been able to get things accomplished through the use of power, but that doesn't make them leaders. Leadership is a strategic process of using influence to create or strengthen dynamic relationships and motivate individuals to achieve the common purposes of both the leader and the people being led.

In 1978, political scientist James MacGregor Burns described leadership in even simpler terms when he wrote one of the definitive books on the subject. In his Pulitzer prize-winning work, which Burns appropriately titled *Leadership*, he argues that leadership is not headship, it is not winning friends and gaining popularity, and it is not power wielding. Leadership, according to Burns, is best understood as a relationship between leaders and followers. Inherent in that relationship is power and how that power is used as it converges with the people, purposes and resources of the relationship determines whether a person is leading or power wielding. To this point, Burns comments, *"To control things – tools, mineral resources, money, energy – is an act of power, not leadership, for things have no motives. Power wielders may treat people as things. Leaders may not. All leaders are actual or potential power holders, but not all power holders are leaders."*[1] Leaders, then, don't use power to control people or make them do what the leaders want them to do. Instead, they influence followers to make the choice to act on purposes or needs that both leaders and followers have in common.

Developmental More Than Dictatorial - I find it interesting that the inability of managers to engage people productively in their work is often blamed on the workers' laziness. The logic of this argument follows that managers need only to dictate what should be done and punish those lazy people who don't or won't comply. While "laziness" may be a factor occasionally, often the lack of engagement and productivity is due to the manager's inability to teach and develop people effectively. According to Dr. Mel Levine, a learning expert, developmental pediatrician and professor at the University of North Carolina, laziness is a myth. Dr. Levine explains that certain neurodevelopmental dysfunctions may cause what he calls "output failures", but he argues convincingly that none of these failures is due to laziness. Through his work Dr. Levine has learned, as he describes it, that *"Laziness is not an innate trait. We are all born with a drive to produce, and like saplings growing in an orchard, we have within us the resources to bear fruit...From early childhood on through our adult years, we want to show what we can do. We gain energy and feel good about ourselves whenever our personal output wins the approval, the acceptance, the respect of our friends, our families, our bosses (or teachers), and, most of all, our own self critical selves. To feel fulfilled in life, it helps immeasurably if you can take pride in your work."* [2]

Assuming that Dr. Levine is correct, and he presents convincing arguments that indicate that he is, then what he says has significant implications for leaders. Though we may be born with the drive and resources to produce, both of these traits need to be cultivated and nurtured for the individual to learn how to produce. The learning "how" is the job of leaders. Since we know that not every person learns the same way, it is incumbent upon leaders to create a developmental culture of teaching and learning that employs various pedagogical models (ways to teach) so that followers can be successful.

In a covenant, part of a leader's coaching role involves making a commitment to teach and develop followers in the same transforming way that Coach Wooden taught and developed his players. How do leaders teach? They teach by explaining, modeling, measuring and by allowing followers to be successful and allowing them to fail. Essentially they create a culture that develops people by fostering an environment of teaching and learning where it is safe to ask questions and safe to take risks.

Within this culture of teaching and learning the lessons must also go well beyond the "how to" of a task. Through covenants leaders create customized learning opportunities where followers can be coached in principles and methods that equip them to handle both the immediate business of work and the longer term business of life. It is part of the transformational component of leadership, that James MacGregor Burns identified, where leaders seek to develop and eventually transform followers by elevating them to higher levels of skill and performance. Sometimes the teaching and learning occur directly between leaders and followers, but they can also occur worker to worker, citizen to citizen or family member to family member. Regardless of how it occurs, it is clearly the leader's covenant commitment and responsibility to create a culture where it can occur.

Humane and Genuine More Than Commodified and Manipulative - When an organization of any kind is said to be humane, it usually means that it has a culture where people recognize the intrinsic worth of individuals and treat each other with genuine dignity and respect. That happens not because of the power, the abilities or the personal attributes of people, but simply because they are human beings and therefore worthy of dignity and respect. Organizations built on the principles of covenant, for example, are ones in which leaders respect and value people intrinsically and therefore are considered humane and genuine.

By contrast, organizations that value people and afford them dignity and respect only to the extent that they can perform and/or produce, are actually inhumane and disingenuous because they are treating their people as if they were commodities. What is a commodity? Investorwords.com defines a commodity as *"A physical substance, such as food, grains, and metals, which is interchangeable with another product of the same type, and which investors buy or sell, usually through futures contracts."* [3] Because corn grown in Indiana is really no different than corn grown in Indonesia, the value of this commodity has been quantified solely by its utility in consumption and is subject to fluctuations based upon the supply and demand of products with similar utility.

The commodities market is clearly of great benefit for investors and producers of goods. It allows farmers in Indiana to sell their corn before harvest time to ensure that better-than-expected production in Indonesia doesn't wipe them out. It allows airlines to buy insurance against the risk that oil prices will skyrocket. It ensures that Ford will have sufficient quantities of steel to continue making cars. But what happens when the concept of a commodities market is extended into other areas of life? What happens when we see the commodification of every aspect of our personal lives?

This was the proposition of University of Chicago professor and Nobel Prize winner Gary S. Becker in his 1972 work entitled, *A Theory of Marriage: Part II.* In it he demonstrates how even the most intimate of human relationships can be commodified and he cautions that *"economic theory may well be on its way to providing a unified framework for **all** behavior involving scarce resources, non-market as well as market, non-monetary as well as monetary, small group as well as competitive . . . marriage is no exception and can be successfully analyzed within the framework provided by modern economics."*[4]

Dr. Becker argues that decisions such as the selection of a spouse, when to marry, how long to stay married, when to remarry if divorced or widowed, whether to have children, and even love itself can be quantified by a series of utility functions which relate such attributes as income level, physical capital, and intelligence to the personal gain from marriage. This does not suggest that vast numbers of people are testing mathematical correlations or creating economic models to select marriage partners. However, it is clear that variables such as these are becoming more prominent in decisions regarding marriage, which is contrary to the idea of marriage as a covenant.

It's no big surprise that if we can see commodification influencing our marriages, we can and surely will see it influence our business relationships with greater frequency. Jeremy Rifkin, author and

President of the Foundation on Economic Trends, speaks of the growing presence of commodification in business relationships. He describes it as an environment or attitude where companies attempt to get a larger share of their customers by becoming trusted advisors and selling them products and services in every area of their lives. According to Rifkin, *"What these ideas boil down to is the commodification of a person's entire lifetime of experiences ... Assigning lifetime values to people with the expectation of transforming the totality of their lived experience into commercial fare"*[5]

Ironically, both the commodities model and the covenant model imply that the type of relationship that accrues the most personal benefit is a covenant. As we have seen from Gallagher and Waite, there is an enormous body of evidence suggesting that being in a committed marital relationship (a covenant) is more rewarding and beneficial than being single or cohabiting. Likewise, a growing body of evidence (much of which we will examine) indicates that the covenant model applied to relationships in business, is far more productive than the commodities model. That's because commodities can be manipulated, but people must be led. It makes sense that individuals would rather be treated with dignity and respect than be commodified.

Nevertheless, many organizations today still cling to a commodities model of just about everything, including human relationships. In such places, the "value" of individuals is often measured by how well and to what extent they can serve the self interests of organizational decision makers. When this attitude pervades an organization, the intrinsic worth of individuals is lost in a culture that puts constant emphasis on performance and production.

But as we have seen from our discussion of the differences between covenants and contracts, a covenantal relationship (though it is arguably the most productive form) can never be achieved if it is entered into for the sole purpose of personal fulfillment or bottom line results. These elements can be optimized by covenants, but the very essence of a covenant means that the people of the covenant genuinely consider the interests of all of their covenant partners.

Hence, if we operate under the commodities model of relationships, which makes self-interest primary, we will never achieve the optimal state intended by the model which ultimately comes from a covenantal existence. Said another way, covenanting with people to achieve a common purpose is far more humane, genuine and productive than commodifying or manipulating them, but one can not enter into or sustain a covenant with purely self-centered motives.

Also, the fact that the covenant model is far more productive than the commodities model begs an important question: If the results of the covenant model are superior to those of the commodities model, then what is the utility of the commodities model of relationships and why bother ever applying it? If by applying its principles, you can never achieve optimal success, then it would seem to defy logic to continue doing so. When relationships and people are treated as commodities, then those relationships become steeped in attitudes of consumption rather than commitment. As that happens, the product of the relationship (what I receive) becomes more highly valued than the individual people of the relationship. Under this model, human interactions are reduced to exchanges of products or resources rather than exchanges in which people are treated humanely and bonded together as they give themselves fully to a cause or purpose. Unfortunately, though it is less effective such commodification is quite common.

Committed To and Valued More Than Used and Consumed - Most people want to be valued intrinsically for who they are and not just what they can do or how they perform for others. This is not to suggest that doing or performing for others in relationships never matters, clearly it does matter. But, sustaining a relationship with any sense of long term commitment requires more than doing and performing.

In covenants leaders demonstrate that they are committed to people and value them irrespective of their level of talent or performance. For example, talent and performance are clearly important in athletics. Yet, the best coaches understand that beyond these two elements there are many more aspects of the player – coach relationship. In fact, given the appropriate amount of direction that is tempered by respect, consideration and caring by a coach, a player is likely to put forth great effort to maximize his or her performance in ways that can sometimes make up for a lack of talent. I had this very experience when I played basketball in college. In my era in the 1970s, freshmen were not allowed to play varsity sports. Instead we played a reduced schedule of 15-20 games, which was intended to help us make an effective transition from high school to college. It was also during an era in which our university was making moves in its athletic program that would eventually find us ranked in the top 20 among Division I basketball teams. Of course, this in no way is a reflection on my ability as a player. In fact, my coach told me one day that the coaching staff had made a decision in a recent meeting that involved me. When I asked the nature of that decision, he said in a matter of fact manner, "We decided that we would recruit at your level of talent and above." The good news was that I was in the mix; the bad news was that I was the bottom standard. Maybe that's why I played the "weak side forward," which is the side that is mostly away from the ball.

Though I was by no means a "star athlete," my coach paid attention to me. He took time to talk to me and engage me both on and off the court. I eventually became a starter, but only as a role player. I wasn't a scholarship athlete, but I still knew my coach respected and cared about me as a human being. In fact, he knew my family didn't have much money, so he went out of his way to help me get plugged into support systems the university offered. He also helped me find some much needed financial assistance for which I was eligible. In other words, my relationship with Coach Ludwig wasn't just about basketball. Though he was plenty tough when he needed to be, he demonstrated that he valued me beyond basketball as a human being, and as a result I worked harder for him than I did for any coach I ever had. In fact, that was pretty much the case with our entire team, as we lost only two games all season.

True, in America most people have come to accept a certain amount of commodification from advertising and marketing firms (though I do see tolerance waning for point of purchase data collection).

However, they do not expect it to come from friends and colleagues in their personal and working relationships. Commodification of individuals can't inspire people to follow but the commitment of leaders can. The problem with commodification of relationships is that it breeds mistrust and short-term commitment. Commodification cannot engage the full person, because it does not seek to meet an individual's deeper needs such as esteem, appreciation, recognition and respect. When followers know, for example, that a leader's primary commitment to them is based on the followers' performance, then the relationships are not likely to survive long-term. In this consumerist model, as soon as someone fails to perform up to expectations, the relationship loses value and therefore can be and often is terminated. People simply are not products to be used, consumed or terminated if their performance slips. They want leaders who are committed to them and value them beyond their immediate performance; leaders who attend to their needs and not just those of the organization.

This is not to suggest that covenants mean a lack of performance or accountability. Though some power wielders might fear that this would be the result, research and anecdotal evidence consistently demonstrate that the opposite is true. When people are treated well, valued and trusted, they tend to heighten performance and assume more rather than less accountability. There can be plenty of accountability in the leader-follower relationship without commodification. In fact, when the focus of leaders is primarily on performance, then it tends to breed competition, fear, defensiveness and a lack of individual accountability.

Consider the case of General Electric Corporation. Under the direction of CEO Jack Welch, the company was one of the most successful businesses in the world. In 1980, the year before Welch took over the reigns, General Electric recorded revenues of about $26.8 billion. By 2000, before he left, annual company revenues had climbed to about $130 billion. In 2004 General Electric was valued at $400 billion, the largest in the world. Nevertheless, the profit did not come without a price. The culture of General Electric had always emphasized cost cutting and high performance among business units and individual employees. However, an extreme form of this came between the years of 1981 and 1985 when Mr. Welch cut 118,000 jobs, earning himself the name of "Neutron Jack". By his own admission, the "Neutron Jack" tag bothered Mr. Welch. Equally disconcerting to him was the 1984 *Fortune Magazine* article that put him at the top of a list of its "Ten Toughest Bosses in America."[6]

Also, in the midst of laying off so many people, Jack Welch spent $75 million on fitness equipment and a major upgrade of the company's management development center. Granted, the investment was small compared to overall company revenues, but it did not endear him to many of the General Electric employees. To his credit, Mr. Welch noted that *"... people weren't buying it. For them, it was a total disconnect. It didn't matter that the money I was investing in treadmills, conference halls and bedrooms was pocket change.... The symbolism of the $75 million was too much for people to handle.... Despite my good intentions with the fitness center, people had trouble seeing the benefits in the face of layoffs."*[7]

Jack Welch freely admits that at times he was, as he describes it, *"too full of myself."* As evidence of this he cites the nearly disastrous acquisition of Kidder, Peabody in April of 1986, despite the dissenters on his Board who advised him not to acquire it. Less than one year later in February federal officers entered its headquarters and arrested several company officials for insider trading. In reflecting on his mistake, Mr. Welch commented, *"There's only a razor's edge between self confidence and hubris. This time, hubris won and taught me a lesson I'll never forget."*[8]

Maybe that explains why General Electric, though it performed at 2.8 times the general market from 1985 to 2000, by comparison did not perform as well as the "Good to Great" companies included in Jim Collins' study. On average, those companies performed at almost seven times the general market for the same period. This is even more interesting in light of the fact that all "Good to Great" companies had what Mr. Collins described as "Level Five Leaders," CEOs who possess a paradoxical blend of personal humility and professional will.[9] While he was arguably a very successful CEO with a strong professional will and plenty of talent, by most accounts Mr. Welch is not known for having a great deal of personal humility.

A 1998 *Business Week* article alleged that Mr. Welch frequently encouraged managers to get rid of what he called "duds" or poor performers. [10] True or not, perception is often reality in business. Even if these allegations about Mr. Welch were unfounded, there are plenty of CEOs who do operate in this manner. Beyond being intimidating, such a mindset conveys a clear message about employee value: "Your value as an employee is directly related to your performance.... Perform better than your fellow workers or you'll be considered a "dud" and be vulnerable to getting fired."

While Mr. Welch has received much acclaim for his achievements at the helm of General Electric, not everyone was enamored with his performance. The same *Business Week* article quoted the United Electrical Workers representative who negotiated a contract for 6,000 General Electric employees as saying, *"No matter how many records are broken in productivity and profits, it's always, 'What have you done for me lately?'"* The negotiator further described General Electric as a place where, *"The workers are considered lemons, and they are squeezed really dry."* [11] Granted, this individual may have had a vested interest in portraying the company in a negative light and a certain amount of friction between companies and unions is all but guaranteed. Yet, more than one critic has commented on the demanding atmosphere at General Electric that was said to emanate from the intense pressure to perform imposed by Mr. Welch. [12]

No doubt, issues are never as black and white as critics make them out to be, but regardless of whether or not these critics are accurate, the fundamental principle is still true. People simply cannot continue to be pushed and/or commodified without compromising the depth of their commitment and the quality of their output. In fact, quality improvement initiatives like General Electric's famous "Six Sigma" program work best when employees are secure and allowed to assume ownership for their jobs. While profit and performance are crucial to long-term success, sustaining them long-term requires leadership and there is more to leadership than bottom line results.

Respectful and Loving More Than Intimidating - One of my favorite authors is the late Henri Nouwen. Among other topics, he wrote about the temptation of leaders to rely on power. In talking of his own struggles as a leader, he noted, *"I still have moments in which I clamp down and tell everyone to shut up, get in line, listen to me and believe in what I say."*[13] Nouwen both posed and answered an important question regarding why so many people resort to power when they try to lead: *"What makes the temptation of power so seemingly irresistible? Maybe it is that power offers an easy substitute for the hard task of love. It seems easier to be God, than to love God, easier to control people than to love people, easier to own life than to love life."*[14] He explains further that many people opt for the power and control method because they do not know how to develop healthy, intimate relationships.[15]

Because of their respect for others, authentic leaders resist the power temptation and tend towards sharing rather than wielding power. That frees them from having to intimidate followers. It also allows them to build relationships and focus on what Nouwen calls, "the hard task of love." Consider the case of Southwest Airlines. Like General Electric, Southwest Airlines is a place where employees are known to work hard but they also have fun while doing it. The company is consistently listed among *Fortune Magazine's* "100 Best Companies to Work For in America." Southwest also has to deal with unions just like General Electric and other companies do, but Southwest executives work hard to make the unions their partner. It makes sense that when the focus in an organization is on building healthy relationships and creating a sense of ownership for the common purpose among followers, then accountability tends to become self-imposed.

The atmosphere at Southwest is due in a large part to Herb Kelleher, the Chairman of the airlines. He is a leader who talks all the time about respecting and even loving his people. Witness the big heart painted on the airplanes symbolizing that love and also the energetic friendly demeanor of employees that reflects it. These and other attitudes at Southwest help explain why the company has lower turnover rates than any other airline in the industry. And evidently, all this talk and practice of love does not compromise profitability. Consider that in 2003 Southwest Air earned more than all of the other major airlines in the United States combined.[16] Despite the turbulence in the airline industry where profits are a rarity, Southwest Air has been profitable every year for more than 30 consecutive years.[17]

Like Herb Kelleher, the founder of Manpower Limited and the Secretan Center for leadership, Lance Secretan, also believes that love is a crucial part of leading people. He commented, *"... if I ask an audience at a speaking engagement whether they want more competition and fear in their lives, not one hand gets raised; but when I ask them if they want more love in their lives, every hand goes up.... The courageous leader comes to terms with that and makes sure that people in the workplace feel they're in a place where they are loved."*[18]

Again, the market concept of commodification certainly works well with the purchase and consumption of actual commodities like groceries, appliances and cattle. However, it is highly inappropriate for developing meaningful relationships in which two or more people give themselves to a common purpose. Commodification is dehumanizing and relies on power, manipulation and sometimes intimidation to move people; leadership is engaging and relies on respect, love and mutual commitment. When commodification is prevalent in relationships, then potentially everyone becomes a free agent looking for the best deal. Such a consumerist mentality applied in personal relationships can be devastating, as evidenced by the high levels of dysfunction and divorce that exist in families today. Likewise, commodification applied in organizations also leads to a form of free agency and self-centeredness that bring organizational dysfunction. Often that dysfunction is manifest in a lack of respect, trust, teamwork and commitment to the organization.

When my value or payoff in a relationship is measured and rewarded by my ability to deliver commodities or perform in ways that serve someone else's self-interest, then my primary focus will be to keep my perceived value high by continuing to perform. The problem is that the higher the stakes the more the dynamics of the relationship lend themselves to deception, manipulation, power wielding and even cheating to enhance my performance and to keep my value high. Consider the results of the increased commodification in the world of professional sports. The growing incidence of illegal steroid use and other forms of cheating may enhance performance short-term, but they injure the long-term health and credibility of the athletes and they diminish the respect of the fans. Witness the rapid decline in popularity of home run king Sammy Sosa after his bat broke and the umpire found cork in it. In the final analysis, it's difficult to embrace a cheater either as a hero or a trusted leader.

Mutually Beneficial More Than Selfishly Prosperous - There is a great deal more to relationships and business and life than making a profit and serving self. In fact, that was exactly the point Charles Dickens made when he wrote about the self-centered Scrooge in *A Christmas Carol*. Jacob Marley is Scrooge's deceased business associate. With the appearance one night of Marley's Ghost in chains, Scrooge is perplexed. As Marley explains his earthly regrets, Scrooge challenges him saying, *"But you were always a good man of business, Jacob."* At this, Marley's Ghost replies, *"Business! … Mankind was my business. The common welfare was my business; charity, mercy, forbearance, and benevolence were all my business. The dealings of my trade were but a drop of water in the comprehensive ocean of my business!"*[19]

In addition to being a beloved and enduring Christmas story, Dickens' work is also a commentary on business and the social conditions that existed in England around the time of the Industrial Revolution. Through the dialogue between Marley and Scrooge, Dickens is pointing out that business exists for purposes beyond just making money for the owner. There is a responsibility for business leaders to attend also to the human needs of workers rather than exploiting or commodifying them. It is only in realizing and acting on the fact that Bob Cratchit is actually a person with a family and needs, that Scrooge finds redemption and becomes a leader. Essentially, Scrooge stops commodifying every aspect of his relationship with Cratchit, and he starts treating him like a person with value beyond what he can do for Scrooge.

In order for leadership actually to be leadership, it necessitates that relationships between leaders and followers address a set of mutual needs and aspirations, not just those of the leader. Scrooge's inability to recognize that point made him a selfish, commodifying power wielder instead of a leader. Certainly heads of corporations can drive performance and profits, but that doesn't make them leaders. As Dickens, Burns, Kelleher and others have expressed it; leadership requires both the absence of commodification and the presence of a common and ethical purpose that promises to benefit everyone involved in its pursuit. Beyond that, leadership is also a relationship in which people are respected, and leaders and followers are both bound together by and freely give themselves to that common purpose. Simply stated, people are not commodities and they cannot be led effectively by treating them as such.

Transformational More Than Exploitative - Finally, leadership or specifically, the leader-follower relationship, is more about transformation than it is about exploitation. Essentially, it is the intentional transformation of people and organizations for the better. That is clearly a theme of Dickens' story. As a result of being led by the spirits of Christmas past, present and future, Scrooge was transformed. These spirits or mentors led him through a series of purposeful and sometimes painful experiences that changed Scrooge and eventually achieved their intended outcomes. Through their guidance he came to an understanding of his own selfishness and the needs of others around him. Scrooge chose to use his resources to transform the lives of others because he himself had been transformed. Using the language of James MacGregor Burns, the kind of relationship that existed between Scrooge and the spirits would be classified as transformational leadership. It is a relationship where leaders recognize higher needs in followers (love, hope, meaning, esteem) and engage their full person by seeking to meet those needs and convert followers into leaders.[20]

According to Burns,

> *"... transforming leadership ultimately becomes moral in that it raises the level of human conduct and ethical aspiration of*

both leader and the led.... Such leadership occurs when one or more persons engage with others in such a way that leaders and followers raise one another to higher levels of motivation and morality. Their purposes, which may have started out as separate but related as in the case of transactional leadership, become fused."[21]

In other words, though leader-follower relationships begin and, to some extent can continue, with transactions, they shouldn't end there. As leaders earn credibility and therefore trust through their transactions with followers, they also gain more power to influence and elevate followers in transformational ways. Using power to influence and elevate followers in ways that transform them or, as Burns says, in ways that move followers "...to higher levels of motivation and morality," is one of the primary evidences that leadership exists. It implies regard and respect for and commitment to followers, apart from which leadership is relegated at best to supervision.

Over more than 2,000 years of history, mounds of convincing evidence indicate that no leader has influenced more people or changed the world more profoundly for good than Jesus of Nazareth. In Jesus we have what is arguably the best example of a transformational leader.

Witness the relationship He had with His disciples. Jesus understood that His followers had both intrinsic value and very human needs. Based on those needs, at the first meeting He engaged them in a transaction that He initiated. He filled their boat with fish in order to gain their attention and gain credibility, both of which they gave to Him. Jesus also made other promises to His disciples, and as He delivered on those promises His credibility grew. Throughout all of His interactions with followers, Jesus related to them and particularly to His close disciples in ways that demonstrated genuine regard for them. That regard was manifest in the many acts of love, kindness and service He extended to them. No doubt, the relationship Jesus shared with His followers was a covenant, a covenant so powerful that it changed their lives permanently.

As a leader, Jesus demonstrated genuine regard for and commitment to his disciples, and it transformed them. As a result of their relationship, these disciples eventually deepened their commitment both to Jesus and to the common purpose they shared with Him. Specifically, by teaching, healing, challenging and loving these mostly uneducated and sometimes cowardly followers, Jesus transformed them into courageous and committed leaders. His mission and values became their mission and values. In fact, so powerful was the disciples' transformation, that they boldly carried on the organizational mission in ways that cost most of them their lives. Yet, the power to lead and transform His followers did not come through any worldly position Jesus may have held. Instead it came through the relationships Jesus shared with His followers and the love, commitment, respect, sacrifice and spirit of Jesus those followers experienced. It is a clear illustration of the fact that leadership is not a position; it is a relationship with enormous potential to achieve and transform for the better.

Finally, to facilitate better understanding and application of the points covered in this chapter, I have created the following matrix. As I mentioned earlier, both leading and power wielding occur in degrees. One good way to use this matrix is to evaluate the current culture of your organization and determine where each of the tendencies lie. If there are more tendencies that fall under the Leader/Follower column, then it is likely that the culture is one where leadership is relational and the principles of covenant are being applied consistently. If, however, more of your organizational tendencies fall under the Power Wielder / Subordinate column, then it is more than likely that your people are not engaged, not achieving maximum capacity and not very fulfilled at work. Fortunately, changing the culture is not impossible, but it does take a leader who is willing to do so. If you are or aspire to be that leader, then the remainder of the book is devoted to helping you learn why and how to achieve that end.

Tendencies / Attitudes Regarding:	Leader / Follower Relationships:	Power Wielder / Subordinate Relationships:
Power	Influential & Dynamic	Positional and Controlling
Management & Supervision	Developmental	Dictatorial
Prevailing Culture	Humane & Genuine	Commodified & Manipulative
People	Committed to & Valued	Used & Consumed
Human Interactions	Respectful & Loving	Intimidating
Rewards & Benefits	Mutually Beneficial	Selfishly Prosperous
Intended Outcomes	Transformational	Exploitative

[1] Burns, J. MacGregor. *Leadership* (New York: Harper and Row, 1978), p. 18.

[2] Levine, Mel M.D. *The Myth of Laziness* (Simon & Schuster; New York, NY; 2003) p. 1.

[3] Investorwords.com: *Commodity*: http://www.investorwords.com/975/commodity.

[4] Becker, Gary S. *A Theory of Marriage: Part II:* Journal of Political Economy, Vol. 82, No. 2, (Mar-Apr 1974) p.S11-S26).

[5] Rifkin, Jeremy. *Customers, Not Products, Are the Chief Commodity of the New Economy*; http://www. commondreams.org/views/032300-105.htm (March 23, 2000).

[6] Welch, Jack with John A. Byrne; *Jack. Straight From the Gut* (Warner Business Books; New York, 2001), pp. 121-123

[7] Ibid. p. 123.

[8] Ibid, p. 229.

[9] Collins, Jim. *Good to Great*. (Harper Business; New York, NY; 2001) p. 13.

[10] BusinessWeekOnline.com; *How Jack Welch Runs GE*; June 8, 1998; www.businessweek.com/1998/ 23/b358/001.htm.

[11] Ibid

[12] Ibid

[13] Nouwen, Henri, J.M. *In the Name of Jesus: Reflections on Christian Leadership* (The Crossroad Publishing Company; New York, 1989) pp. 74-75.

[14] Ibid; p. 77.

[15] Ibid; p. 79.

[16] Gittell, Jody Hoffer; *The Southwest Airlines Way*; (McGraw-Hill; New York, 2003).

[17] Ibid.

[18] DeGiorgio, Rich. *Thought Leaders: Lance Secretan, Developer of Higher Ground Leadership, Inspire! What Great Leaders Do*; http://www.hr.com/hrcom/index.cfmlweeklymag/FD2C4120-7389-4746- A1368F2531A43196?ost=wmfeature.

[19] Dickens, Charles; A *Christmas Carol*. In *Charles Dickens, Four Complete Novels*; (Bantam Classic, 1990).

[20] Burns, J. MacGregor. *Leadership* (New York: Harper and Row, 1978), p. 18.

[21] Ibid. p. 20.

Chapter 2
Leadership Evaluation and Action Discovery (LEAD)

Evaluate the kind of relationship dynamics that exist in your organization by completing the following checklist regarding your culture:

A. Evaluate the kind of relationship dynamics that exist in your organization by checking the answers that best describe its culture:		YES	NO
1.	Rather than trying to control people through power and authority, leaders in our organization try more to listen to, influence and persuade them.	❏	❏
2.	For the most part people in our organization try to be genuine and treat each other humanely rather than trying to manipulate and use each other.	❏	❏
3.	Leaders in our organization commit to and value people rather than use them to achieve selfish purposes.	❏	❏
4.	Leaders in our organization encourage and build confidence in people by demonstrating respect for them rather than intimidating them through disrespect and power wielding.	❏	❏
5.	Consistent efforts are made to benefit most people in the organization rather than just a few.	❏	❏
6.	Consistent efforts are made to develop people and even transform them into leaders rather than just exploit them.	❏	❏
7.	Leaders in our organization tend to trust in the talent and abilities of people.	❏	❏

B. If you checked one or more "no" answers, there is a high probability that your organizational relationships and culture are not as effective as they could be. Therefore, according to the findings of several key studies the likelihood is high that your people are less engaged and less productive and your enterprise is less profitable than it could be. With that in mind, please answer the following:		YES	NO
1.	Do you see the need to change the relationship dynamics?	❑	❑
2.	Do you believe that your organization can change in ways that your people can become more engaged in their work and more productive and your enterprise can become more profitable?	❑	❑

PART TWO

II. Understanding and Leading by the Principles of Covenant

Introduction

While the purposes and people of a covenant may vary, the principles and characteristics are fairly consistent. As defined in the previous section, a covenant is a relationship in which two or more people who *trust* and respect each other; willingly bind themselves together in pursuit of a *common and ethical purpose*. They are guided in that pursuit by a set of ethical *core values* with which their behavior is aligned. The lack of *alignment* is where ethical breaches occur and the covenant is broken. That's why covenant partners display an almost unwavering *commitment* to the core values of the covenant as well as the people, the purposes and the *common good* the covenant serves.

If the relationship is truly a covenant, it will benefit all the partners. Of course, achieving that assumes that the pursuit of both the common purposes of the covenant and the common good it serves will be based on principles or some notion of *objective truth* and not just preference or power. Also, where covenants do exist, the people of the covenant will derive a sense of *meaning and momentum* and ultimately hope from both the relationship and the larger purpose it serves. Certainly there are challenges associated with maintaining the covenant and the trust that supports it requires ongoing *recognition* of the value and the contributions of the covenant partners. It also demands a willingness of those partners to embrace a *self-imposed accountability* for keeping the covenant.

Finally, living and working within the context of a covenant is not simply a multi-step linear process that comes from the application of a few techniques. Developing human relationships is never that simple because people are complex beings with a variety of needs and desires. In much the same way an effective coach must adjust and adapt his or her methods in order to accommodate different personalities, engage players and build a team, so too must an effective leader adjust and adapt to achieve the same with followers. Embracing the concept of covenant is first and foremost a *choice* of both a lifestyle that is driven by specific values, principles and obligations and a worldview that influences everything a person does. Making that choice is not always easy in the fast paced, immediate gratification, "keep your options open" culture in which we live. Living contrary to the prevailing culture always has and always will require thoughtfulness, character and ultimately leadership to achieve. To help readers better understand what that choice involves, I have included in this next section both a more in-depth discussion of the chief principles and primary characteristics of a covenant, and I have provided real life examples and illustrations of those principles and characteristics in action.

Chapter 3

Understand and Serve Your Common Purpose

In the latter part of the 19th Century, acclaimed Russian novelist Leo Tolstoy made some important observations about the crucial nature of having a sense of purpose. At one point in his career, despite the great fame and success he had achieved, Tolstoy was despondent and empty. He came to the conclusion that life was without purpose and meaningless, and that led him to frequent thoughts of suicide. With his rational mind Tolstoy searched for a sense of purpose beyond his immediate circumstances and his substantial material wealth, but he could find nothing. He explained, *"Rational knowledge brought me to the recognition that life was meaningless, my life stopped and I wanted to destroy myself."* [1] Tolstoy continued to search and eventually he found a sense of transcending purpose in faith, but getting to that point was a long and painful struggle that almost destroyed him.

In *Man's Search for Meaning,* psychiatrist Victor Frankl also explains the importance of purpose by providing a vivid look at his three year struggle for survival in several Nazi prison camps including Auschwitz. He noted that in the midst of such a dehumanizing captivity, it was important for him and other prisoners to have a strong sense of purpose and to allow that purpose to transcend their immediate circumstances. Frankl explains that Nietzche captured the essence of his point about the importance of purpose to survival when he said, *"He who has a why (a purpose) to live for, can bear with any how."* In a chilling account, Frankl described the fate of prisoners who lost their sense of purpose while they were in captivity, "Woe to him who saw no more sense in his life, no aim, no purpose, and therefore no point in carrying on. He was soon lost." [2]

Surviving and Prospering with Faith and Vision - Understanding and then serving a common purpose require a certain amount of faith, faith in an idea, faith in a person or persons, faith in an institution, faith that the purpose being served is worthy of the effort, and more. But as important as faith is to purpose, so too is vision. Vision provides hope that something better can and will happen in the future.

Consider the experience of my father-in-law, George Rogers, during World War II. In 1941 as young men all over America were being drafted into the service, George decided to enlist in the army. He arrived at his hometown recruiting office in St. Louis, and the major in charge of recruiting convinced him that the Philippine Islands were a poor man's paradise. George enlisted and shortly thereafter he was shipped out to the west coast. As political tensions and aggression heated up, things moved quickly and about one month later his unit was receiving a final medical inspection before boarding a ship to embark for the Philippines. They arrived in October, and he and six other men were assigned to the 4th Separate Chemical Company. As it turned out, George was the only one of the seven to survive.

Two months later, on December 7th, the Japanese attacked Pearl Harbor. Then on December 8, the Japanese continued their assaults and landed on an island off the northern coast of Luzon, in the Philippines. The Chemical Company was ordered first to Manila and then to Bataan. In early January, thousands of Filipino and American troops retreated under heavy fire. On April 9, 1942, after fierce fighting, General Edward P. King, Jr., surrendered to the Japanese.

Subsequent to General King's surrender of Bataan, the surviving forces, which according to most estimates numbered about 76,000 Americans and Filipinos, were taken prisoner and forced to march over 100 kilometers. The trip lasted several days and took place in scorching heat, with no planned food or water stops. Since the troops had been on limited rations for three months as they resisted the Japanese, they were already weak, tired and suffering from sickness. Men carried their sick friends but often as they fell, they would be shot, stabbed with a bayonet or run over by tanks. By the time they finally arrived several days later in San Fernando, an estimated 10,000 men had died and the survivors were hungry, sick and exhausted. Immediately, George and the rest of the survivors were loaded into steel box cars and shipped to Camp O'Donnell by rail in temperatures that reached an estimated 110 to 120 degrees. But the death did not stop when they reached the camp. Within the first 40 days after the march 1500 additional Americans died and by July of 1942, 25,000 Filipinos had died.

George and most of the other prisoners were eventually shipped to Japan. He was forced into hard labor in a steel mill. In his 3 1/2 years in Japanese prison camps, George was put on a starvation diet that left his 6'3" frame weighing only 85 pounds. In addition to the hard work and poor sanitary conditions, he endured beatings, humiliation, malaria, dry beriberi, amoebic dysentery, quarantine and isolation, loneliness, helping bury 1,600 Americans, and much more at the hands of his captors.

Nevertheless, despite these circumstances; he was not defeated and he never lost hope. Not only was George able to survive, but also he has prospered. When I asked him what sustained him during his years in captivity, he replied that two things had helped him survive. Interestingly, both of these things were ideas, ideas that shaped his thinking, added meaning and purpose to his life and thereby bolstered his mental state. First, George believed in God and he had a strong sense of who he was in relation to God. That faith bolstered him with an understanding that despite his circumstances, God cared about what happened to George and he still had a purpose for him even in the midst of these terrible circumstances. This faith and understanding also led George to believe that God could and would see him through his trouble one day at a time. The confidence and strong sense of self this gave him, allowed George to choose to be optimistic and choose not to be bitter or defeated. He also noted that the prisoners who lacked a sense of transcending purpose tended to be quickly overwhelmed by their circumstances and they often gave up and died.

Second, as a result of those beliefs and his sense of purpose, George developed a vision for the future that added even more meaning to his life. That meaning allowed him to transcend his present circumstances as he planned for the future. After the war, he would go back to his home town of St. Louis, date and then marry Barbara Randall. Then he would go on to college, get a degree from St. Louis University, secure a good paying job and help raise a large family. George thought about that vision and discussed it frequently with a friend who was also from St. Louis. His friend actually planned to marry Barbara's sister Carol, and as a result their common purpose and vision for the future bonded them together in an even tighter friendship. Unfortunately George's friend succumbed to sickness and died, but George continued to work the vision out in detail and keep it alive. Clearly, the meaning it provided helped sustain him:

> *"You have to have something to look forward to," said George. "We had on a day to day basis, nothing to look forward to. Our news was six months to a year old. And we didn't get any correspondence. Yes, having something to look forward to was very helpful. And, of course, having someone to talk to who knew the Randall family helped. We talked about the Randall girls who were very beautiful, and I said that I was going to, if she were still available, why I would certainly make Barbara my wife".* [3]

After George was liberated but before being released to civilian life, he and the rest of the former prisoners received a pep talk of sorts, from a team of doctors who addressed them as a group.

> *"They said that I would probably be dead before age 45," George recalled. "Don't bother to go to school because I would be unable to keep up the grades. Don't think about having children because I think that they thought it would be impossible. They said my eyes would be gone, my teeth would be gone, my hair would be gone. Well they were wrong in every*

respect. I graduated with honors from St. Louis University, taking a four year course in three years. I married Barbara and had five wonderful children with five wonderful spouses and 14 grandkids. I still have my teeth, I still have my eyes and I still have my hair. Of course, I didn't dwell on the fact that I was going to be dead at age 45, you can bet on that! I just took the positive approach. [4]

The experience of George Rogers offers a powerful illustration of how a strong sense of purpose, bolstered by faith and a clear vision for the future, can sustain a person in the midst of some very bleak circumstances. George's vision of what could be and his faith-based philosophy of life have not only helped him survive, they have also allowed him to build a successful family and a business career that continues today (at his choice) as he approaches 90 years of age.

Whether it's in a family, a friendship, a prosperous career or a prison camp, people need a sense of purpose to flourish. However, that sense of purpose can not endure apart from some sense of faith and vision that pursuit of the purpose will make things better. As Frankl, Tolstoy, George Rogers and others have demonstrated, understanding and serving a common purpose are crucial not only to the success but also to the survival of individuals and relationships. Interestingly, what these people have observed about the importance of purpose to the survival of human beings, we have observed about the survival of businesses and many other kinds of organizations. When a sense of purpose is lost, it's not long before people reach a point of fragmentation, apathy and despair and sometimes the organization dies.

Asking and Answering Key Questions - For covenants to develop, there must be an understanding among the covenant partners of the purposes around which their relationships were formed. No matter how large or small a group is, it is virtually impossible to lead or follow effectively in it without first understanding the group's purpose or mission. That's why when our company facilitates planning; we begin with the purpose statement. If they do not have a purpose or mission statement, we help them create one by asking and answering, in concise fashion, two questions about the organization: *Who are they? and Why do they exist?* Though the statement is rarely longer than one or two sentences, it is important that everyone involved understand it. Everything that is done within the organization should flow in some way from that purpose statement. Also, if the purpose is to be meaningful, then the process of discovering or understanding it can not be self-focused. Regardless of whether it's an individual or organization doing the asking, the answers to these questions must always be considered in relationship to other people.

This is exactly the point made by Victor Frankl when he described life in Nazi prison camps and talked about the sustaining nature of purpose. Surviving meant that the prisoners had to change their attitudes. He explained, *"We had to learn ourselves and, furthermore, we had to teach despairing men, that it did not really matter what we expected from life, but rather what life expected from us... Life ultimately means taking the responsibility to find the right answers to its problems and to fulfill the tasks which it constantly sets for each individual."*[5]

Assuming that Frankl's observations are correct, then common purposes that sustain both individual and organizational life, are ones that provide answers to problems and/or fulfill responsibilities in relationship to other people. Fully understanding our common purpose in this context, implies that leaders ask and answer at least three additional key questions as they create and pursue a common purpose: *What problems will we solve? What responsibilities will we fulfill?* and *Who will we serve in the process?*

Adding Knowledge to Your Understanding – Leadership, particularly in the context of a covenant, involves more than just understanding the purpose of an organization; it also involves understanding the people who have that purpose in common with one another. As a leader that means I must add knowledge about the people I lead to my understanding of the purposes we share. Accordingly, if I know the people and understand the purposes of our organization, then that should influence both the way I pursue those purposes and the way I relate to others in the process. This comes full cycle because, if I endeavor to lead by the principles of covenant, then my relationships must be based on more than just the pursuit of my own selfish purposes that promise to serve only me. Instead, covenants are based on the pursuit of common and ethical purposes that promise also to serve the mutual needs and goals of all the stakeholders. But to serve the stakeholders, leaders must know them. Who are the stakeholders? They are any people who have a stake or interest in the successful future of the organization. In a business that includes leaders, partners, employees, customers, stockholders and vendors; in other kinds of organizations it includes donors, members, students, clients, volunteers, patients, alumni and more. Whoever the stakeholders are, knowing them requires a consistent effort on the part of the leader to communicate with them.

Essentially what binds stakeholder relationships together in any setting are the purposes stakeholders have in common with the organization and the degree to which those purposes are served. That is essentially what James MacGregor Burns meant when he said that relationships are nothing apart from being linked by common purposes, ones that are bigger and more meaningful than our own selfish purposes[6]. Relationships, if they are to be meaningful (and effective), are formed by the convergence and subsequent fulfillment of individual and organizational purposes. Therefore, one of the first responsibilities of a leader is to understand and help define the purpose or purposes of the group being led. Beyond that it is also crucial for a leader to know and understand the needs and aspirations of the organizational stakeholders. Of course, in most cases among the chief needs of stakeholders is to be known and appreciated by the leader. Finally, once the leader achieves appropriate levels of knowledge and understanding regarding both the purposes and the people, he or she must then communicate those purposes and pursue them in ways that are clearly understood and embraced by the stakeholders. That doesn't just happen by chance. As you will read in the examples that follow, it takes a deliberate and strategic effort on the part of a leader.

Operating like a Pastor - It's not uncommon for pastors to be admonished to operate more like a CEO of a business or large nonprofit organization, but seldom if ever is a CEO admonished to operate more like a pastor. At first glance it would not appear that pastors and CEO's have much in common. Yet, if they are effective, the best pastors and their churches have a clear sense of purpose and therefore a great deal to teach CEOs. For example, in 2006 Bob Russell retired as pastor at Southeast Christian Church in Louisville, Kentucky after serving in that capacity for more than 40 years. During his tenure the church grew from about 50 members who then met in the basement of a home, to more than 20,000 members who meet today in a state-of-the-art 9,700 seat sanctuary on a 100 acre campus. His last decade of service brought heightened visibility from the outside world. Bob would often be interviewed by people asking about the Church's secrets to success. In most cases Bob said simply that it was a result of Providential blessing and the efforts of the church leadership to "keep the main thing (preaching and teaching the Gospel and ministering to people) the main thing." In other words, Bob is saying that an important part of success is to understand the purpose of the Church and to keep that purpose in the forefront as the primary driver of everything that is done.

Bob clearly understands the purpose and the people of the church, and for many years he and the church elders have communicated and pursued that purpose in ways that are commonly understood and embraced by a large majority of the members. The mission statement is printed in much of the literature, and it is posted in several locations around the church. Also, the pastor and others regularly preach and teach on the scriptural basis of the mission, and all of the church ministries are organized around it. To ensure that the congregation understands the mission and values of the church, the ministerial staff offers a series of eight one hour classes entitled, "What We Believe," for all prospective and/or new church members. It covers lessons on the mission, guiding principles and key doctrines of the church as well as the practical application of core Gospel values that the people of the church are encouraged to emulate. Through these sessions not only do people learn more about the "who we are and why we exist" of the church community (the common purpose); they also learn both what is available to and expected from them as members. Bob commented, that through the series he intends,

"...to tell people up front what they can expect from this body (church)...It gives them an opportunity to plug into what the values of this church really are. And we say, 'Ok, here's what we stand for; here's where we're coming from; here's what you can expect from the pulpit.'"[7]

Just like they do in other kinds of organizations, people join the church with different intentions and needs as well as different individual purposes they hope to fulfill. That's why, to accommodate those needs, there are so many different programs and ministries; but individuals are also encouraged to give back to those ministries by volunteering. Each year there is actually a campaign where church members are asked to sign up to volunteer their time in such ministries as childcare, teaching, foreign missions, recreation and sports, music, medical missions, counseling and much more. In essence, they are being encouraged to use their talents and resources to help in achieving the common purpose of the church. It is truly amazing to see the thousands of people who volunteer many hours each year. Beyond the participation and volunteer hours, church members further demonstrated their commitment to the common purpose by contributing $77 million in capital funds, over and above their regular offerings between 1995 and 2005. Total church giving for that same period is close to $250 million, a clear indication that church members understand and enthusiastically support the common purpose.

With some 20,000 members and more than 300 employees, the church long ago outgrew this pastor's ability to control everything. To be successful in achieving the common purpose Bob explained that he has had to adapt and change. He commented,

"When I started off I was the pastor. I had 125 people. I can visit the hospital, counsel in the marriages. I can be there when the kids are playing baseball. I know everyone's names. And then it starts growing beyond my control. Now I can either panic and feel like I am losing it and try to smother it, or I can let it grow and change with it... and so I had to change from

> *being a pastor to being an administrator and then eventually*
> *to being a shepherd of the staff and the leaders of the church."*[8]

Bob noted that another important part of accommodating the growth of the church while maintaining the same focus on achieving the common purpose, is recruiting the right volunteer leaders and staff and then giving them freedom to use their talents. He explained,

> *"...90% of leadership is hiring (or recruiting) the right people.*
> *You get the wrong person and it does not matter how much*
> *oversight, how much direction you give. But you get the right*
> *person and give them the responsibility and the resources and*
> *encouragement and its amazing what they'll do. You try to*
> *smother these people and box them in much, and they're going*
> *to work to please you rather than please the Lord and fulfill*
> *their giftedness. So I really believe in hiring (good) people and*
> *then giving them the freedom to do what they are gifted to*
> *do."*[9]

Granted, the mission and dynamics of a church are different from those of other kinds of organizations and, there are probably as many power wielders in the pastorate as there are leaders. Nevertheless, as far as the processes of communicating (or sometimes preaching), building consensus and leading around a common purpose are concerned, CEOs could learn a thing or two from effective pastors like Bob.

Of course, this also assumes that both the purposes and relationships of the organization and the people who lead it are ethical. By being ethical I am not suggesting that it has to be faith-based in the same way a church is. I am saying that ethical means that organizational purposes and relationships are not only bound by common interests and goals, they are also governed by principles that serve both the law and the norms of the larger society. While this alignment is an important responsibility of leaders, it is not their only responsibility. There are additional responsibilities related to the pursuit of a common and ethical purpose that influence relationships and help define what it means to be a true leader.

Recognizing Responsibility to Others – Sacrificing Self-interest - As a leader it should go without saying that understanding and then pursuing a common purpose will also serve my own self-interests in ways that are personally gratifying. But the benefits of pursuing a common purpose in a covenant always extend beyond self to the other people involved in the relationship. By definition, a common purpose must consider both responsibility to and consideration for the interests of the other people of the covenant. If being a leader means that at some point I need to engage followers, then it makes sense that my interests must extend beyond self and sometimes my gratification must be delayed. Simply stated, in defining and pursuing a common purpose, leaders must recognize their responsibility to and for others. That means demonstrating a commitment not only to the organization's well being, but also to the personal and/or professional well being of the stakeholders.

For example, in 2005, the Chicago White Sox won a World Series, and the New England Patriots won three Super Bowls in four years by focusing on team rather than individual performance. Not that individual performance is unimportant, but it must be tempered and balanced with what is best for the team. In the case of these two sports teams it meant that at times a star receiver had to serve as a decoy or a power hitter had to lay down a bunt. As the saying goes in sports, both of these are examples of "taking one for the team." It means that players are willing to sacrifice individual glory for overall team performance. In order for that to happen, leaders must create a culture of "sacrificing self interest" to achieve a greater good. That usually occurs first by leaders modeling that attribute themselves in their daily actions; finding others in the organization who will follow that lead and then rewarding people when they do so. It requires leaders to be strategic in their actions and to strike a balance between their own self interest and their responsibility to and for others.

For a leader to achieve that necessary balance and build such a culture requires a certain amount of selflessness and even humility. That's exactly what researcher and author Jim Collins discovered in his study of "Good to Great" companies (eleven companies that returned an average of $471 for every $1 invested over 35 years). He found that the most effective leaders (what he calls level five leaders) are a *"paradoxical blend of personal humility and professional will."* In talking about "personal humility," the author does not mean weakness. Instead he is referring to leaders who are secure enough to check their egos at the door and then do what is best for the organization. In other words what happens in high performing "Good to Great" organizations is not always about accommodating their leaders and raising their individual profiles. It's about advancing the organization and its well being first. According to Collins, the lack of humility among high profile level 4 leaders with big personalities is why they were not nearly as effective as the level 5, "humble" leaders of "Good to Great" companies.[10]

What Collins is demonstrating in his research is simply that in order to achieve long-term sustained results, leaders will have to become more focused on the larger mission of the enterprise and less focused on themselves. Recognizing and acting on one's responsibility to others and to a larger mission is an essential part of establishing a covenant; it is also how leaders build credibility and motivate people to follow them. It sometimes requires them to sacrifice self-interest in favor of the common purpose and/or to delay immediate gratification in favor of longer term success.

For example, while there may be a few dissenters, the vast majority of Americans and historians would agree that our founding fathers were leaders who covenanted together and sacrificed their self-interest in favor of the common good. Consider just the cases of John Witherspoon, Abraham Clark and Richard Stockton, New Jersey delegates who signed the Declaration of Independence. Mr. Witherspoon, who had been president of a college that eventually became Princeton, fled with his family as the British occupied the college buildings and burned the library that held many of his most prized books. Abraham Clark had to leave his wife's sick bed to flee from the British and when he returned his farm was destroyed, his wife had died and his children were gone. Richard Stockton had been a well-esteemed, distinguished and wealthy man. He went into hiding but an informant told the British where he was. They dragged him out in the middle of the night, stripped him and took his property. The British destroyed his home and threw him in prison in New York where he was malnourished and regularly exposed to the cold weather. As a result, he contracted a disease that eventually killed him. Towards the end of his life when his fortune had been depleted, he had to rely on friends for accommodations and he suffered from depression.[11]

It would have been easy for these and others of our founders simply to ignore the quest for liberty. Many of them were wealthy and they lived quite comfortably. Still, wealth was not their primary motivator; it was the common and ethical purpose of liberty for all Americans that bound them together in a covenant and led them to sacrifice their self-interest in favor of achieving this larger purpose. When leaders recognize their responsibility to others and sacrifice some of their self-interest in favor of a common purpose that serves the common good, it inspires followers to serve that same purpose in ways that endure.

Going Beyond Performance to Service – When one refers to the "common purpose" of an organization, it assumes that many and not just a few people will be served by that purpose. Though the language of "common purpose" is used, sometimes the organizational reality can be quite different. For example, there are occasions when our company works with individual clients who have "big personality" leaders at the top. It's not uncommon for us to hear these CEOs talk of things like "team" and "shared vision". Yet, the culture they create is something quite different from that. Instead of a covenant, their approach to leadership is more like a self-serving contract that encompasses a series of performance and power-driven transactions and even manipulations between the person in charge and the rest of the team. Here the notion of common purpose is lost because everything and everyone in the company seem to serve the "leader's" immediate purposes, often without regard to the long-term cost.

True, individuals "in charge" can wield power and, in the short-term, achieve high levels of quantitative success, but they are not necessarily leading. While leadership cannot be separated from performance, it also involves more than just a simple performance contract or a series of transactions. In fact, leaders understand that "hitting the numbers" at any cost may not be in the long-term best interest of the company or the common purpose it serves. As Collins' research demonstrated, leadership is about building credibility, using influence, demonstrating commitment and serving others both inside and outside the company to achieve its common and ethical purpose.

In this context, leadership has very little to do with charisma and very much to do with setting the example and building trust as the leader and followers work toward the common purpose and serve others both inside and outside of the organization. For leaders in particular that requires a conscious effort to go beyond the basic performance expectations of the job and serve the purposes and people of the organization. In the 1970s former AT&T executive, Robert Greenleaf, made this very observation when he began writing about the concept of servant leadership. He noted simply that the best way to build trust with people and get them to follow is to serve them.[12] Servant leadership does not exclude performance, but it does recognize that performance is enhanced when followers are served by the people who lead them. It means that leaders build credibility by making and keeping their promises to stakeholders; promises that allow the leader to serve both the common purpose and the stakeholders simultaneously.

In the same way it occurs in the Greenleaf Model, where effective leaders serve their followers, so too do covenant partners serve each other. Like the leader-follower relationship, covenants do not exclude performance; they enhance it as the covenant partners freely give to and receive from each other. However, covenants are about far more than performance and so is leadership. In life and in work most of us aspire to achieve not only success but also respect and fulfillment as we relate to other people. Getting to that point requires that we live and relate in reciprocal relationships, giving to others and not just receiving from them. In a covenant, partners must work towards understanding and then achieving a common purpose. However, at some point they must also go beyond simply performing their duties if they intend to achieve the full benefits of the relationship.

Essentially in a covenant each partner serves not only the common purpose of the covenant but also the other person or persons of the covenant. Over time this builds trust and causes the bonds of the covenant relationship to be tightened and the people to be supported in ways that can be transformational. Understanding the common purpose in this way enhances both the achievement of that common purpose and the growth and fulfillment of the covenant partners. At its best that is exactly what effective leaders do or at least aspire to do.

In a business setting people may come together seemingly for the purpose of making widgets for a profit. But beyond the activities of widget making, leaders also understand that they have a responsibility to meet the needs of both the people making the widgets and the people buying them. In that way the common purpose and the promise of the business go beyond profit to that of serving mankind. That's exactly what Henry Ford meant when he said, *"For a long time people believed that the only purpose of industry is to make a profit. They are wrong. Its purpose is to serve the general welfare."*[13]

Sometimes serving the general welfare requires that the leader sacrifice some self-interest to serve the needs of others both inside and outside of the organization. That's because relationships can't always be about the leader's needs, especially if the leader hopes to maintain credibility and continue leading. When leaders are able not only to recognize their responsibility to and for others but also to help their followers embrace the same, then covenants develop among stakeholders. Consequently those covenants allow stakeholders to pursue the common purpose freely and without restraint because they can trust that others in the covenant have their best interest in mind. It makes sense that when people are served by the covenant, it frees them to reciprocate in like manner by serving the people and the purposes of the covenant. As an entire group of people understand and pursue the common purpose and serve the general welfare by making widgets or anything else, they can do so with a spirit of cooperation and an eye on excellence because of the covenant they share.

Elevating Followers - Leaders create opportunities for followers to experience a sense of individual purpose by helping followers understand the larger mission of the organization and then allowing them both to align with it and to use their gifts in pursuing it. This kind of covenant leadership often has a transformational effect in ways that elevate the awareness, motives, values and behavior of those followers. Abraham Lincoln was a transformational leader because of how he pursued the ideals set forth in the Declaration of Independence and how he related to others when he did it. Donald Phillips, author of *Lincoln on Leadership*, notes that Lincoln worked to *"motivate and mobilize followers by persuading them to take ownership of their roles in a more grand mission."*[14] In his service as president, Lincoln was able to elevate and transform followers and eventually an entire country because, as Phillips observed, *"He treated everyone with the same courtesy and respect.... He lifted people out of their everyday selves and into a higher level of performance, achievement and awareness. He obtained extraordinary results from ordinary people by instilling purpose in their endeavors."*[15]

Perhaps the greatest example of a servant leader who understood the purpose He had in common with His followers, established a covenant with them, and thereby elevated and transformed them; is found in the person of Jesus of Nazareth. Greenleaf described Jesus as *"... a leader, as I see it, in the fullest meaning of the term."*[16] Likewise, leadership guru and author, Ken Blanchard said, *"After studying both the theory and practice of leadership for more than 35 years, I have found that Jesus is the greatest leadership model of all times."*[17]

Though He was an acclaimed and revered teacher and prophet, Jesus lived a humble life of service and commitment to His disciples. He had a clear purpose for His followers and He made that purpose well known: *"I have come that they may have life, and that they may have it more abundantly."*[18] They would experience that abundant life by believing in Jesus and His promises, living by the principles He taught and spreading the Gospel to the world. He invested time and energy in teaching and mentoring the apostles, and as a result they were eventually transformed into leaders. Through Jesus' revolutionary teaching, His life of service and ultimately His death, He established a common purpose and a new and powerful covenant with His followers that was based on that purpose. Further, as a result of Jesus' elevating and transforming leadership, not only did He help His followers understand and embrace the common purpose, but also He inspired such a strong commitment among His closest disciples that all of them were willing to suffer persecution, and all but one of them died for the cause.

Similarly, when leaders make and keep promises in pursuit of the common purpose, promises that serve both the organization and its people, it builds credibility and trust, and it demonstrates the leader's integrity. It also makes it safe for people to follow and thereby be transformed. Peter Drucker (2001) put it this way:

> *"The final requirement of effective leadership is to earn trust. Otherwise, there won't be any followers – and the only definition of a leader is someone who has followers. To trust a leader, it is not necessary to like him. Nor is it necessary to agree with him. Trust is the conviction that the leader means what he says. It is a belief in something very old-fashioned, called 'integrity.' A leader's actions and a leader's professed beliefs must be congruent, or at least compatible."*[19]

Attending to Process, Not Just Outcomes - Certainly, Mr. Drucker's comments imply that leadership is a bit more complex than completing tasks, fulfilling contractual obligations or reaching numeric goals. Those may be by-products of effective leadership, but they do not capture its essence. A leader's effectiveness in pursuing a common and ethical purpose is determined as much by the process of how he achieves something as it is by what he achieves. Hitler was certainly charismatic and he achieved a great deal. Yet, in the language of Peter Drucker, he was a "misleader" because of all the evil and suffering he inflicted.[20] In the end, his "mis-leadership" or "power-wielding" was far more about his own selfish purposes than it was about the common and ethical purposes of the German people. To Hitler people became objects to be used and manipulated for his own purposes, or destroyed and discarded at his whims. Their value was not intrinsic but solely utilitarian and those attitudes led to the

Nazi concentration camps. The barbaric and inhumane treatment that Victor Frankl and millions of others experienced is a horrifying example of taking such attitudes to an extreme but in some ways logical conclusion.

The intrinsic worth and humanity of individuals should cause leaders to serve people as well as receive from them in the process of pursuing a common purpose and achieving desired outcomes. Whenever that concept of worth is forgotten or even discarded as it was in Hitler's case, then it's easy for people simply to become commodities or objects available for the selfish exploitation and manipulation of those in power. In some respects Hitler delivered on his contractual promise to elevate Germany, but the process of fulfilling that contract lacked an ethical base. It was brutally enforced through power wielding, deceit and intimidation, and because of that, eventually Hitler failed. Apart from a relationship based on common and ethical purposes and a process that demonstrates a concern for individuals as people with needs instead of commodities, leadership cannot exist. That's why it is usually the case that the more the selfish purposes of the "mis-leader" are served, the more power, deceit and manipulation are required to keep people serving those purposes.

It is clear from the experiences of Frankl, Tolstoy and many others that having purpose in life is crucial to long term survival. The same is true in organizational life. To sustain long term health and well being, the purpose of the organization must be clearly understood. Beyond that, the purpose must transcend individual preferences and immediate circumstances; it must serve and elevate others and finally, it must be pursued in an ethical manner. No doubt, achieving all of that requires a strong sense of purpose but it also requires leaders who are able to build enduring and productive relationships.

---

[1] Tolstoy, Leo. *Faith Provides Life's Meaning,"* from *Classical Philosophical Questions,* (James A. Gould, editor; Prentice Hall, Englewood Cliffs, New Jersey, 1994 p. 627-638.

[2] Frankl, Victor E. *Man's Search for Meaning*. (New York: Beacon Press, 1992) p. 84-85.

[3] Rogers, George. Interview with Len Moisan, February 2007.

[4] Ibid.

[5] Frankl, Victor E. *Man's Search for Meaning*. (New York: Beacon Press, 1992) p. 85.

[6] Burns, James MacGregor. *Leadership*. (New York: Harper and Row, 1978) p. 18.

[7] Russell, Bob; Interview with Leonard J. Moisan, July 16, 1996.

[8] Ibid.

[9] Ibid.

[10] Collins, Jim. *Good to Great*. (Harper Business; New York, NY; 2001) p. 13.

[11] Nathaniel, Dwight. *The Lives of Signers*. (1876). In *Our Sacred Honor: Words of Advice From the Founders in Stories, Letters, Poems and Speeches* (William J. Bennet, editor; Broadman & Holman Publishers; Nashville, Tennessee; 1997) pp. 30-32.

[12] Greenleaf, R. K.; *Servant Leadership* (New York: Panelist Press; 1977).

[13] Ford, Henry; *Corporations and Morality*; Thomas Donaldson (New Jersey: Prentice Hall; 1982) p. 57.

[14] Phillips, Donald T.; *Lincoln on Leadership* (New York, New York: Warner Books; 1992) pp. 172-173.

[15] Ibid.

[16] Greenleaf, Robert K.; *On Becoming a Servant Leader*; Edited by Don M. Frick & Larry C. Spears (Jossey-Bass, San Francisco, 1996) p. 325.

[17] Blanchard, Ken; Lead Like Jesus 3; www.ccn-tv/programming/event/evt_18nov04.htm.

[18] Scripture taken from the New King James Version, (John 10:10) Copyright © 1979, 1980, 1982 by Thomas Nelson, Inc. Nashville, TN, Used by Permission. All rights reserved.

[19] Drucker, Peter F.; *The Essential Drucker* (New York: Harper Business; 2001) p. 271.

[20] Ibid., p. 270.

Chapter 3
Leadership Evaluation and Action Discovery (LEAD)

In any kind of organization what binds stakeholder relationships together are the purposes they have in common with the organization as well as how well those purposes are served. Leadership expert, James McGregor Burns, noted that not only is leadership a relationship, but also a relationship is nothing apart from being linked by common purposes. Using the information in this chapter, please answer the following questions:

	A. In no more than two sentences (preferably one), describe who you are and why you exist as an organization:
1.	The _____ is ... *(organization name)* We exist to
2.	Who are your stakeholders (people, groups who have a stake in the future of your organization – i.e., customers, employees, etc.)? _____ _____ _____ _____ _____ _____ _____ _____ _____ _____ _____ _____ _____ _____ _____ _____

3.	What purpose or purposes does your organization have in common with these stakeholders? Stakeholder Common Purposes _____ _____ _____ _____ _____ _____ _____ _____ _____ _____ _____ _____ _____ _____ _____ _____ _____ _____

B. Using information from Chapter 3, please answer the following questions:

1.	How can we as an organization or team better serve these purposes?
2.	What responsibilities do I have to other stakeholders in the organization?
3.	In what ways do I or can I sacrifice some of my self-interest in order to serve better the interests of and my responsibilities to stakeholders?

Chapter 4

Identify the Common Good that Purpose Serves

There is a great tradition in America of pursuing individual success in ways that are balanced by serving others. Sociologist Robert Bellah talked about this balance in his best selling book, *Habits of the Heart*. Bellah's work is actually a study of American society in which he examines both individualism and commitment in American life. Success, according to Bellah, is quite different from happiness and joy. The former is an individualistic pursuit that comes from free competition in an open market. In that competition, the ones who come out ahead are the ones who are considered to be successful. By contrast, joy and happiness come not from competition but from giving oneself to the service of others without counting the cost. [1]

Bellah argues that success and joy *"complement and counter balance each other."* He explains, *"The self interest demanded by individualistic pursuit of success needs to be balanced by voluntary concern for others."* [2] Bellah's point is that in America there has always been an unresolved tension between the individual pursuit of success (private interest) and the community concern for others (common good). Even though society holds very dear the notion of private interest and the individual pursuit of success, to maintain civility and order individuals living in a free society must also assume responsibility to manage this tension and attend to the needs of others. Bellah explains, *"...in a free republic, it is the task of the citizen, whether ruler or ruled, to cultivate civic virtue in order to mitigate the tension and render it manageable."* [3]

Beyond the tension that Bellah describes, private interest and common good are also linked because the pursuit of one should serve the other. For example, if the pursuit of my private business interests is done in ways that voluntarily serve the common good and cultivate civic virtue, then I help create an environment that is less restrictive, more trusting, more civil and more conducive to the further pursuit of my private interests. By contrast, if in the pursuit of my private business interests, I ignore the common good and civic virtue; then I help create an environment that is more restrictive, less trusting, less civil and less conducive to the further pursuit of my private business interests.

Said another way, when I ignore or violate the common good and pursue purposes in ways that primarily benefit me; I create mistrust and invite resistance of some kind. That resistance can come in many forms including increased transaction costs, a loss of customers, diminishing cooperation, more government regulation, increased crime and more. True, some individuals violate the common good and pursue their private business interests with apparent impunity, but that approach is usually short-sighted. Even the people who are able to get away with this, weaken the system of voluntary compliance with common values and invite resistance for everyone else. Witness the exponential growth in government regulation in certain business sectors and the resulting increases in compliance costs due to the indiscretion of a few individuals. And that represents just one form of resistance that comes as a result of ignoring or violating the common good.

The essence of a covenant is recognizing that at times private-interest and success are better served long-term by giving up some individual rights, comforts or interests in favor of a greater or common good. It is an acknowledgement that we are linked to each other by common purposes that are sometimes more important than our own individual purposes. But common good goes beyond the idea of common purpose. In a sense it is the end that a common and ethical purpose serves. For example, on September 11 of 2001, the terrorists who attacked America were linked by a common purpose, but that purpose was clearly unethical because it violated the law and had as its end destruction and evil as opposed to good. True, there are some relativistic thinkers who might argue that one man's evil is another man's good. However, taking that thinking to its logical end, any behavior could be rationalized as "good", and as a result there would never be any basis for justice. Thus, by "good" I assume an objective, absolute definition of the term and not a relativistic one. Whether it's in a marriage or a much larger group, it is an understanding that the purpose by which we are linked will go beyond our own self gratification and contribute in some way to the health, well-being, quality of life or advancement of mankind. If common purpose binds people together, then common good fuels their passion and their commitment. It is for this reason that serving a common good is such a crucial part of a covenant. It is really the end goal to which the common and ethical purposes of a covenant are directed.

An example of leaders who were passionately committed and bound together by this concept of common good is found in the lives and relationships of America's founding fathers. They all had a clear understanding of their common purposes to resist and defeat the tyranny of Britain and the common good of liberty that purpose served. The common purposes they pursued and the experiences they shared in those pursuits bound them together in a covenant. Even though some founders may have had philosophical differences, they never allowed those differences to get in the way of achieving the larger common good that their covenant served.

Building Strong Relationships - The kind of relationships that exist in an organization determine how well people are able both to achieve consensus on and to work toward a common purpose that serves a common good. For example, where there are self absorbed and shallow relationships in a group, trust, communication and respect for individuals are usually lacking. Instead of creating an environment of cooperation and teamwork, those kind of dynamics tend to create an environment where a lot of individual purposes compete with each other. The concept of "good" is relegated solely to what's good for me, with very little consideration for the organization and the purpose and people it serves. Conversely, strong relationships in an organization, where trust, respect and communication abound;

go a long way toward helping people work together toward the common purposes and the common good they serve. Accordingly, an important responsibility of a leader is to help facilitate the development of strong, cooperative, and functional relationships among the people of the organization.

Consider the case of John Adams and Thomas Jefferson. In *Founding Brothers*, Pulitzer Prize winning author, Joseph Ellis, discusses both their friendship and their philosophical differences. He comments, *"There were to be sure important political and ideological differences between the two men.... But as soul mates who had lived together through some of the most formative events of the revolutionary era and of their own lives, Adams and Jefferson bonded at a personal and emotional level that defied their merely philosophical differences. They were charter members of the 'band of brothers' who had shared the agonies and the ecstasies of 1776 as colleagues. No subsequent disagreement could shake this elemental affinity. They knew, trusted, and even loved each other for reasons that required no explanation."* [4]

In other words, the strong bonds that were created by the covenant they shared, allowed John Adams and Thomas Jefferson to mitigate their differences. Once the covenant commitment was made and the bond was established, despite any differences they could continue to lead by pursuing both the common purposes and the common good for the people, the country and the principles they served. This also does not mean that covenants require people to give up the pursuit of their own self-interests. Certainly Jefferson and Adams and the other founding fathers didn't believe that. On the contrary, they believed that the pursuit of the common good of liberty would serve everyone's private interests, including their own. They also demonstrated that the ability and even the desire of people to pursue that common good are greatly assisted when there are bonds and even friendships among the people involved.

Organizationally applied that means that leaders can enhance cooperation, teamwork and success in pursuit of both common purposes and the common good they serve, by creating opportunities for their people to build and strengthen bonds among them.

Sometimes those opportunities occur at work in a formal setting, but they also occur in informal social or volunteer settings. For example, Intuit, the inventors of financial software such as Quicken and Turbo Tax sponsor Friday afternoon socials, summer cookouts and beach parties to build camaraderie and celebrate the end of tax season. The Fuqua School of Business at Duke University offers Fuqua Fridays. The events are sponsored by a club, association or sometimes a corporation and provide opportunities for MBA students to socialize, partake of food and refreshments and get to know fellow classmates outside of formal studies. The idea in both of these organizations is certainly to have fun at these social gatherings but also to build camaraderie and teamwork that will transfer to the work and learning environments.

Sometimes corporations structure more formal opportunities for employees both to bond outside of work and to serve the common good while doing so. For example, Timberland Corporation's slogan "Make it better" applies both to the way they make their products and the way they live in the community. The company provides time for employees to serve as volunteers and in so doing serve the common good. According to their website, Timberland leaders endeavor to forge, "...powerful partnerships that create positive sustainable impact in our world." CEO Jeffrey Swartz notes that responsible corporate citizenship is one of Timberland's core values. Evidence that this value is aligned with corporate behavior is found in the fact that employees have contributed nearly 300,000 hours partnering with nonprofit organizations. Mr. Swartz explained, "We recognize the vast potential of like-minded individuals united for the common good..." He acknowledges further that company sponsored volunteer activities, "...align us more closely with partners as we share the same goal of increasing our collective impact through service." [5]

Uniting in a Shared Vision - The process of identifying the common good a purpose serves is often enhanced by creating a shared vision that articulates how achieving it will serve others. For example, the vision of achieving the American dream is a "common good" upon which most people would agree. Certainly there are many people who have not achieved it, but it is clearly a vision that unites us because it is shared by most people. The pursuit of a better life or enhancing one's position in society (success in Bellah's terms) have always been keys to the entrepreneurial spirit that has enabled many of us to create wealth and achieve the American dream. Realizing this kind of success has proved beneficial both for private interests and the common good. Those benefits are manifest in advances in technology, creation of jobs, improvement of pay and benefits, strengthening of our economy, increases in philanthropy and much more. However, leading and living by the principles of covenant is about more than just the pursuit of certain benefits. A covenant is a relationship of individuals united by a shared vision that is beneficial to everyone involved. Covenant partners recognize that the self-interest served by the covenant is sometimes enhanced and even enabled by cooperating with others and working towards a common good (articulated sometimes as a vision) that is larger than self and adds value to others outside of the immediate relationship.

But for a vision actually to be shared, demands that people understand it, become vested in it and work to make it a reality. That really is the essence of the World War II generation, people who served and fought and sometimes died to preserve the common good of freedom. They were ordinary individuals who bought into the vision of resisting and defeating our enemies and thereby preserving our liberty so their generation and future generations could prosper. They recognized that their individual futures (private interests) were linked to those of others and would be best served by cooperating, joining forces and pursuing the common good in a just war. In much the same way they did with the World War II generation and many generations before and after them, covenants unite people in a shared vision and compel them to work toward the common purposes and common good the covenant serves.

If leaders in any context intend to build a high level of cooperation in pursuing common purposes and the common good those purposes serve, it helps if they can create a shared vision of what will be achieved and how it will benefit people both inside and outside of the organization. Again, as people share a vision and a purpose, it creates an incentive for them to work together. That happens best when the vision, its meaning and its intended outcomes are clearly understood and include the input and interests of others besides the leader.

This notion of people working together to create and achieve a shared vision goes directly to the heart of what a covenant is. Essentially it is a relationship in which the covenant partners are bound together by a common and ethical purpose that is "bigger and more important than any one individual purpose, and it provides meaning and hope for everyone involved." Helping people understand that purpose, experience that meaning and realize that hope are greatly enhanced when leaders can create a picture (a vision) of what people will experience, achieve or become as a result of their efforts.

Superseding Self-interest With Human Obligation - The problem with cooperating to achieve a common good that benefits humanity, is that today it is becoming increasingly more difficult for people to agree on what is "good." Again, the absence of common values to help define "good" and guide people, often leads them to pursue their own self-interests. As they do, it frequently sets up competition and arguments that can create rifts. Settling those rifts often requires either the intervention of law enforcement officials or some form of litigation. While law enforcement or litigation may promise some immediate relief for an individual, it shows little or no regard for others. Whether it's in an organization or a community, as people rely less on common values and more on the law to define good and mitigate differences, trust and civility normally decline. It is a clear sign that leadership is lacking. By contrast, when leaders create a culture guided by common values and some concept of "common good" (or as Bellah called it 'cultivating civic virtue'), then it helps mitigate the unfettered pursuit of self-interest and the power driven, legalistic control of others that emerge in the absence of any sense of human obligation. True, the self-interests of individuals may be served temporarily by power and control motivations, but such motivations are detrimental to the preservation of the common good and the proliferation of covenants. That's because both power and control are often guided by an assumption of mistrust.

In order to build the kind of trust that sustains a covenant and encourages people to serve a common good, leaders must supersede some self-interest (and power) with common values that support the notion of human obligation. Leaders who embrace the concept of human obligation are acknowledging that people and organizations exist in an interdependent state. It is an understanding that because we are served by that interdependence, we also have an obligation to serve others. But human obligation goes beyond the selfish idea that attending to it serves one's own self-interest. Certainly that is true, but it is not an end in and of itself. The idea of human obligation also embraces the principle that obligating oneself to others because they are individuals made in God's image and therefore have intrinsic value, is what preserves our culture and distinguishes us as human beings. Apart from that it's easy for people to pursue their own self-interests at the expense of others and thereby lose any sense of trust, civility or human obligation.

Whatever the cause, in an environment that does not value trust, civility and a sense of human obligation, people quickly become more territorial and legalistic and less willing to give of themselves and their talents. If it's all about self, then you get a lot of independent selves competing with each other to get ahead. There's no sense of mutual obligation to each other or to mankind and therefore, no sense of shared vision. When that happens, people are less likely to share resources, defend or support one another or commit to common goals, and that operates contrary to the success of any organization.

In 1978, author Alexander Solzhenitsyn prophetically cautioned the Harvard graduating class that a society (or any organization for that matter) that is devoid of trust and based primarily on the letter of the law, and not the common good, creates an atmosphere of mediocrity. It misses the full range of human potential because legalism stifles a person's inclination towards risk, virtue, duty and eventually greatness. Solzhenitsyn warned, *"It is time, in the West, to defend not so much human rights as human obligations ... destructive and irresponsible freedom has been granted boundless space. Life organized legalistically has thus shown its inability to defend itself against the corrosion of evil."*[6]

Creating a culture where Solzhenitsyn's concept of "human obligation" permeates an organization requires first that leaders embrace the idea of their own obligation to the organization, its people and the common purposes they serve. That happens most effectively with leaders who are guided in both their decisions and their actions by values that have their basis in some notion of objective truth and not power or personal preference. As leaders align their behavior with these values, it enables them to set the pace and model the way for their followers. Where this concept of "human obligation" is modeled in the organizational culture, it makes leaders and followers much more inclined to obligate themselves to each other and to the purposes they serve. In this sense, leadership is also about helping people understand and embrace their human obligations. It involves using influence to move individuals beyond their own self-interest in pursuit of a common good. When it's done right, it binds people together in relationships we call covenants.

Balancing Profit With Human Obligation - For a business, the idea of human obligation must be balanced with the profit motive or the company will cease to exist. Yet, there are times when the sense of human obligation is so strong that it compels individuals and corporations to serve the common good first and worry about profit later. A case in point is Dynamic Orthotics and Prosthetics. The Houston Company, which is owned by Tom DiBello, clearly exists for the purpose of making a profit. However, the purpose goes well beyond making prosthetic devices for profit. The larger purpose of the company is to improve the quality of life for people who, because of an accident, disease or the horrors of war, have experienced the pain of losing a limb. That purpose is linked to the common good of serving mankind which is based in the truth that all human life is valuable.

Mr. DiBello demonstrated the company's commitment to that common good when he heard the plight of seven Iraqi merchants. These men lost their hands and forearms through forced amputations ordered by Saddam Hussein because they used American currency in their businesses. When Mr. DiBello heard about their predicament, he arranged for one of his suppliers, Otto Bock Healthcare of Germany, to donate their most sophisticated prosthetic devices. In addition, several well known surgeons volunteered their services as did the Houston Medical Center, the Methodist Hospital, the Institute for Rehabilitation and Research, several occupational therapists and Continental Airlines, who flew them over and back free of charge.[7]

In this case, human obligation and commitment to the common good were so compelling that they superseded the profit motive. These leaders demonstrated a covenant commitment to the people they served, a commitment that sacrificed self-interest in favor of the common good. This same commitment and sense of human obligation are evidenced in the estimated $13.8 billion that American corporations gave in 2005 for philanthropic purposes. [8]

Keeping the Covenant, Not Compromising Integrity - When Jim Bakker started in ministry and then founded PTL in 1974, no doubt it was for the purpose of serving God. Many people who shared those same purposes joined him in that work both as employees and as donors. The ministry espoused Biblical principles and projected an image consistent with high ethical standards. They also frequently highlighted the good they were doing. Thousands of people put their trust in Jim and Tammy Faye Bakker and in a very real sense they made a covenant commitment to the ministry. In fact, PTL referred to its friends and donors as partners.

It's hard to say exactly when Mr. Bakker began to lose sight of his obligation to the organization, the people and the common purpose he was supposed to be serving. It became clear in 1987 when he resigned as head of the ministry after admitting to an extramarital affair and a financial scandal, that the covenant he shared with his wife, his employees and his partners had been broken, and his integrity had been deeply compromised.[9]

Two years later when he was indicted on eight counts of mail fraud, 15 counts of wire fraud and one count of conspiracy, it became even more evident that Mr. Bakker was not being guided by the principles he espoused but by his selfish personal preferences and his power. Eventually he was convicted of all 24 counts in defrauding his followers of more than $150 million.[10] As a result of his mis-leadership, the noble purpose of the ministry and the common good it was designed to serve were lost.

Jim Bakker served five years of an eight-year sentence and was eventually released for good behavior. The lesson of leadership that this case offers is poignant. People at the head of most organizations have power. How that power is used, and the degree to which it is aligned with the principles designed to guide the organization, is the degree to which organizational heads are leaders as opposed to power wielders. In Mr. Bakker's case he abused the power of his position, compromised his integrity and violated the trust his followers gave him, all for the purpose of serving his own self-interest instead of the common good. He chose preference and power over truth and principle and a lot of people got hurt. As a result, he violated the covenant and forfeited both his credibility and his opportunity to lead.

For effective leadership to exist, principles and not power or preference must guide the leader's actions and behavior regardless of the circumstances he or she faces. Apart from that, it is impossible to achieve an environment of trust or a system of mutual accountability that are typical of covenant relationships. Likewise, achieving an understanding of common good is an exercise in futility without having some transcendent moral truth to help define that good. That was exactly the point upon which the civil rights movement was built in the 1960s. In his *Letter from Birmingham Jail*, Martin Luther King, Jr. said simply that: *"...A just law is a manmade code that squares with the moral law or the law of God. An unjust law is a code that is out of harmony with the moral law."* Dr. King argued further that God's law is objective moral truth, and therefore authoritative and superior to man's law.[11]

Relying on Transcendent, Not Situational Truth – Natural law, or as Dr. King called it, moral law is based on the notion of absolute or objective truth. It postulates that something is true because it transcends time, place and circumstances. For the most part, post modern thought dismisses the idea of objective or absolute truth as an impossibility. Proponents of the post modern view of life argue that truth is relative and absolutes are mostly the product of wild-eyed religious zealots. Yet, even though they deny it, these same people are governed by natural law and absolute truth daily. For example, farmers in Iowa plant their crops in the spring after the last frost. They do this because those farmers are absolutely certain of the truth that if they plant them any earlier the crops will die. In this sense natural law dictates their behavior.

Similarly, if a person chooses to jump from the balcony of a 30-story building without a parachute, he or she will fall to the ground 100% of the time. Regardless of how strongly you might believe to the contrary of this absolute, if you jump off the balcony you'll still hit the ground. Apart from suicide, attempting this would mean that you are trying to operate contrary to the natural law of gravity, an action that would be both self-destructive and counter-productive no matter how popular it was.

Just as there are natural laws that govern the physical universe, there are also natural laws or moral absolutes that govern human behavior. Like it is with the law of gravity, whether we understand and embrace them does not change the fact that these absolutes exist. And when we operate contrary to these moral absolutes (as in the case of murder, theft or the kind of exploitation of humans Dr. King resisted), we sow the seeds of disorder.

Whether it's in a business, a charity or in a larger community, people rely on ethical standards to govern behavior and bring order. And what is considered to be ethical and responsible behavior in a given environment, is measured by how it aligns with common values that serve the common good. However, as we discussed earlier, if values and common good are relative terms or if they are defined by comfort, preference or personal gain and not by transcendent moral truth (absolutes), then what is considered "ethical" and "good" changes based on the individual and the situation. Applying these assumptions, if the civil rights movement were occurring today instead of the 1960s, its leaders would not have the basis for achieving moral high ground that they did then when they relied on moral absolutes. Those absolutes were gleaned from what the movement considered to be Biblical truth, and leaders like Martin Luther King used that truth to justify and support their mission. Therein lies the problem. In post-modern America transcendent moral truth constitutes an anathema of major proportions. In fact, the post-modernist would argue that agreeing on a common good is an impossibility because at best truth, good and evil are all relative terms and responsibility to others does not supersede responsibility to self.

One of the most prominent post-modern philosophers of our day, Richard Rorty, put it this way, "*... our responsibilities to others constitute only the public side of our lives, a side which competes with our private affections and our private attempts at self-creation.*" Rorty suggests further that "moral obligation" is but one of many considerations for an individual and it does not trump all other considerations in motivating behavior.[12] In Rorty's world, as a person of power, I have the right to do just about anything I desire. But that raises an important question. If moral obligation does not trump private affections, then what happens to justice or civility when my "private affections" lean towards hate or racism or my "attempts at self creation" find me trying to dominate others unfairly or accumulate wealth without the slightest regard for my employees or stockholders? Ask the eight million Iraqi people who risked life and limb and walked miles to exercise their newly acquired right to vote if "moral obligation" should "trump" private affections. For 30 years they suffered under the despotism of Saddam Hussein who pursued his "private affections" without any restraint of moral obligation. Leaders simply cannot be leaders and operate with impunity in an environment of relative good that they define and enforce. They are power wielders and dictators but they are not leaders.

Defining Obligation with Moral Truth not Personal Power - If Rorty is correct, then human obligation (manifest in the idea of corporate responsibility) will always clash with what he calls "private affections," because at times fulfilling the community norms or human obligations requires a certain amount of self-denial. Also, if the notion of objective moral truth is unattainable, and truth, good, evil and even ethical are all relative terms, then the only things left to define obligations or mitigate differences are law and power. The logical creation of an organization or a society in such a state is an environment where mistrust, power and the pursuit of individual interest dominate. Taken to the extreme, we get Iraq under Hussein or Nazi Germany under Hitler. In business, that kind of logic is what brings us some of the corporate scandals and CEO abuses that are so prominent in the press. Unfortunately, all too often with the ascendancy of the individual comes the decline of civility and the common good, and that's exactly the point Solzhenitsyn made at Harvard in 1978. If there is no ability to define what is moral, then there is no way to align behavior and no justification for any concept of common good.

For any grouping of people that operates under Rorty's assumptions, the potential for covenants is lost in the clash of competing self-interests. Because "good" or "moral" is primarily the construct of the individual (according to the post modernist), there can be no transcendent moral truth to mitigate differences of opinion or reconcile competing goods. Simply stated, if my opinion of good differs from yours, then we are left to fight it out in a Darwinian form of organizational gamesmanship. Instead of voluntary covenants (guided by core values based in moral truth) arbitrating individual preferences and maintaining the common culture, people must rely on either the legal system or the brute force of power. Those without power who choose not to comply with the rules of the common culture or the prevailing power of an organization (regardless of how "immoral" or "unethical" either may be) are punished, ostracized and often eliminated. Hence, compliance is logical for the individual only inasmuch as it aids in self-preservation and/or the accumulation of power. Consequently, the primary end of competing individuals in such an organization is not the betterment of the organization but the acquisition of power. One is no longer bound by any rules apart from those that serve one's personal benefit. In essence, in Rorty's organizational world, everyone becomes a free agent.

In applying this logic to business, it follows that it is the CEO's prerogative, without any moral obligation to the company or its workers, to use power any way he pleases to achieve personal gain and personal preference. When people with power adopt such behaviors, the only "good" they serve is their own. Instead of pursuing a common good that serves others, they act in a manner consistent with the 16th century philosophy of Niccolo Machiavelli espoused in *The Prince*. Machiavelli viewed people as mere objects to be manipulated with power and fear solely for the benefit of the prince without any concern for moral obligation. He commented,

> *"Here the question arises; whether it is better to be loved than feared or feared than loved. The answer is that it would be desirable to be both but, since that is difficult, it is much safer to be feared than to be loved, if one must choose. For on men in general this observation may be made; they are ungrateful, fickle, deceitful, eager to avoid dangers, and avid for gain, and while you are useful to them they are all with you, offering you their blood, their property, their lives, and their sons so long as danger is remote, as we noted above, but when it approaches they turn on you.... Men have less hesitation in offending a man who is loved, than one who is feared."*[13]

Also, because preferences vary with the individual, it's not surprising that rules, values and cultures often change with a new CEO. That's why it is more common today than it was even a decade ago to see CEOs of unprofitable or even failing companies receiving multi-million dollar salary and benefit packages. Consider the case of Gary Winnick, founder of telecommunications giant, Global Crossing. According to a *Fortune* magazine article, within a year of going public in 1997 the company was worth more than $38 billion, and within two more years it collapsed. During that time *Fortune* noted that Winnick treated the company as his own private cash cow, earning exorbitant fees from consulting and real estate deals between Global Crossing and his own private investment company. In total, Mr. Winnick kept $735 million from the sale of his stock and continued to receive $10 million a year in salary. By the time Global Crossing filed for bankruptcy in 2002, the company's market valuation had dropped from $47 billion to $70 million. Investors and creditors lost some $20 billion.[14] By definition Mr. Winnick appears to have been not a leader but a misleader, since his actions led away from the primary goal of returning value to the shareholders of Global Crossing.

By contrast, when leaders attend to obligations that are based in moral truth, they build trust and credibility in ways that make it easier for them to define and then serve the common good. Because of relational dynamics that are so central to a covenant, having a strong bias towards this concept of obligation is fundamental to covenant leadership. That is not to suggest that covenants lack personal power. In a covenant, leaders have plenty of power, but they use it to achieve the common purposes, attend to the needs of followers and serve the common good.

Forming Culture With Common Values, Not Preference and Double Standards - A culture that is formed by the consistent alignment of behavior with common values based on unchanging moral truths or principles, brings stability to organizations. Conversely, creating culture by substituting core values with preference and power brings arbitrary change and instability. While the double standards that often accompany the latter conditions may be well within the boundaries of the law, they do not serve the common good nor are they well received by anyone other than the individuals who are accommodated by them. It's important to note here that such power driven, double standard cultures are not peculiar to the business sector. There are plenty of examples in schools, nonprofit organizations and even churches where these conditions exist and people have been hurt as a result. The problem is that when individuals in top positions violate the common values and therefore the common good as everyone understands them, it often has devastating effects. Consider the thousands of people influenced by the decisions of the WorldCom, Enron and Arthur Andersen executives.

Much has been written in attempt to understand such abuses of power by CEOs. In one now classic *Business Week* report, "CEO Disease," John Byrne, William Symonds and Julia Flynn cited examples of many CEOs who seemed to change dramatically once they came into power. The authors explained the seductive nature of the self-serving power shift that often has a negative influence on the company, *"Pampered, perked and protected, many American CEOs have developed an unhealthy love of power which threatens their companies' well being."* They note further that the power to control this "CEO disease" rests with the shareholders, but often by the time it gets to the shareholders the damage is irrevocable.[15]

It shouldn't surprise us when we hear of corporate heads abusing power to serve their own purposes. Absent the notion of human or moral obligation that is grounded in true, unchanging principles and the values that flow from them, values that define common good and help guide behavior, we are left with a Nietzschean type culture driven by preference and power. Consistent alignment of behavior with values allows people to focus on achieving the common purpose and serving the common good because those actions help create a culture that brings stability to organizations and communities. Conversely, when individuals operate counter to the prevailing culture it creates a certain amount of disruption and instability. We will discuss such alignments further in chapter six. But what I find interesting is the fact that while some people seemingly have difficulty defining or agreeing on common good in public discourse, they appear to achieve consensus about it quickly once that common good has been violated. It offers compelling evidence that individuals may postulate in the public square as if common good, moral obligation and absolute truth do not exist, but they order their lives and their expectations as if they do. And when leaders operate contrary to the culture and core values of an organization, not only do they operate under a double standard, they create organizational instability. That instability inhibits the achievement of both the common purpose and common good the organization purports to serve.

---

[1] Bellah, Robert N.; *Habits of the Heart* (Harper & Row; New York; 1986).

[2] Ibid pp. 199.

[3] Ibid pp. 270.

[4] Ellis, Joseph J.; *Founding Brothers* (Alfred A. Knopf; New York; 2001) pp. 163-164.

[5] Swartz, Jeffrey B. *Message From our CEO* Inform (September 25, 2006). www.timberland.com/timberlandserve/content.jsp?pagename=timberlandserv.

[6] Solzhenitsyn, A. (June 8, 1978). Quote from his address at Harvard College.

[7] Fullen, Meredy; *"Houston Health Professionals Help 'Merchants of Baghdad'"* The *OSP Edge*; www.oandp.com/edge/issues/articles/2004-07_07.asp.

[8] Giving USA 2006, The Annual Report on Philanthropy for the Year 2005. Brown, Melissa; Managing Editor. (Giving USA Foundation, Glenview, IL, 2006) p 94.

[9] Peifer, Justice Paul E.; *Jim Bakker's Federal Court Appeal*; (Supreme Court of Ohio; Office of Public Information; Column for April 12, 2000) http://www.sconet.state.oh.us/Communications_office/Justice_ Pfeifer/2000/jp041200.htm.

[10] Ibid.

[11] King, Martin Luther Jr.; *Letter From Birmingham Jail*; in *Why We Can't Wait*, ed. Martin Luther King Jr., 77-100, 1963;

[12] Rorty, Richard; *Contingency, Irony and Solidarity* (Cambridge: Cambridge University Press, 1989) p. 194.

[13] Machiavelli, Niccolo; *The Prince*; translated and edited by Thomas G. Bergin (New York: Appleton – Century – Crafts, 1947) p. 48.

[14] Creswell, Julie with Nomi Prins; "Global Crossing The Emperor of Greed;" (*Fortune*, June 9, 2002).

[15] Byrne, John A. , William C. Symonds, Julia Flynn; "CEO Disease;" *Business Week* (New York: McGraw-Hill, Inc.; April 1, 1991).

Chapter 4
Leadership Evaluation and Action Discovery (LEAD)

The notion of common good acknowledges that the purposes by which we are linked extend beyond our own self-gratification and contribute in some way to the health, well being or advancement of mankind. It is the end goal to which the common purposes of a covenant are directed. Using the information in Chapter 4, please answer the following questions:

A.	**What larger common good does your organization serve or in what ways would your clients or customers or community be lacking if your organization ceased to exist?**
B.	**To what extent has this "good" become a part of your organization's shared vision and how can it become a more prominent part of the vision?**
C.	**What are your moral obligations to stakeholders?**
D.	**What safeguards do you have to help ensure that you keep the covenant, align behavior with core values, avoid double standards, and not compromise integrity?**

Chapter 5

Give and Build Trust Around You

In the 1990s Don Peppers and Martha Rogers took the marketing industry by storm with what some people considered to be a new and revolutionary concept. Instead of promoting the "larger market share" concept; they proposed that companies seek a larger share of the customer. In *One to One Future* Peppers and Rogers made a compelling case for using a one-to-one marketing strategy that focused on building relationships one customer at a time. The authors demonstrated that by doing so companies could sell more goods to fewer people in ways that made them more profitable. Their approach is based on building trust in relationships with customers by collaborating with them to meet their needs. They noted, *"If you and your customer are collaborating, you are friends. And the essential ingredients for any friendship are dependability and trust. They can count on you… It is possible, in fact, to make more money, more efficiently, by increasing the level of trust enjoyed with every customer relationship."* [1]

The relationship dynamics, results and particularly the trust that Peppers and Rogers intend for companies to create with customers are similar to those that come as a result of covenants. Essentially the authors encourage companies to build stronger relationships with customers because they recognize the great potential it offers. No doubt, people do business frequently with companies they trust. For example, my wife and I have a couple of favorite restaurants, and we keep going back to them. Certainly the food is good, but the draw is the attention they give us. They know us and our children and

91

though we are customers they treat us like family. Therefore, when we have an event to celebrate or people to entertain, we go there because we trust them to help us do it right. They have earned our loyalty because they have worked hard both to develop a relationship with us and to serve us.

Approaching leadership as a covenant is demanding because making covenants functional requires time and effort to establish relationships and build a foundation of trust that will sustain those relationships. On the practical side, that translates into leaders earning trust through consistent and ethical actions over time. But it also involves giving trust in meaningful ways by allowing people to do their work, make contributions and participate with the leader in keeping the covenant. Of course, trust is not without tangible benefits. An International Association of Business Communicators (IABC) Research Report clearly demonstrates the value of organizational trust. In "*Measuring Organizational Trust: A Diagnostic Survey and International Indicator,*" researchers found that the ability to form trusting relationships within an organization is a strong predictor of its effectiveness. The study demonstrated that trust is strongly related not only to organizational survival, but also to increased profits, innovation, effectiveness, job satisfaction and successful international business.[2] These benefits alone provide ample justification for leaders to make building trust a leadership priority.

Creating the Norm of Reciprocity – Effective leaders often build trust by giving to others in some way. Why did Warren Buffett, one of the richest men in the world, announce that he would give away most of his $44 billion in Berkshire Hathaway stock to charity? He explained that he and his wife Susie, "*...were totally in sync about what to do with it – and that was to give it back to society.*" "*In that*", said Mr. Buffett, "*we agreed with Andrew Carnegie who said that huge fortunes that flow in large part from society, should in large part be returned to society.*"[3]

What Mr. Buffett did is just one example of a whole system of reciprocity or "giving back" that exists in America, and creating an organizational environment and expectation of reciprocity is one way leaders build trust. In *Bowling Alone*, Robert Putnam provides an explanation of reciprocity and an analysis of the collapse and revival of American community that are almost laser-like in their accuracy. Like Tocqueville did in the nineteenth century, Putnam observed today that Americans trust and help each other in a reciprocal fashion because they find that in so doing their own self-interests are served. Essentially, when we rake our leaves so they don't blow in the neighbor's yard, when we keep an eye on our neighbor's house or kids, when we take turns buying lunch we participate in what Putnam calls "the norm of generalized reciprocity." This "norm" not only helps create a nice environment in which to live and work, it also helps us build trust which prospers us economically.[4]

As Francis Fukuyama argues in *Trust*, the presence of trust in society creates social capital. When people give back (reciprocity) and learn to cooperate with others beyond their immediate families, as volunteers serving on a church committee or in the Rotary Club, they also learn to trust each other. That trust allows them to cooperate and get things done in communities and organizations. Fukuyama notes that the social capital created from trust becomes economic capital because the trust that develops with others outside of a person's family transfers into the workplace. By way of contrast, when trust declines so does our wealth. That's because we are forced to spend more time and money on things like insurance, legal protection, surveillance equipment, government regulation and more.[5]

Putnam also makes a convincing case for the importance of trust and reciprocity in our society. He cautions that declines in each of these areas have diminished our quality of life and increased our costs of doing business. He notes that, *"when each of us can relax her guard a little, what economists term 'transaction costs' – the costs of the everyday business of life, as well as the costs of commercial transactions – are reduced…. A society that relies on generalized reciprocity is more efficient than a distrustful society…. Honesty and trust lubricate the inevitable frictions of social (or organizational) life."*[6]

To Putnam's point, in another study of supplier-automaker relationships in the U.S., Japan and Korea, Jeffrey Dyer and Wujin

Chu found that trust reduces transaction costs and increases information-sharing and other forms of reciprocity in supplier-buyer relationships. Their findings indicate that trust translates into a substantial economic value. For example, they note that the automaker that was found to have the least trusting relationships with suppliers, also had five times the procurement costs and spent twice as much in face-to-face time on writing contracts, assigning blame and haggling compared to the most trusted automakers. Presenting at the 2002 annual meeting of the Academy of Management in Denver, the authors pointed to new research suggesting that trust may reduce the cost of making a car by as much as 10 to 15 percent. Equally impressive is the fact that the same research revealed that parts purchased at the least trusted of the companies averaged just over $2 million while the parts purchased from the most trusted company was about $12 million or six times as much.

No doubt, trust works both ways, but these findings have major implications for rethinking relationships in the auto industry as well as other industries. The authors note that, *"The arms-length, hard nosed approach has historically been most associated with General Motors, which has seen its market share in the United States drop during the past 40 years from over 50 percent to about 28 percent. Of course, there have been many factors in that. But, based on our findings, it's hard to believe that trust hasn't been an important one."*[7]

It's important to note that the norm of reciprocity and the trust that it creates are not things that come automatically, and establishing them requires time and effort, particularly in an environment of declining trust. To that point, a recent Gallop poll demonstrated that the percentage of Americans who believe most people can be trusted has declined from 55 percent in 1966 to about 30 percent today.[8] Accordingly, as leaders attempt to lead, they often must spend a great deal of energy breaking down cynicism and mistrust in their organizations. That is part of the reason why it is often much easier to engage people contractually with a straightforward and simple transaction: *"If you will perform this task in this way, I will compensate you in this manner."* While contracts and transactions of this type allow organizations to achieve certain tasks at a basic level, they do not build the kind of reciprocity and trust that encourage ownership and maximize productivity as people perform those tasks. Creating a norm of reciprocity in an organization requires leaders who are willing to initiate it by giving to and serving others. In other words, leaders create a culture of reciprocity and the trust that comes from it, first by modeling reciprocity and then rewarding it in others. Absent of such a culture, leaders simply can not expect people to trust them, nor can they expect to establish covenants.

Giving Meaningful Work ... Valuing and Empowering People - The literature is replete with studies demonstrating that trust, high productivity and attitudes of ownership are not only related, they are interdependent. In a large part they come from simply giving people meaningful work to do and treating them well as they do it. Giving people meaningful work to do is a manifestation of trust. It involves helping people understand both how their specific jobs are related to the larger mission and goals of the organization and why those jobs and their personal contributions are important. When leaders take time to do this, they communicate to people that their work is meaningful and that they are important to the success of the organization. As workers begin to understand these things, they are likely to see themselves as valued members of a team, individuals who have been entrusted with something to do that makes a difference. This kind of trust tends to breed more trust and good will among the people who receive it.

Successful coaches provide excellent examples of leaders who are able to build trust, maximize productivity and encourage ownership for tasks and outcomes among their players. For players to follow a coach, they must believe that the coach is competent and that he or she has their best interests in mind. Beyond that, every player also wants to know that his or her role as a team member is an important part of the overall team success.

During my brief career as a college basketball player, I was what is known as a role player. According to our coach, my role was to rebound and play defense. It wasn't necessarily a glamorous role, but the coach spent a lot of time talking to me about the importance of my role to overall team success. He also demonstrated in several ways that he was interested in me as a person and not just as a player. The job that was given to me was meaningful because I understood its importance and I also felt that I was a valued member of the team. As a result, I assumed ownership for my role by working hard and getting better at it. Along the way the coach also exhibited trust in me, as several times I was assigned to guard our opponent's best player. In turn, I trusted my coach because I knew he had my best interest in mind.

Effective leaders in organizations build trust and ownership in the same way effective coaches do. They must clearly communicate to people the importance of their work. Beyond that, building trust and ownership requires that leaders also give trust to people without hovering over them as they do their work. This means that leaders must provide necessary resources, remove barriers, empower people to make decisions and recognize them appropriately as they make contributions.

Acknowledging Contributions - What may start as a trusting relationship often begins to fail when people take each other for granted. For example, higher turnover rates among employees can sometimes signal a lack of appropriate recognition. While taking people for granted comes in a variety of forms, it usually boils down to a failure to acknowledge the value and contributions of another individual. As previously mentioned, building a foundation of trust requires not only giving people meaningful work to do but treating them well as they do it. An important part of treating people well is making an effort to acknowledge their contributions.

John Wooden is arguably the most successful college basketball coach ever. In the 1960's and 70's he guided UCLA to an incredible ten national championships in eleven years. When I interviewed Coach Wooden, he explained to me that he believed it was essential to acknowledge the contributions of all players on his team, regardless of how small their role was. He illustrated this point by sharing an analogy he used with his players,

"I would say, 'We're like a powerful automobile and this player, for example, maybe it's Jabbar, is the powerful engine. You now, are only a wheel; and you over here are only a nut that holds that wheel on. Now which is most important? What good is that engine if we don't have wheels? What if you don't have the nuts holding that wheel on? You also need somebody behind that wheel, inside, directing it or you'll go in circles. You all have an important part. You all have a role to play.' And I made a special effort at practice to let those who aren't playing very much know how much I appreciated them."[9]

Appropriate recognition can be verbal or written, but to be effective occasionally it must go beyond that. Sometimes it means allowing people who make significant contributions to share in the profits of their labor. For example, in December of 2003 the San Antonio Shoe Company in Pittsfield, Maine made national news when owners of the privately held company decided to recognize employees in a special way. At about 2:30 in the afternoon the management team gathered employees and announced that they each would receive a one-time bonus of $1,000 for every year of continuous service. In their announcement, they thanked employees for their loyalty and dedication and for helping make the San Antonio Shoe Company a success.[10]

In the case of one married couple, each spouse had worked for the company for 19 years, which meant together they received $38,000. While that level of profit sharing is not always possible, in this case it went a long way towards acknowledging the contributions of the workers and building good will and trust. In other words, assuming that a leader endeavors to actualize the potential of workers or associates, that leader will have to give something to the people he or she seeks to actualize. Getting more out of a relationship in any context requires giving more, and when people begin to trust and give freely they start to move out of the realm of a contract and into the realm of a covenant. In this sense, covenants are far more complicated than contracts. They require a willingness on the part of leader and follower alike to respect and trust one another and to give to rather than just receive from the relationship. In essence, it means acknowledging the contributions of each other, but it also means sharing talents, resources, work, problems and even revenues in ways that create an environment of mutual trust.

Benefiting Mutually - When trust is high in an organization, then benefits are shared, meaning that they flow both ways. If benefits are perceived to flow just one way, then trust dissipates and the sharing declines. For example, of a 2002 *Wall Street Journal* article read, "On Factory Floors, Top Workers Hide Secrets to Success." In the article, author Timothy Aeppel provided examples of exemplary workers who refused to share with their companies the "tricks" that enabled them to "out produce" peers. One highly productive, manufacturing worker explained his reluctance. This veteran employee of 24 years commented that if he gave the company his secrets, he feared they would use them to "speed things up" and increase work demands for everyone.[11] In other words, this worker's experience taught him not to trust management and therefore not to share his knowledge and talent with them. Mistrust like this costs untold millions and possibly even billions in lost productivity each year, and productivity is clearly a leadership issue.

Though covenants take time and energy to develop, and in some ways make people more vulnerable, because they are built on trust and engage people more deeply, they also promise higher productivity and greater rewards. However, for a relationship to be a true covenant, the benefits and/or rewards (as I explained earlier) must flow both ways. People must believe that they receive benefits from their associations or they are not likely to trust, nor are they likely to give or commit very much to them. For example, consider the case of the manufacturing worker who refused to share his secrets. He may have had full knowledge of the importance of his job and may have been freely trusted and empowered to do it. Had he been able to share in some of the profits from his ingenuity without fear of excessive workloads, then he might have been more inclined to share his knowledge. It is precisely because the benefits of covenants flow both ways, that they tend to create a culture of trust and a spirit of cooperation where people are more willing to share. Also, since covenants are flexible enough to accommodate a variety of circumstances, they don't have to be renegotiated like contracts do when conditions change. The trust that exists in covenants, allows such relationships to be far more adaptable, forgiving and resilient than contracts, and all of these elements are essential to success in the 21st century.

Sharing Information - Sometimes a lack of trust comes simply from people not having enough information. While the issue is easy enough to resolve, left unattended it can push a company to the brink of failure. Consider the case of a small telecommunications company that came to us for help a few years after I started my business. They were having trouble motivating workers to go the extra mile and produce high quality work. Competition was increasing and profit margins were quickly declining, so the owners brought in a new CEO and management team to turn things around. Both the industry and their company had experienced a great deal of change in the mid to late 90's. The new leadership group needed to pull the workers together, but the workers resisted their efforts. Regardless of how hard they tried, getting people to come together and assume ownership for their work and for the welfare of the company proved to be a daunting task for the new management team.

As we interviewed the workers, we found that many of the former managers refused to share crucial information about the company and its financial health with them. Essentially, they kept workers in the dark and tried to drive them to higher levels of productivity. These managers had been taking a strict contractual approach with people...one that was *inflexible, unforgiving* and rife with *mistrust.* In the absence of information, workers were left to make assumptions about both the management team and the company. One such assumption that emerged was that the managers themselves really didn't care about the company or its mission; they were simply trying to drive workers and bleed the company for their own benefit. In this case, credibility had eroded, a foundation of trust was missing and the negative results were quite predictable.

If people in an organization can't trust each other, it's just a matter of time before that organization begins to deteriorate. At this telecommunications firm, it took the new CEO months of hard work and information sharing to begin regaining the trust of his workers. Trust is always a leadership issue because leaders are the ones responsible for initiating and creating the culture. Quite predictably, when leaders fail in an organization, it's often because of their inability to engender a trusting environment where people are willing to cooperate in achieving a common purpose. Hoarding information and not answering questions in relationships tells people either that they are not respected or they can't be trusted, or both. A meaningful and productive relationship simply cannot develop if people are not trusted and respected.

On a larger scale, the same thing is true of trust in our society. In his best-selling book, *Trust*, author and social philosopher, Francis Fukuyama, compared what he called, "high trust societies" with "low trust societies." He demonstrated how trust in American society gives American business a strategic advantage that is absolutely critical to our economic prosperity. As we discussed earlier, when we work together towards common purposes in clubs, social service agencies, religious groups and communities, we learn to trust people outside our families and develop skills that transfer into the workplace.[12] In part, what demonstrates that trust and is simultaneously a result of that trust is the free flow of information that exists in America. The converse of that is also true. Declining trust also invites costly government intervention and regulation of the kind American business has experienced in the wake of corporate scandals at companies such as WorldCom, Tyco, Enron, Adelphi and others. Those companies decided to hide and even distort information and the customers, investors and the rest of American business paid the price. In addition to a loss of jobs, investments and general credibility that their indiscretions caused; the annual costs for Sarbanes-Oxley compliance, the legislation that came as a result of their actions, are estimated to be nearly $6 billion and rising.

Eliminating Unhealthy Competition - We live in a highly competitive society, and where there is competition there are winners but there are also losers. Politicians, journalists, athletes, business executives and more all compete to win out over their rivals. The culture of individual winning and success (private interest) that has been so admired and rewarded in our society can also permeate organizations in unhealthy ways. Sometimes it pits executive against executive, teammate against teammate and worker against worker. When that happens it diminishes trust and cooperation and, while someone usually wins (at least temporarily), someone else loses.

As a parent, it would seem a bit absurd if I created a family environment where I put my children in competition with one another. Consider the results of my recognizing only the "winner" or the "most productive" child with rewards of attention and money. Such an atmosphere would likely create division, anger and frustration among my children. Ultimately it would make both our family and our children far less functional and productive than they could be. Though it is clearly self defeating behavior, corporate managers and even CEOs do this regularly, hoping that somehow this kind of internal competition will make their people more productive and their companies more profitable.

This is not to suggest that competition is bad. On the contrary, competition in the marketplace can clearly benefit consumers, particularly as it results in higher quality, lower prices and scientific advancements. When athletes compete, the play elevates and fans get a better performance; when school systems compete, the students get a better education; and when businesses compete, the customers get better products and services. It must be noted though, that competition is healthy only in the proper context. For example, a company that purposes to gain a competitive advantage and a superior brand in the external marketplace needs to foster a spirit of cooperation internally among its employees as they work toward those purposes. A spirit of internal competition can distract the external focus of the company in ways that diminish the quality of products and services delivered to customers. Additionally, intense competition among colleagues can be quite costly, because it tends to focus people on their own self-interests and their own welfare in ways that inhibit teamwork and divide the organization. Instead of trusting, supporting and cooperating with one another, employees tend to horde information, cover their own backs and pursue their own purposes. To build trust in any group, leaders need to work on eliminating unhealthy competition and bringing people together.

John Dalla Costa, President of The Center for Ethical Imperative, explains it this way, *"Unbridled competition creates conditions for a much more dangerous inequity that finally provokes all parties into separate corners of self-interest."*[13] By contrast, he notes that, *"Cohesion provides the opportunity of the whole being greater than the sum of its parts, but also requires ... a community held together by trust, mutual respect, shared values...."*[14]

Facilitating Cohesion and Cooperation – Both cohesion and cooperation result in and are the result of trust. But those things don't naturally happen inside organizations. Creating the conditions that allow for cohesion and cooperation to flourish requires leadership. Specifically, this means that leaders must trust people and use their resources and ingenuity to create a cooperative culture. Of course, this assumes that leaders will also create incentives and hold themselves and others accountable for behavior that is consistent with the desired culture.

After taking over as president in 1964, the late Ken Iverson, a self proclaimed "business maverick," created a culture at Nucor Steel that, according to him, accounted for 60 percent of their competitive advantage. He achieved this by opening up lines of effective communication, breaking down traditional hierarchies, decentralizing operations and incentivizing team performance. Instead of using traditional methods of compensation, at Nucor teams and their managers were rewarded based on what they produced as a unit. Iverson's approach seeks to align the purposes and goals of the employees, the corporation and the customers. He believed strongly in the importance and value of his people and trusted both their abilities and intentions. That's one of the reasons why, during the steel industry slowdowns of the 1980s, when his production was down 50 percent, he didn't order any layoffs. Instead, Iverson cut hours and salaries for everyone including himself. All of his efforts and those of his people brought the company from the brink of bankruptcy to doing over $4 billion per year.[15] He produced a great reservoir of trust and cooperation among employees and a lasting legacy in the company. That's because as a leader Mr. Iverson trusted people and served them, not as employees but as valuable covenant partners. In a sense he built trust by giving trust and the relationships and sense of common purpose that resulted prospered everyone involved.

Becoming Vulnerable - When individuals trust each other, they become vulnerable. That's why people run from commitment all the time. Commitment involves human beings trusting and making themselves dependent on and therefore vulnerable to one another. Where individuals harden themselves to any kind of vulnerability, their relationships with others are at best shallow. And, even when they do commit, there is no guarantee that their commitment will be long-term, which tends to build cynicism among the people around them.

In *Happiness is a Serious Problem,* author and radio talk show host, Dennis Prager, comments that people sometimes fail to commit by trusting and becoming vulnerable in a relationship because of fear and pain avoidance. He uses the example of a typical 40-year-old bachelor to illustrate his point. He notes that even though dating may be providing increasingly less satisfaction for the bachelor, he remains single because he fears the potential pain and vulnerability that may come with a permanent commitment. Prager explains further that learning to deal with pain (and the vulnerability that it brings) is a crucial part of achieving happiness. Unfortunately, many of us are so pain averse that we miss opportunities for fulfilling long-term relationships. Of course, we learn to avoid pain from our parents, who do whatever they can to shield us from it. *"But,"* said Prager, *"the purpose of life is not to avoid pain. That is the purpose of an animal's life – but animals cannot know happiness."*[16]

It follows then, that one way for us to avoid pain is to make shallow or conditional commitments in our relationships. For leadership actually to be leadership, at some point the leader must demonstrate belief in and commitment to followers. That means trusting people and becoming vulnerable by giving to them. What do leaders give? First, they give themselves and their talents. But beyond that, leaders also give power and meaningful work and recognition and more. Whether it's in a marriage or a multinational corporation, covenants cannot occur apart from willingness for people to trust and give to each other in this manner. By doing so they are trusting that the principles of the covenant when applied will work and that the people of the covenant, when trusted, will reciprocate. In a sense, leaders in an organization are a lot like partners in a marriage. To make it work, they must abandon themselves to the people and purposes of the covenant and in so doing make themselves vulnerable. However, in order to make the covenants effective and functional, leaders must also trust that their vulnerability will not be violated.

Forgiving Mistakes - I have had the good fortune of reading and seeing both the movie and the Broadway production of Victor Hugo's classic novel, *Les Miserables*. It is a moving story of both the healing power of forgiveness and the self destructive nature of vengeance and bitterness that come from an unforgiving heart.

The story opens with Valjean being released after serving a 19-year sentence in prison for stealing a loaf of bread. Homeless and destitute, Valjean is a hardened and bitter man. His fortune changes when a kindly and gracious bishop provides him food and lodging. Evidently, the Bishop's kindness is of little consequence to Valjean, because he steals his silverware and flees. He is soon caught by the police, but the Bishop covers for Valjean and tells the police it was a gift. This hardened and bitter man is transformed by the Bishop's act of grace and forgiveness.

Valjean gives up his hardness and bitterness, moves away and leads a humble and transformed life. He changes his name, builds a successful business and becomes mayor of a small town. However, due to a police oversight, he is alleged to have violated parole and the vengeful police inspector Javert sets out in pursuit of him. All is well until the new police inspector (Javert) arrives in town. It is Javert who recognizes Valjean from his previous life and plots to expose and capture him. Instead of succumbing to capture and prison, Valjean escapes to Paris with Cosette, the young daughter of one of his employees who had died. Valjean had raised Cosette as his own daughter and he loved her. But as she approached adulthood, Valjean was forced to let her go with a young revolutionary she loved because Javert was fast in pursuit. The story takes an interesting twist as Valjean extends kindness to Javert, and he helps him escape from the French revolutionaries.

The movie shows the contrast between Valjean who has been transformed by the grace and forgiveness of the Bishop and Javert who has a compulsive black and white view of justice that quickly becomes a distorted form of vengeance. While Javert's demand for justice and his need for vengeance make Valjean's life miserable, eventually Valjean's kindness overcomes the inspector's lack of forgiveness and Javert commits suicide rather than respond in kind. In this sense, forgiveness is as much about leaders giving up their right to vengeance as it is about giving the gift of forgiveness to others. Javert could not give forgiveness because he could not give up his right to vengeance and it eventually destroyed him.

What I find interesting is the fact that when mistakes are made inside organizations, CEOs or key managers sometimes act like Javert and refuse to give up their right to vengeance. This is particularly true when the CEO and/or managers perceive that they have been hurt in some way. Instead of forgiving the offending party, they get angry, seek revenge and demand justice in a manner that is designed to make the offender pay. Of course, payment can be extracted in a variety of ways including hurting the offender's career, assaulting his or her character or even excluding the person in a spiteful way. Whatever form the payment takes, it still comes from an unforgiving heart that demands vengeance. But this inevitably causes relational rifts and, in particular, inhibits the possibility of covenants developing; because it is difficult to form a covenant and trust someone who chooses not to forgive. For leaders to build long-term success, they must recognize that every person has flaws and sooner or later everyone makes mistakes. Since people spend almost half of their waking hours at work, it is probable that at least some of the mistakes they make will occur there. Modern day organizational Javerts who fix blame and demand retribution are incapable of leading or inspiring others to greatness. Instead they would rather wield power and control people through fear and intimidation.

Leaders, who endeavor to maximize the potential of individuals, must also give those individuals the freedom to take risks and make mistakes without having to pay or be lambasted every time they try something that fails. Like the kind Bishop in *Les Miserables*, leaders, if they are to be effective in transforming followers and maximizing their potential, must be willing to forgive and have some tolerance for mistakes. It is only when they do so, that people will feel safe enough to trust, become vulnerable and take risks. Forgiveness builds trust and cohesion because it draws people together rather than separates them. In contrast, demanding justice and seeking to extract payment for an offense like Javert did, not only pushes people apart, it can also destroy the person who refuses to forgive. Again, this is particularly true with power wielders. They would rather make people pay for mistakes and risk ruining the organization, than forgive and fix mistakes. Leaders are able to move past mistakes by giving up their right to vengeance or retribution and focusing on the potential of individuals to build and grow the organization.

Admitting Mistakes - In addition to forgiving mistakes, leaders must also be willing to admit mistakes and be transparent. That too becomes a form of trusting and giving. Essentially leaders are trusting in the integrity and good will of others not to violate the leader's transparency. They are also giving followers an honest and realistic view of themselves in ways that build credibility. For example, Stan Gault was clearly one of the premiere CEOs of the 1980s and early 1990s. At Rubbermaid his leadership helped generate 40 consecutive quarters of earnings growth. After completing the successful turnaround of Rubbermaid, he did the same thing at Goodyear. A *Forbes* article suggested that Mr. Gault was a "tyrant," to which he responded that, while he agreed that can be a tyrant, he also noted that he is a "sincere tyrant."[17] However, even this self-proclaimed tyrant (a label I find hard to justify after talking with him and hearing his appreciation for employees and his philosophy of leadership) expressed the danger of too much ego and noted the importance of leaders being willing to admit mistakes:

"No one is always correct and there isn't anyone who always has all the bright ideas. I don't think that one has to encourage conflict, but by the same token, you cannot shy away from it. I think that many times a position, top management or an individual has taken, could be the result of poor information that was originally used to support the hypothesis. There could have been an unexpected and significant change in the market, or in competition and therefore, what was right or correct back a few months ago, may not be the appropriate course of action today. You have to be willing to step back and say things have changed and we must change our direction, move forward and not get hung up emotionally. That you can't afford. Sometimes your ego won't permit you to either admit you made a mistake or that you should be changing course."[18]

Deepening Relationships Through Grace - Grace is often manifest in forgiveness and tolerance. It is by definition unmerited favor, and giving it is crucial both to covenants and to leadership. When leaders extend grace to others, it increases trust and good will and deepens relationships. A clear example of a leader trusting and giving the kind of grace that is manifest in forgiveness is found in a story about two of our country's most esteemed leaders, John Adams and Thomas Jefferson. Even though they had a lifelong friendship, they had many differences, and for a period they were estranged. However, they were reconciled towards the end of their lives and began a series of 158 correspondences between 1812 and 1826 that are now famous.

Evidence of the strength of their friendship is found in an incident that occurred in 1823. A series of letters that Adams had written earlier in his career were reprinted in the newspaper. In these letters Adams was less than complimentary of Jefferson, calling him a *"duplicitous political partisan."* The newspaper was obviously trying to stir up trouble between the two men, but Jefferson responded with grace and forgiveness by writing the following words to Adams, *"Be assured, my dear sir, that I am incapable of receiving the slightest impression from the effort now made to plant thorns on the pillow of age, worth, and wisdom, and to sow tares between friends who have been such for nearly half a century. Beseeching you, then (I ask you) not to suffer your mind to be disquieted by this wicked attempt to poison its peace, and praying you to throw it by."[19]*

So relieved and pleased was Adams at Jefferson's graceful words, he insisted that Jefferson's letter be read aloud at breakfast to his entire family. Jefferson had given a gift of grace to his friend and that gift was motivated by his love and admiration for Adams. Jefferson's actions depict what good leaders do; they forgive by disassociating actions or mistakes from the value of the person. It reminds me of what philosopher Soren Kierkegaard said in *Works of Love*:

> *"Through forgiveness love covers a multitude of sins. Silence really takes nothing away from the multitude of notorious sins. … forgiveness takes away that which still cannot be denied as being sin. So love strives in every way to hide the multitude of sins; but forgiveness is the most outstanding way."[20]*

What leaders do when they forgive or tolerate mistakes, is to demonstrate that they value this person and the relationship they share beyond this immediate action. In a very real sense, they are extending the gift of grace to people and grace tends to break down barriers and deepen relationships. Using Kierkegaard's description of forgiveness, Jefferson demonstrated not only that he valued Adams, but also that he loved him. Ultimately, the most effective leaders embrace grace and demonstrate in their ability to forgive, a form of love. That doesn't negate accountability between leaders and followers, but trusting people and giving them grace also builds trust and increases the likelihood that the accountability for actions will be self-imposed.

Demonstrating Compassion - As the head of Nucor Steel, the late Ken Iverson contended that his decision to buck the downsizing trend in the steel industry was a smart business move. History has clearly proven that he was correct. Beyond his shrewd business acumen, as a leader Mr. Iverson demonstrated compassion for the people who worked for him, and compassion is another way to build trust. It is also an antidote for self-centered, competitive environments that destroy trust. Though its origin is unknown, this often used saying is true for leaders: *"People don't care how much you know until they know how much you care."* In order to build covenants of trust, leaders must demonstrate care and compassion for the people they lead.

The late Henri Nouwen noted that compassion is in great demand and short supply in today's world. He explained, *"While in our intensely competitive society, the hunger and thirst for friendship, intimacy, union and communion are immense, it never has been so difficult to satisfy this hunger and quench this thirst.... As insecure, anxious, vulnerable and mortal beings ... competition seems to offer us a great deal of satisfaction.... It is not in 'excelling' but in 'serving' that makes us most human. It is not proving ourselves to be better than others but confessing to be just like others that is the way to healing and reconciliation."*[21]

Leaders are most effective when their followers or partners cooperate to achieve the purposes they have in common with the leader. That happens best in relationships based on trust where there is a culture of cohesion, cooperation and compassion. When the leader is able to establish such a culture and demonstrate compassion to and for followers, it increases the levels of trust that exist among them. It also represents a form of giving to followers that results in reciprocity, shared benefits and the potential for covenants to emerge among the people involved. Covenants naturally address our need for compassion, and that's part of the reason why they also create the synergy and power necessary for leaders to overcome great obstacles and to achieve great rewards.

Keeping Promises...Sharing Success and Hardship - When Kouzes and Posner conducted their study of 2685 managers, they found that the number one characteristic followers want from their leaders is honesty.[22] That's not surprising; because it's difficult to follow someone you have trouble believing. One of the chief areas in which leaders demonstrate honesty and gain and lose credibility is in how well they keep their promises. Simply stated, when leaders keep their promises to followers they gain credibility and when they break their promises they lose it.

Committing in a covenant and walking the talk of values also involve keeping the covenant promises regardless of the circumstances. That means aligning your behavior, keeping your promises and being willing to share the success but also the hardship. Apart from that, it simply is impossible to keep a covenant and when covenants are broken, it's usually because one person puts his or her interests and comfort ahead of those of others. Frank Layden is the former president of the Utah Jazz of the NBA. In a conversation I had with him about covenants, he commented:

> *"The minute the covenant is broken is when I say I'm more important than you are and that my goals are more important than yours and that the reason we are doing this is for my benefit or for the benefit of the few. And I don't think we should be able to do that. What we should rather say is that if we have a contract, then that contract is supposed to be fair to both of us."*[23]

A real life example of taking action consistent with the principles and keeping the promises of a covenant is found in the story of J. Robertson McQuilkin, President Emeritus of Columbia International University. For 22 years he served as the University's President, and his tenure was arguably one of the most productive of any president in the South Carolina school's history. By his own admission, this was his "dream job."

On a vacation to Florida, McQuilkin noticed that his wife, Muriel, began to repeat stories that she had just told only minutes before. It was a pattern that eventually would lead to a diagnosis of Alzheimer's. As the disease advanced, McQuilkin was faced with an important decision. His wife was obviously growing less and less conscious of both the people and the circumstances around her. The doctors advised him that regardless of the person providing care for her, her condition would likely deteriorate to the point where she would not recognize who it was. Therefore, he could just as easily continue as University President, achieving the vision of the University and taking care of his wife by providing full-time nursing care for her.

Despite the doctors' counsel, McQuilkin's covenant with his wife was much stronger than his loyalty to the University. He commented, *"When the time came, the decision was firm. It took no great calculation. It was a matter of integrity. Had I not promised 42 years before, 'in sickness and in health ... till death do us part?'"* President McQuilkin eventually resigned his position to care for his wife. In speaking of his action and his commitment to his wife, he said simply, *"This was no grim duty to which I was stoically resigned; however, it was only fair. She had, after all, cared for me for almost four decades with marvelous devotion; now it was my turn."*[24]

In his actions, J. Robertson McQuilkin demonstrated his commitment to and his belief in the principles and the concept of the covenant he shared with his wife. The same is true in organizations. Leaders are not only responsible for embracing and articulating a belief system, they must demonstrate commitment to those beliefs through their actions. Apart from that kind of commitment (the absence of action) they only create cynicism. It makes perfect sense that if I as a leader espouse the value of covenants, but I don't initiate actions consistent with the principles of covenant, I will lose credibility. In other words, as a leader I must continue to act in ways that are consistent with the trust, respect, good will, positive recognition and other common values implied in the covenant, regardless of the circumstances I face or what it may cost me personally in a given situation.

[1] Peppers, Don and Rogers, Martha. *The One to One Future.* Currency Doubleday, New York, 1993, pp. 328.

[2] Shockley Zalabak, Pamela, Ph.D.; Ellis, Kathleen, PhD; Casaria, Ruggerio. *Measuring Organizational Trust: A Diagnostic Survey and International Indicator.* IABC Research Foundation Report; 01, January, 2000; IABC.

[3] Loomis, Carol J.; *Warren Buffett Gives it Away"*,(Fortune; July 10, 2006) p. 60.

[4] Putnam, Robert D.; *Bowling Alone* (Simon and Schuster; New York, New York; 2000).

[5] Fukuyama, Francis; *Trust* (The Free Press; New York, New York; 1995). Also in: Howard, Philip; *The Death of Common Sense.*

6 Putnam, Robert D.; *Bowling Alone* (Simon and Schuster; New York, New York; 2000) p. 35.

7 Dyer, Jeffrey H.; Chu, Wujin; *The Determinants of Trust in Supplier-Buyer Relations in the U.S., Japan and Korea*; "Journal of International Business Studies Volume 31, Issue 2; April, 2000; pp. 259-285.

8 Jones, Jeffrey M., *Americans Express Little Trust in CEOs of Large Corporations or Stockbrokers: Four in 10 believe most people can be trusted; teachers are most trusted group*. http://www.gallop.com/poll/releases/pr020717.asp.

9 Wooden, John; Interview with Leonard J. Moisan; September 6, 1995.

10 Grard, Larry. Kennebec Journal Online, Morning Sentinal, Central Maine. com/news/local/250188.shtml, December 16, 2003.

11 Aeppel, Timothy. *Tricks of the Trade:On Factory Floors Top Workers Hide Secrets to Success*. (The Wall Street Journal; July 1, 2002) pp. A1, A10.

12 Fukuyama, Francis. *Trust: The Social Virtues and the Creation of Prosperity*. (New York: The Free Press; 1995).

13 Dalla Costa, John; *Ethical Imperative: Why Moral Leadership is Good Business* (Addison-Wesley; Reading, Massachusetts; 1998) p. 27.

14 Ibid, p. 27.

15 Iverson, Ken; *Plain Talk: Lessons From a Business Maverick* (Wiley, John & Sons, Inc.; 1997).

16 Prager, Dennis. *Happiness is a Serious Problem* (New York: HarperCollins Publishers, 1998) p. 54.

17 Gault, Stanley; "Sincere Tyranny," Forbes, January 28, 1985, p. 54.

18 Gault, Stanley; Interview with Leonard J. Moisan; August 6, 1996.

19 Jefferson, Thomas; Letter to John Adams; October 12, 1823 in: Ellis, Joseph J. *Founding Brothers – The Revolutionary Generation* (Alfred A. Knopf, New York, 2001) p. 224-225.

20 Soren Kierkegaard in: Bretall, Robert. *A Kierkegaard Anthology* (Princeton University Press; Princeton, New Jersey, 1946) p. 318.

21 Nouwen, Henri; *Here and Now* (Crossroad Publishing; New York, New York; 2000) pp. 98-99.

22 Kouzes, James, and Posner, Barry. *Credibility* (Jossey-Bass, Inc.; San Francisco, California; 1963).

23 Layden, Frank; Interview with Leonard J. Moisan; November 7, 1996.

24 McQuilkin, Robertson; *Muriel's Blessing, Christianity Today*, October, 1990.

Chapter 5
Leadership Evaluation and Action Discovery (LEAD)

Trust is an essential part of a covenant and research consistently demonstrates that the presence of trust in stakeholder relationships can greatly enhance profitability, innovation, organizational effectiveness, job satisfaction and more. Using the concepts presented in Chapter 5, please answer the following questions:

A. Do the following relationships between the people of your organization and stakeholders have a high level of trust?		YES	NO
1.	Relationships with employees	❏	❏
	Why or why not?		
2.	Relationships with customers	❏	❏
	Why or why not?		
3.	Relationships with suppliers	❏	❏
	Why or why not?		
B. What can you do to enhance trust with:			
1.	Employees:		
2.	Customers:		

3.	Suppliers:

C. Besides pay and products, what benefits flow to your stakeholders as a result of their relationship with your organization?

1.	Employees:

2.	Customers:

3.	Suppliers:

D. What promises have you or your organization made to key stakeholders (what do they expect?) and how can you better keep those promises?

1.	Employees:

2.	Customers:

3.	Suppliers:

Chapter 6

Identify Your Core Values and Align Your Behavior

Trust and cooperation in American life and work have traditionally been supported by and aligned with a set of core values. Values create the context in which relationships are established and common purposes are pursued. Until recently, those values were agreed upon and deemed important by most Americans. To this point, one of the conditions that Tocqueville found "astonishing" about America was what he called "the strange stability of certain principles". According to Tocqueville, as he traveled across America in the 1830's, he observed that these "principles" or core values were embraced broadly by most Americans. *"In the United States..."*, said Tocqueville, *"...general doctrines concerning religion, philosophy, morality and even politics do not vary at all...".*[1]

The reason Tocqueville found such stability and consistency of core values among Americans is due to the fact that they were taught in their homes, churches and civics classes. Those values guided the behavior of Americans and both created and preserved a uniquely American culture. This process of aligning behavior with core values continues to be an essential task of leaders and a crucial part of the covenant that Alexis de Tocqueville observed.

Moving Away From Legalism - It is not unusual for people to assume mistakenly that law brings order and stability. While that may be true in theory, for the most part order comes from our voluntary compliance with the common purposes and values that we share.

This is exactly what Tocqueville observed when he noted the "strange stability of certain principles" that were operating in America. True, the law sets limits, but the core values of most people have helped them live life well within the limits of the law. If this were not the case, there simply would not be enough police to enforce compliance.

We find today that those values and the culture they have created are changing and, to some extent, our relationships, our communities, our businesses and our organizations have suffered as a result. We now experience less of a consensus regarding our common values, and therefore less of a basis for trust and cooperation. We have replaced the flexible concept of covenant with a rigid concept of contract and, instead of values like integrity and commitment binding our agreements, it is either now the law or the threat of legal action. To this point Robert Putnam explains with a slight hint of sarcasm that, *"One alternative to generalized reciprocity and socialized honesty is the rule of law – formal contracts, courts, litigation, adjudication, and enforcement…If the handshake is no longer binding and reassuring, perhaps the notarized contract, the deposition, and the subpoena will work almost as well."* [2]

But building meaningful and productive relationships (covenants) based primarily on legalism is virtually impossible. It certainly makes leading and agreeing on values much more of a challenge. That's because the by-products of this emerging culture of legalism are increasing rigidity, growing disagreements and a focus on self, all of which represent the antithesis of a covenant. In his work on trust, Mr. Fukuyama cautioned that a legalistic preoccupation with individual rights in the U.S. undermines American economic interests because it dissipates trust.[3] That dissipation is evidenced in the growing frequency with which people today break commitments and look to the courts and to government to solve their problems.

Consider that since 1950 tort costs as a percentage of GDP in the U.S. have more than tripled, going from .62 percent of the GDP to more than 2 percent today. Total court costs are expected to exceed $300 billion in the coming years and have increased at an annual rate in excess of 9 percent since 1975. Medical malpractice tort costs are even more alarming as they have increased at a pace of nearly 12 percent per year during the same period.[4]

In December of 2004, President Bush traveled to Madison County, Illinois. It is a place that the American Tort Reform Association called the nation's top "judicial hellhole." The county judicial system is known for making big awards and allowing lawsuits that would otherwise be thrown out. Evidently the county has earned its reputation fairly. Over a two-year period more than 1400 asbestos cases and 179 class action suits were filed in Madison County.[5] Such legalistic thinking and the tort actions that follow are causing people across America to perform in a defensive posture because they fear being sued. At some point we have to ask where that takes us as a society. Already we are seeing that increases in tort action have caused an alarming number of physicians to drop their practices and businesses to close their doors. The 2000 presidential election gave us a taste of what life and decision-making are like in a legalistic society that values winning at any cost and requires trial lawyers and judges to arbitrate differences.

Though it definitely appears to be heightened in recent years, this rise in legalism is not exactly a new trend. So concerned was trial lawyer Philip Howard about the proliferation of litigation and regulation in the 1980s and 90s, that he wrote a best selling book entitled, *The Death of Common Sense: How Law is Suffocating People.* I had the opportunity to speak with Mr. Howard about the increases in litigation and regulation that America is experiencing. He noted that these conditions have continued to become the norm along with what he called the degradation of the legal profession. Elaborating on these points, Mr. Howard commented,

> " ... *What's happened to the profession is sort of like erosion. Slowly, year after year, the standards are getting lower and lower. What people get away with, what people are willing to say, arguments they are willing to make, writing briefs to say something that is literally accurate but conveys what they know to be an untruth.... And everyone keeps going down to*

the lowest common denominator ... and the result is general degradation."[6]

Howard believes that this increased litigation is hurting initiatives and paralyzing our ability to get things done, not to mention the damage that it's doing to relationships. This is clearly true in business where compliance costs and regulation are stifling, but Mr. Howard also explains that despite these conditions people still have not shirked their responsibilities. On the contrary, he believes there are plenty of people willing to assume responsibility and take initiative, but the bureaucratic systems we create constrain them. He noted,

> *"Many people are more than willing to or even anxious to take responsibility," he said, "but we've created systems which out of distrust of others taking responsibility, we have basically allowed no one to take responsibility . . . . I think it's less a fear of ourselves taking responsibility than it is the fear of other people taking responsibility and having authority. Whether it's teachers in the classroom . . . or doctors in a hospital using their best judgment, or inspectors or foremen or whomever it is in society."*[7]

Ultimately, the lack of trust emerging from this heightened legalism and regulation is making our relationships and our organizations less functional and less profitable in just the way that Mr. Fukuyama prophetically predicted it would. People, organizations and societies simply function better in an environment of trust, where values and not litigation and fear guide behavior. In fact, Mr. Fukuyama's observation regarding the relationship between trust and success is almost instinctive with effective leaders. Consider what the former head coach and president of the Boston Celtics, the late Red Auerbach, said about his now legendary run of success. In an interview he gave in the 1980s on leadership, Auerbach explained that trust and loyalty were central to his philosophy, and those values were applied in his relationships with workers and players in ways that helped the Celtics win 16 world championships. Auerbach also commented on the lack of ingenuity and productivity that come from fear and mistrust:

"If you have employees who work through fear, you're not going to get any ingenuity out of them ... all you'll have are robots that are going to do their jobs, have a low-key approach, stay out of trouble."[8]

True, legalism and regulation can hold people in check and may even intimidate them into compliance, but they are limited. They cannot, for example, bring people together in a cooperative effort or inspire them to greatness. Those things happen only when there is strong leadership, common purposes, an alignment of behavior with core values and a solid foundation of trust.

No doubt, leadership is an essential part of the equation for moving our organizations and our society away from this trend of legalism and towards a trend of trust. However, for leaders to create or gain trust, they must be willing to give it. How do leaders give trust and move away from legalism? They do it by relying less on laws and rules that control behavior and more on core values and principles that guide it.

Walking the Talk - Unfortunately, in just about every sector of society there are organizations rife with mistrust and operating in the legalistic, contractual manner that Messrs. Howard, Fukuyama and Auerbach all warn against. Again, this does not mean that we can or even should eliminate the use of contracts. Our modern world sometimes demands that contracts be used as a standard part of doing business. But this also does not justify operating in a strictly contractual manner towards each other. For a contract to work well it requires an assumption of good faith among the people involved. That good faith is based on some underlying values such as integrity, trust, cooperation, a sense of common purpose and respect; values that are shared and therefore central to the relationship.

Of course, it will not do simply for organizations to have stated values. There must be alignment between those values and the daily practices within the organization. In fact, misalignment between values and practices often is where the seeds of an ethical breach take root and the covenant begins to be broken. That's why leaders must assume responsibility for ensuring that relationships are respected and that the core values are aligned with practices and lived daily.

Consider the case of the Enron Corporation. Boldly stated in their company literature were their core values of *Respect, Integrity, Communication and Excellence*. No doubt, when these values were developed they were intended to guide their company's operations. However, at some point something caused the company decision makers to operate quite contrary to the stated values. Even as the company was deteriorating, the founder and corporate chairman, Kenneth Lay, continued to tout those values and encourage people to buy Enron stock. In fact, at the same time he was telling employees that the stock was an "incredible bargain," he and about two dozen senior executives were cashing in more than $1 billion worth of that same stock. Two days before filing bankruptcy, Enron gave $55 million in retention bonuses to "key managers," yet they refused to provide severance pay to the 4,500 employees they laid off of work. In total, the company's indiscretions caused 15,000 employees to lose $1.2 billion, and the CFO alone to be charged with 109 counts of fraud, money laundering, conspiracy and obstruction of justice. Eventually, in May of 2006 the late Ken Lay was convicted on all six counts brought against him including conspiracy to commit securities fraud. Likewise, CEO Jeff Skilling was convicted on 19 counts of conspiracy and fraud. [9] Had the Enron executives taken their stated values more seriously and aligned their practices with those values, there would not have been an ethical breach or a violation of the covenant that was implied in the values they had publicly stated.

Maintaining a Culture - To be effective, particularly in building and maintaining covenants, core values cannot be just words. Since core values represent the spirit of the covenant, they must be shared and they must reflect the culture or ethos of the organization. According to philosopher Immanuel Kant, *"Culture restrains and informs personal desires so that individual expression binds people together in a community of shared values."* [10] Creating a culture with core values that are shared and applied daily is the responsibility of leaders, and adherence to those values is an essential part of keeping the covenant. Core values help build credibility and confidence so that, regardless of how difficult the circumstances might become or how "iron clad" a contract may be, ultimately the people involved can trust each other because the core values will guide their actions. Though that sounds simple enough, maintaining the culture by aligning daily practices with the stated core values does not automatically happen. It requires hard work and vigilance on the part of leaders and the presence of at least three conditions:

(1) First, the values must have some basis in objective or universal truth. If they do, then the values are transcendent and applicable in all situations; if not, they are relative and applicable only in some situations. Cicero noted that true law (or what we would call objective principles), *"is right reason in agreement with nature; it is of universal application, unchanging and everlasting; it summons to duty by its commands, and averts from wrongdoing by its prohibitions."*[11] Thus, if our values are based on true *"unchanging"* principles, then what to do or not do in a given situation becomes more obvious. For example, if respect and integrity are relative truths, then it is up to me as an individual to decide when and where to apply them. Accordingly, it is a short step of rationalization for me to accommodate disrespect and dishonesty of the kind that led to Enron's downfall. Conversely, if those truths are universal, then they apply in all situations for everyone, not just in situations where applying the values serves my own self-interest.

(2) Second, those values should be widely communicated and commonly understood. For example, my youngest son was a scholarship athlete at the University of Notre Dame. For each of his four years of eligibility, he had to attend an orientation/ training session that is mandatory for all varsity athletes. At these all-day meetings the President, the Athletic Director and other university officials discuss the values of the Notre Dame athletic program and the behavioral expectations of Notre Dame athletes in alignment with those values. Among other

things, they learn about the code of ethics (or as they call it at Notre Dame, *The DuLac*). They are taught how to deal with members of the press and appropriate manners for dining and traveling. They learn that there is zero tolerance for fighting, drug and alcohol violations and premarital sex. In addition, these athletes learn that they have academic expectations that supersede their athletic commitment and that they are considered Notre Dame athletes with behavioral expectations 24 hours a day, seven days per week and 365 days per year. Since these values are widely communicated and commonly understood, there is no excuse and little tolerance for any behavioral misalignment.

(3) Third, leaders must demonstrate a strong commitment to hold themselves and others in the organization accountable for aligning their behavior with those values. Values are intended to help create an organizational culture. At Notre Dame there are no double standards in holding athletes accountable for the stated values and expectations. In fact, several times in the past decade well-known star athletes have been dismissed from the University as a result of a failure to align their behavior with the values. In many cases, after sitting out for a period, these athletes have been able to amend their behavior, return to the university and go on to graduate successfully. It is a system that balances accountability with a sense of grace; a culture in which athletes can learn, contribute and achieve success in ways that will equip them for life.

Eric Guerra, the Coordinator of Student Development, works primarily with student athletes at Notre Dame. He noted that leaders at The University take the core values quite seriously and they try to lead by example, aligning their own behavior with those values. He commented, *"It starts with Father Malloy (former President) and his example. He lives in Sorin Hall with the students and he teaches. It is very much a model of servant leadership.*

> *Then the coaches and the rest of the university officials all try to live by the spirit of 'DuLac.'"* Mr. Guerra explained further, *"I feel the responsibility myself. We believe we are compelled to be what we represent and therefore everyone is held to that same high standard."*[12]

This is not to suggest that the core values at Notre Dame are never violated, either by students or by faculty and staff. In a community that large there are bound to be misalignments. However, when those misalignments between the stated values and practices do occur, they stand out as a sharp contrast to the norm, and the violators are usually held accountable.

In a corporate setting core values make statements about how we will do business, how we will deal with our customers and how we will treat each other. If the culture does not reflect the values, then it's usually because the "leaders" do not consider the values serious enough to hold themselves or others accountable for them. Again, had the senior executives at Enron "walked the talk" and aligned their behavior with their stated values of respect, integrity, communication and excellence, they never would have considered deceiving their employees or shareholders in the first place.

Doing What is Right - In discussing the concept of leaders aligning their behavior with a set of reasoned and ethical core values, what I am really talking about is leaders doing what is "right" and not just what is "legal." The problem for many leaders is that within the complexity of every day life, sometimes what is right is a lot different than what is legal. That's because law often sets the bar for action at its lowest tolerable point, rather than it's highest. Certainly what is right in a given circumstance should always meet the test of being within the limits of the law. But if something is "right," it should also be consistent with our core values and beliefs. It is this latter test of consistency that often restrains people from taking certain actions that might be "legal" but not necessarily moral or ethical.

That is exactly the point Alexis de Tocqueville made in the 1830s when he observed, *"... while the law allows the American people to do everything, there are things that religion (values and beliefs) prevents them from imagining and forbids them to dare.*"[13]

What Tocqueville observed was a way of life where most Americans were holding to a standard of right that was much higher than what was legal. By contrast and with increasing frequency, we now rely much more on the law to guide and regulate our behavior than we do on trusting people to do what is right. As Philip Howard has observed, the consequence of our reliance on the law is hurting our ability both to relate to one another and to get things done. On this point he cautioned that,

> "*law cannot save us from ourselves. Waking up every morning, we have to go out and try to accomplish our goals and resolve disagreements by doing what we think is right. That energy and resourcefulness, not millions of legal cubicles, is what was great about America. Let judgment and personal conviction be important again. There is nothing unusual or frightening about it. Relying on ourselves is not, after all, a new ideology. It's just common sense.*"[14]

Restoring the importance of judgment and personal conviction so that covenants can flourish will require leaders who are committed to leading based on doing what is right.

Continuing the Legacy - In *Leadership is an Art*, Max DePree, author and Chairman Emeritus of the Herman Miller Company, notes that leaders are responsible for leaving behind them assets and a legacy.[15] No doubt, the strength of the balance sheet as reflected in physical and financial assets is an important concern for leaders. But an equally important concern for leaders is the question of who will lead when they are gone. That concern is what DePree calls a leader's legacy, the responsibility to develop new leaders who will grow the assets, teach the values, align the behaviors and perpetuate the culture. It's an important part of the leader's covenant commitment to the people and the organization.

A few years ago I had the good fortune to speak with New York Yankee's great Bobby Richardson. He explained that when he played, the older Yankee players took responsibility for passing along the Yankee values or what he called the "Yankee culture" to the younger players during the "golden years" of the New York Yankees:

> *"I know if a younger player came in who didn't have the tradition (habits, values) the Yankees had, the older player would step in and say, 'Hey, listen, that's not the way we operate here, we do it this way; we're a team; we don't play as individuals.' And so I saw in my time with the Yankees, just a real, real togetherness and a bonding around common values and goals."*[16]

In a sense the leadership responsibility and eventually the legacy are both wrapped up in the establishment, strengthening and continuation of the organizational culture. How well the leader aligns behavior with values and how well he or she keeps the covenant will determine how enduring the culture is and, therefore, how strong the leadership legacy is.

---

[1] Tocqueville, Alexis. *Democracy in America*, J.P. Mayer and Max Lerner, eds. (New York: Harper & Row, 1966).

[2] Putnam, Robert D.; *Bowling Alone* (Simon and Schuster: New York, NY; 2000) p. 144-145.

[3] Fukuyama, F. *Trust: The Social Virtues and the Creation of Prosperity* (New York: The Free Press; 1995).

[4] Tillinghast - Towers Perrin; *U.S. Tort Costs: 2004 Update Trends and Findings on the Cost of the U.S. Tort System* (January 14, 2004) p. 2.

[5] USAToday.com; *Bush to highlight tort reform in Illinois*; January 4, 2005; www.usatoday.com/news/Washington/2005-01-04-bush-tort_x.htm?esp=36.

[6] Howard, Philip; Interview with Leonard J. Moisan; September 12, 1995.

[7] Ibid.

[8] Weber, A. M. "Red Auerbach on Management." *Leaders on Leadership: Interviews With Top Executives.* Warren Bennis, ed. (Boston: Harvard Business School; 1987).

[9] Sunseri, Gina and Rottman, Sylvie; *"Enron Verdict: Ken Lay Guilty on all Counts, Skilling on 19 Counts*; May 25, 2006; abcnews.go.com/Business/ LegalCenter/Story?id=2003728&page=2; see also Emshwiller, John R. and Smith, Rebecca; *24 Days* (New York: HarperCollins Publishers; 2003).

[10] Kant, Immanuel; *Lectures on Ethics*, "The General Principle of Morality;" ed. Nelson, Benjamin (trans. Infield, Lewis); Harper and Row; New York, 1963.

[11] Keyes, Clinton Walker (ed.); Cicero: Deke Publica De Legibus (Cambridge, Harvard University Press; 1952) p. 211.

[12] Guerra, Eric, Telephone interview with Len Moisan; August 5,

[13] Tocqueville, Alexis de. *Democracy in America*. J.P. Mayer and Max Lerner, eds. (New York: Harper & Row, 1966).

[14] Howard, Philip K.; *The Death of Common Sense* (Random House; New York; 1994) p. 187.

[15] DePree, Max; *Leadership is an Art* (Dell Trade Paperback; 1989).

[16] Richardson, Bobby; Interview with Leonard J. Moisan; January 8, 1996

Chapter 6
Leadership Evaluation and Action
Discovery (LEAD)

At Enron Corporation their core values were respect, integrity, communication and excellence. They were wonderful core values, but the core values did not guide the operations and leaders were not held accountable for aligning their behavior with the values. Using the information in this chapter, please answer the following questions:

A. What core values guide your organization?
B. How are those core values communicated now and how can they be communicated more effectively in the future so they are widely understood by stakeholders?

C. How or to what extent are people held accountable to ensure that values and behavior are aligned?

D. How can the core values be used to reduce legalism and increase trust and freedom in your organization?

Chapter 7
Create Meaning and Momentum

Relationships without meaning are usually short lived. That's because we want our affiliations and our efforts to matter, and we grow impatient when we sense that they don't. Meaning comes from having a sense of purpose and then pursuing that purpose, usually in an alliance with other people. But meaning is not just about having and pursuing a purpose; it's also about making meaningful contributions in that pursuit and being a valued and trusted member of the group. Also, the larger the purpose, typically the greater the meaning associated with the pursuit of it.

As people contribute talent, effort and/or money to the group in pursuit of a purpose larger than their own individual purposes and they make progress on that purpose, they also gain meaning and a sense of momentum. This is particularly true as individuals can see the influence of their efforts and investments on others. That's why the pursuit of a larger purpose is rarely done in isolation. In fact, most of the time larger purposes are achieved through alliances of two or more people. At their best, those alliances become covenants.

Sometimes people, and in particular would-be leaders, miss opportunities to gain meaning and experience the benefits of a covenant because they are too focused on themselves. Rather than making a commitment to a larger purpose or person, they keep their options open looking for the best deal. Often the only value they see in relating to others is what the relationship can do for them personally. But that is no way to try and create strong bonds with other people or to build a sense of meaning in life. Regardless of the environment in which relationships develop (work, church, community, etc.) in order to sustain them and eventually maximize their potential; they must have a clear and ethical purpose. However, to create meaning the pursuit of that purpose should also make a contribution beyond the private interests of the individuals involved. When that happens it tends to create a sense of meaning and momentum, particularly in an organizational environment. However, achieving that state requires certain actions and attitudes on the part of the leaders.

Losing Free Agency - Meaning comes not just from what we do, but from what we do in relationship to and with other people. Even the person who works in isolation can derive meaning from knowing that his work will serve others. For individuals and particularly leaders to be successful in building covenant relationships with meaning, it's important for them to start with an understanding that we all work and live in relationship to and with other people. By coming to this point of understanding, leaders are acknowledging that in some ways they are also dependent on other people. The baseball industry realized painfully in the aftermath of its mid 1990s strike, that ultimately none of us is a free agent. The erosion of their fan base demonstrated that point quite vividly for the baseball players and owners alike. We are all part of something bigger than ourselves whether we acknowledge that fact or not. It might be a larger organization, industry, group of people, community, or even an idea, but that "something" does exist and we simply cannot function effectively independent of it. Though we like to think of ourselves as independent and self-sufficient, in reality we are not even close to being free agents. When individuals cling to free agency or independence at any level of any group, it isolates them from others in ways that make them less effective. This is particularly true of leaders in an organization. One of the myths of leadership is that it's "lonely at the top." The reality is that loneliness is a choice. The late Henri Nouwen explained it this way,

> *"Much of our isolation is self chosen. We do not like to be dependent on others and, whenever possible, we try to show ourselves that we are in control of the situation and can make our own decisions. This self-reliance has many attractions*

130

*... a sense of power ... the satisfaction of being our own boss
... it promises many rewards ... (but) the underside of this
self-reliance is loneliness, isolation and a constant fear of not
making it in life.*"[1]

While effective leaders have an almost innate understanding of this
fact, power wielders have difficulty admitting their dependence on
anyone but themselves. That's because realizing our interdependence
and acknowledging the fact that we are linked to others by a common
purpose, "something bigger than us," requires a level of humility
that power wielders typically lack. When we are humble enough to
recognize our interdependence, then people become less expendable
and more valuable to us intrinsically. It better equips us to establish
covenants with one another and deal with both prosperity and
hardship more effectively. That's because in and through these
common connections, we can gain an understanding not only that
we have a purpose but also that we are not alone in that purpose.

In *Man's Search for Meaning*, psychiatrist and survivor of Nazi war
camps, Victor Frankl, noted that happiness and success do not occur
as they are pursued by an individual for individual consumption. He
argued that sometimes the more intensely a person pursues them, the
more elusive they become. Frankl observed further that happiness
and success often occur as a person gets lost in the service of another
or in the pursuit of a purpose with a larger meaning. He explained it
this way, "*A man who becomes conscious of the responsibility he bears
toward a human being who affectionately waits for him (a covenantal
connection and commitment), or to an unfinished work (a larger
purpose), will never be able to throw away his life. He knows the 'why'
for his existence, and will be able to bear almost any 'how.'*"[2]

Accommodating Heroism ... Building Something That Lasts - In the
now classic work, *The Denial of Death*, Ernest Becker argued that
because the world is terrifying, particularly as we contemplate our
inevitable death, the motivation for a great deal of human behavior
is to make sense of our life by finding ways to deny or transcend
death. He notes that man is typically absorbed with himself and,
as Aristotle noted, most people view luck as someone next to them

getting hit by an arrow. One of the ways men and women try to transcend death and gain meaning is in their attempts to become heroes. Becker explained, *"Tell a young man that he is entitled to be a hero and he will blush... (Yet) we disguise our struggle by piling up figures in a bank book to reflect privately our sense of heroic worth, or having only a little better home ... a bigger car ... brighter children."*[3]

Like Victor Frankl, Becker argues that if man believes what he is doing has the potential to be meaningful and to last beyond himself, then he is capable of great endurance and some incredibly heroic acts. Becker's concept is grounded in the idea that people gain meaning by being a part of something with meaning and having the opportunity to contribute to that something in meaningful ways. He comments,

> *"Man will lay down his life for his country, his society, his family. He will choose to throw himself on a grenade to save his comrades; he is capable of the highest generosity and self sacrifice. But he has to believe that what he is doing is truly heroic, timeless, and supremely meaningful."*[4]

What Becker is really talking about is a person's need to contribute and achieve and, in so doing, accomplish something of potentially heroic proportions. Most people want and even need to be a hero at some level. Leaders understand this need and they allow people to make meaningful contributions to something bigger than themselves. It takes a conscious commitment on the part of the leader to allow someone other than himself to become a hero and be celebrated as such. Often this happens in an organization as leaders enlist the help of followers in building something that lasts. Again, Ernest Becker explains that people are able to earn a sense of the "heroic" by creating something that, *"... reflects human value: a temple, a cathedral, a totem pole, a skyscraper, a family that spans three generations (and I would add a team, an organization or some kind of legacy). The hope and belief is that the things that man creates in society are of lasting worth and meaning, that they outlive and outshine death and decay, and finally that man and his products count."*[5]

In a covenant then, leaders help their people derive meaning. They achieve this by providing followers with opportunities to participate in building something that has the potential to grow beyond their individual capacities and last beyond their individual lifetimes. In providing those opportunities, leaders also empower people to take risks, to make contributions through heroic efforts and to receive recognition for their contributions.

Giving, Not Just Receiving - In the movie, *Fever Pitch*, actor Jimmy Fallon plays Ben, a high school teacher who falls in love with Lindsey, a businesswoman who is played by Drew Barrymore. The relationship blossoms until the spring of 2004 when Ben's passion for the Red Sox begins to compete with his affection for Lindsey. During a late winter, pre-season cookout in the park, Ben tells Lindsey about his passion for the Red Sox, explaining that he enjoys being part of something bigger than he is. In other words, Ben's passion gives him a sense of meaning. As the movie progresses, it becomes evident that Ben and Lindsey both want their relationship to progress to marriage. But for the covenant to work, Ben must give more of himself to Lindsey than to the Red Sox. The conflict between Ben's passion for the Red Sox and his new passion for Lindsey eventually gets resolved, but he first had to realize that life committed to Lindsey in a covenant offered a much more fulfilling and meaningful life and future than a life committed to the Red Sox.

In Victor Frankl's terms, having a larger meaning or a sense of purpose helps us define who we are and why we exist, and it also enables us to cast a vision for the future. Whether our larger "meaning" is found in God, work, family, relationships, community, or an integration of any or all of these elements, we rely on it to help us make sense of the world and to sustain us in times of hardship. In part, "making sense" means recognizing and working towards a common purpose. It also means knowing that as we work we are connected to others in what are now or what promise to be healthy, prosperous and fulfilling relationships. That demands also that we acknowledge our interdependence and give back to those relationships rather than just receive from them. In the final analysis it became obvious to Ben that his passion for the Red Sox was a poor substitute for the potential of his relationship with Lindsey. To restore and build that relationship, Ben had to give to it and not just receive from it. Giving in this case meant that Ben had to demonstrate to Lindsey that she was more important to him than the Red Sox. Accordingly, he took steps to sell his season tickets, tickets that had been bequeathed to him. Making the relationship work really meant that Ben had to give up his free agency and commit more deeply to Lindsey. When he did give in this way, their relationship was restored and their bond tightened.

There is probably no industry where the concept of giving is more alien and free agency is more prevalent than professional sports. Though there is a desire to perform well and win in most athletes, free agency is much more about "receiving" a big contract and much less about "giving." Yet, despite operating in such an environment, professional football player Pat Tillman demonstrated his understanding of these concepts of giving back and gaining meaning. In the wake of the 9/11 attacks on the World Trade Center, he gave up a lucrative career with the Arizona Cardinals to enlist in the Army. At the time of his enlistment, Tillman commented, *"My great grandfather was at Pearl Harbor, and a lot of my family has gone and fought in wars, and I really haven't done a damn thing as far as laying myself on the line like that."*[6] Pat Tillman derived meaning from knowing he was connected to his ancestors and fellow Americans by the ideals they embraced. His understanding of this connection and the larger meaning of the ideals, gave him momentum and compelled him to give back rather than just receive from the covenant they shared. Unfortunately, Pat Tillman paid the ultimate price when he was killed in Afghanistan, fighting for the ideals in which he believed and giving so that others might be free.

Giving in a covenant is giving to preserve and strengthen the relationship and not just to receive from it. Like Pat Tillman and many other leaders have done, it necessitates that we put aside some of our immediate selfish interests (our free agency) or gratification and initiate action that serves the interest of someone or something else. That also requires a certain amount of trust, trust in the importance of the mission and trust in the people we serve. However, as we do trust others and rely on the pursuit of something with a meaning larger than ourselves to motivate and direct us, it makes it easier to give. Covenants also assume the good will of others not to take advantage of us as we give. As leaders that doesn't mean that initiating covenants requires us also to be naïve about people. Clearly at some point we are likely to encounter people and circumstances that will test our resolve in these matters. But being a covenant leader means understanding that despite the potential problems associated with trusting and giving to people, the meaning, momentum and other potential benefits of the covenant are well worth the risk.

Mitigating Individualism with Purpose and Vision - The individualism manifest in the quest for either free agency or sovereignty within an organization creates barriers that tend to stifle momentum. When people understand that a certain person is out for herself and her own welfare above all else, then they tend to cooperate less with her. Conversely, as a person cooperates and gives in working with others toward a common purpose and vision, it mitigates such individualism and creates momentum. Momentum that flows from working with others who share the same sense of purpose and vision bonds people together and offers them a larger meaning. That meaning is reaffirmed and reassured by the unselfish acts of leaders who model the way in giving and working toward the same ends as followers. That's why sustained momentum doesn't come from power wielding. It comes from leading, leading in ways that keep the common purpose and vision in front of followers and set the tone for cooperating and working together. Actually, it is this kind of cooperative pursuit, combined with the benevolent acts of leaders, that enable those leaders to build trust, cast a common vision and give the organization direction. When those elements are present, they mitigate individualism and help provide the meaning and momentum that are so crucial to long-term success.

In *Leadership Is An Art*, Max DePree notes that helping create meaning and momentum is the responsibility of leaders. He explains how momentum, common purpose and vision work together to help people derive meaning: *"Momentum in a vital company is palpable.... It is the feeling among a group of people that their lives and work are intertwined and moving toward a recognizable and legitimate goal (common purpose). It begins with competent leadership.... Momentum comes from a clear vision of what the corporation ought to be, from a well thought out strategy to achieve that vision, and from careful conceived and communicated directions and plans that enable everyone to participate and be publicly accountable....*[7]

People who are engaged in ways that simultaneously benefit them and allow them to contribute to a larger purpose and vision, are able to build fruitful partnerships (covenants) as they work. Those partnerships allow them to derive meaning in much the same way as Victor Frankl described it. No doubt, in the midst of everyday battles, it's quite easy to lose sight of the essentials we have in common with others. It takes a leader to keep the team members focused on their common purposes and not on their individual agendas or differences. Therein lies an important part of the leader's role in creating momentum and nurturing covenants with and among followers.

Planning to Achieve the Purpose – Though it is by no means original with me, one of my favorite adages is, *"Failing to plan is planning to fail."* Implied in that sentence is the fact that even if a person succeeds without planning, success is short-lived. A general lack of planning can and often does lead to such problems as a lack of unified purpose, poor communication, the pursuit of a lot of individual agendas, low morale, heightened conflict, declining cooperation and eventually failure. By contrast, having a plan to achieve a purpose, helps enhance a sense of meaning, momentum and hope about the future among the people of an organization.

Consider the experience of a small engineering firm I worked with for about a year. Originally, the CEO sought help from our firm because in a five-year period his company grew from $5 million in sales and a 20 percent profit margin, to $25 million in sales with a zero percent profit margin. Needless to say, this raised more than a little concern with the CEO; but as far as we could tell at the time, the CEO was one of the few people concerned about the future of the company. In part, that was due to the fact that the CEO did not allow others to share his concerns; nor did he allow them to help find solutions and thereby become involved in meaningful ways.

We began our work with interviews of senior staff and a review of some key reports, and then we followed up with employee and customer surveys. After a few weeks, the critical issues became apparent. Among the most obvious were a lack of planning, a lack of meaningful involvement in decision making and a lack of effective communication. As it often does in organizations, this caused increasing frustration for employees, heightened conflict among managers and a growing lack of confidence in the company leaders. In response, we helped organize and then facilitate a planning process, working with a cross-functional planning team. Through this process, the team created a mission, vision and core values; identified critical issues; established goals to address the critical issues and achieve the vision; developed and prioritized strategies and action plans to achieve the goals and then developed a process both for implementation and evaluation of the plan and its progress.

As the plan was implemented, the entire company appeared to gain a much better sense of purpose and direction. In addition, momentum started to build, morale improved and within about 18 months the profit margin increased to almost 20 percent on $25 million in sales. The planning process allowed people to clarify the organizational purpose and to get a greater sense of meaning and momentum because they were directly involved both in the plan's creation and implementation. They knew that what they said and what they did mattered.

Acknowledging Interdependence - The process of creating meaning and momentum described by Max DePree takes a deliberate effort on the part of leaders. It involves building synergy by creating an environment that acknowledges interdependence in the pursuit of a common purpose. It is quite contrary to a power driven environment where organizational heads try to assume a certain amount of organizational sovereignty. In fact, for individuals or groups to assume they are sovereign usually means that they also assume they are independent of all others and above all others. In this kind of environment the concept of "larger meaning" and the sense of momentum derived from pursuing a common purpose are lost. Power wielding may work for a short period of time but, as Jim Collins discovered in his research in *Good to Great*, to build companies with sustained results (and momentum) over a long period requires that leaders engage the talent and energy of the people they lead.[8]

The improvements and increased profitability the small engineering firm experienced, came as a result of the CEO humbling himself, asking for help and engaging the talent and experience of his people. True, some corporate "heads" at times act as if they are totally self-reliant. Yet, people and corporations who operate as if they themselves are the only ones who can sustain their long term existence, eventually collapse under the weight of their own egos.

Creating Conditions for Peak Performance...Supporting Flow - It is not uncommon for athletes to talk of peak performance as being in the "flow" of the game, meaning that their performance was at a very high level and the game came easy. With athletes who do perform at such a level, it's not unusual for them to elevate the play of everyone on the team. For example, it was frequently said of Michael Jordan that he elevated the play of everyone on the basketball court, teammates and opponents alike. The same thing is also true of peak performers in just about any kind of organization; they elevate the productivity of the people around them. Whenever that happens it proves to be meaningful and fulfilling for everyone involved. Equally important is the fact that it is virtually impossible in organizations or in team sports, for individuals to get into the flow of what they are doing and experience peak performance without certain conditions being present and without assistance and cooperation from their teammates.

For more than two decades Mihaly Csikszentmihalyi, a professor and former chairman of the Psychology Department at the University of Chicago, conducted research on the "optimal experience," times when people experience states of deep concentration, high productivity and considerable enjoyment. He called these states of peak performance "flow," a condition where people are so focused that they become absorbed in an activity and they describe themselves as being in control, alert, at the peak of their abilities and highly fulfilled as a result of what they are doing.[9] When "flow" exists in any kind of organization, not only do the people involved achieve high levels of productivity and enjoyment, they also achieve meaning in their work. While most leaders desire to have peak performers, they do not always provide the conditions necessary for it to occur. Consequently because these conditions are missing, work is not nearly as meaningful or productive as it might have been.

From his studies, Professor Csikszentmihalyi observed that "flow" requires at least three conditions, the first of which is *having and understanding a common or unified purpose*. According to Csikszentmihalyi, "a unified purpose gives meaning to life," and it is in pursuit of and commitment to a unified and worthy purpose (whether it's winning a championship, building a company or serving mankind) that people are able to gain a sense of meaning in what they do and eventually to experience "flow." Helen Keller explained it this way, *"Many persons have a wrong idea of what constitutes true happiness. It is not attained through self-gratification, but through fidelity to a worthy purpose."*[10]

On this point, the author also cautions that it is not enough just to have a purpose; people must also carry through with action and overcome the challenges of achieving that purpose. Accordingly, *resolve* as Csikszentmihalyi describes it, is the second condition necessary for flow and it must translate into appropriate action, or what the author calls "resolution."[11] Resolution becomes the vehicle for pursuing and achieving the purpose. For example, if asked, most coaches and players will tell you that they endeavor to win championships. Yet, very few are willing or even able to carry through on that purpose with the preparation and resolve to take appropriate action and overcome challenges. The same is true of individuals and organizations.

The final condition necessary for flow that Csikszentmihalyi discusses is *harmony*. Harmony comes when the thoughts, actions and focus of the organization or the individual are centered on achieving the purpose with resolution. He explains, *"When an important goal (purpose) is pursued with resolution, and one's varied activities fit together into a unified flow experience, the result is that harmony is brought to consciousness. People who understand their common purpose and work with resolve to achieve that purpose, can also reach a point where their feelings, thoughts, actions and focus are congruent with one another. When that kind of congruence exists, the individuals and the team usually achieve a certain amount of harmony."*[12]

Energizing Individuals With Meaningful Work, Increased Responsibility and Greater Empowerment - For people who do experience flow, it doesn't mean the absence of hard work. On the contrary, individuals who have a fulfilling "flow" or peak experience often exert efforts of heroic proportions to achieve a common purpose or goal. Csikszentmihalyi's observations of such heroic efforts also implies that the goal or purpose should be challenging enough or large enough to require the focus of all or at least a larger part of a person's energies. Accordingly, where there is a challenging purpose that stretches people, along with resolution (action) and harmony; there is also a great deal of meaning associated with the work and at least the potential for a peak performance or "flow" experience. While true "flow" experiences are not always the same, they are closely related, particularly in the sense of the enjoyment and fulfillment that each kind of experience brings.

For example, in August of 1982, 33-year-old Tom Mendenhall was an eager and energetic assistant treasurer for cash and banking at Martin Marietta Corporation. His boss at the time, Bob Powell, happened to be out of town and Chief Financial Officer, Charlie Leithauser gave Tom the responsibility of raising a total of $930 million over one weekend. The funds were used to counter Bendix Corporation's unfriendly attempt to purchase Martin Marietta. Instead of his company submitting to a hostile takeover, Tom's work over the weekend and then over the next month helped Martin Marietta purchase the larger Bendix Corporation, thus forming the now famous "pac man" strategy. According to Tom,

"I was working consistently 16-18 hours a day and I loved it. The action and the responsibility energized me and I couldn't get enough of it. Hard work and long hours weren't ever an issue. Besides, I was part of a team and we all respected and supported each other. At times, we were all physically exhausted and we made mistakes, but we covered for one another. For the first time, I was on the front line doing something I knew was critically important, and I was willing to do just about anything I had to do to deliver. Not only did I enjoy it, but I have gone the rest of my career trying to replicate that experience. Sure, I worked a lot harder, but I was willing to do it because what I was doing was meaningful and important. I felt good and my work was fulfilling. You can't imagine the feelings of exhilaration and satisfaction we experienced the day we went in to City Bank in lower Manhattan and actually bought the Bendix stock."[13]

Similarly, retired executive Edie Stein described what she considered to be one of the peak experiences in her career at UPS. She was part of a group that proposed to senior executives that the company start their own airline. Though the company owned some planes prior to that period, UPS had also been contracting a substantial portion of their work with outside carriers. In the 1980s the business continued to grow and, according to Edie, the year they made their proposal they had close to 90 aircraft, so the proposal made sense. In August of 1987 the UPS Board of Directors accepted the proposal and by September the team began to work with a target date for completion by December 31 of the same year.

During that period, the team of 12 people worked tirelessly to hire and train mechanics and pilots, bring in a management team to run the airline, and put together all of the documentation to register and certify the airline which by itself was extremely tedious and time-consuming. In fact, according to Edie, the standard joke in airline certification is that when the maximum gross weight of the paperwork was equal to the maximum ramp weight of the airplane, then the airline was just about ready to be certified. She explained that the team put in an incredible 21 man years of work in three and one half months, working nearly 18 hours a day, and often seven days per week.

Surprisingly, instead of being tired, Edie said that she and the rest of the team members performed at very high levels and for the most part they were energized and fulfilled by the very meaningful work:

> *"We had a blast. We had a goal, we were excited about the goal; we were completely empowered to get the job done. We enjoyed the heck out of working with each other; we took care of each other in ways that were really kind of heartwarming, in a sense. because there would be days where it would be very, very, very stressful. There was a tremendous amount of challenge from the FAA office because ... what we had experienced ... in our industry in the past, was not the way that we decided that we wanted to continue to operate an airline. There were better ways to do it. So we were pushing the envelope of their comfort zone and saying we needed to try these new things."[14]*

Edie also noted that the stress and hard work did not diminish their performance or their energy, despite the fact that at times they were stretched. She explained how the challenges brought the team together, how they dealt with stress, and how they felt fulfilled when the goal had finally been realized:

> *"There were times also when we were stretched absolutely to the max to meet our own deadlines ... We would see that somebody was really having a hard day and the whole team would kind of take it upon themselves, I mean unspoken, to just take care of that person that day. ... We'd haul them off and go drink hot chocolate for a while and then come back. There were just ways that we would look out for each other and it was just a full team effort and we were absolutely empowered to do it and we did it. We were energized by it. That doesn't mean that sometimes we weren't very tired, but we were energized by the experience. We had two DC-8s, 800 and 819, and they were our first two aircraft departures out of Louisville on February 1st of 1988. One went to Milwaukee and one went to Chicago.*

And I'll tell you what, that was one incredible day when we watched those airplanes take off under the UPS certificate. The whole team was out there - kind of on the ramp, watching the airplanes taxi out. When they went into the air, everybody was cheering, it was like, hooray! It was great."[15]

What I found interesting is that Tom and Edie were given significantly more responsibility and at times they were taxed nearly to the limit. Yet, as both of them shared, through the experience they were not drained but energized and highly motivated. They didn't seem to mind working 18 hour days, because despite some challenges they had real meaning in their work and to some extent they were experiencing flow. Essentially, they had a purpose; they were empowered to take action on that purpose and as they did take action, the team worked in harmony because their goals, thoughts and actions were in congruence. Also, because the work each person was doing was considered important and meaningful, both Tom and Edie were valued for their contributions. Edie discussed the importance of meaning in work and how leaders can provide it:

"It should be the commitment of employers to provide work that is meaningful. Now by meaningful, I am saying that I would know exactly how my task fit into the big picture, what its meaning was relative to the customer. And maybe I would have the opportunity to have interface with the customers so that I would have a better feel for what their needs and wants are, what their expectations are. I'd have a much better understanding of how maybe what I had perceived as my boring little job might be of tremendous importance. I would also begin to understand how my own thoughts and ideas were of great value because my management team showed that they valued me as a team player and that they saw me as an intelligent, responsible, creative adult in the workplace. Those kinds of things I think bring meaning to our work environment. And I think they bring meaning to our overall lives because we feel valued."[16]

In a covenant, leaders help people achieve meaning. They accomplish this first by linking the purposes of the individuals of the covenant with the larger purpose of the organization. Of course, that linkage of individual and organizational purpose is facilitated as leaders energize people with meaningful work and increased responsibility and then as they empower them to take cooperative action that is focused on that purpose. Finally, as all of this happens in a caring, respectful and challenging environment; meaning comes to the people involved. In choosing to operate this way, leaders also bring the organization and its people together and position them both to achieve peak performance and to experience what Csikszentmihalyi calls flow.

In a sense, experiences like these where people are engaged, productive and fulfilled in their work are what individuals seek from organizations and what organizations seek from individuals. Covenants create natural conditions for partners to be trusted with meaningful work to do and to experience fulfillment in the process. But even where covenants have not existed in the past, when people are energized and empowered like Tom and Edie were, it strengthens relationships and creates conditions for covenants to develop.

So why aren't there more people engaged and fulfilled in their work? In part it's because leaders don't always give their people meaningful work, increase their responsibility or empower them to be successful. But it's not all one-sided. Sometimes people lack engagement and fulfillment because they are not always clear about their purpose or not always consistent in pursuit of it. Still, the process and conditions necessary for people to be energized and engaged like they were at UPS and Martin Marietta, are created by leaders, leaders who build strong covenants with their partners and therefore provide an even greater sense of meaning and momentum.

---

[1] Nouwen, Henri J., *Here and Now* (The Crossroad Publishing Company; New York; 1994) p.42.

[2] Frankl, V. *Man's Search for Meaning* (New York: Simon and Schuster; 1946).

[3] Becker, Ernest, *The Denial of Death* (The Free Press; New York, New York; 1973) p. 6.

[4] Ibid, p. 6.

[5] Ibid, p. 5.

[6] MSNBC News; *Ex-NFL Star Tillman Makes Ultimate Sacrifice*; George Lewis, Jim Miklaszewski, Alex Johnson, AP and Reuters Contributors; <u>www.msnbc.msn.com/id/-44k</u>; June 7, 2004.

[7] DePree, Max; *Leadership is an Art* (Dell Trade Paperback; 1989) pp. 17-18.

[8] Collins, Jim, *Good to Great* (Harper Business; New York, NY; 2001) p. 54.

[9] Csikszentmihalyi, Mihaly, *Flow* (Harper & Row; New York; 1991).

[10] Morris, Tom, Ph.D., Helen Keller in *"True Success"* (Berkley Business Books, New York; 1994) p. 278.

[11] Csikszentmihalyi, Mihaly, *Flow* (Harper & Row; New York; 1991), p. 217.

[12] Ibid, p. 217.

[13] Mendenhall, Tom; Interview with Leonard J. Moisan; June 11, 1996.

[14] Stein, Edie; Interview with Leonard J. Moisan; June 5, 1995.

[15] Ibid.

[16] Ibid.

Chapter 7
Leadership Evaluation and Action Discovery (LEAD)

Meaning comes from having a sense of purpose and then pursuing that purpose in alliance with other people. In a sense all organizations are alliances of one sort or another, but the very best alliances are covenants that provide a sense of meaning and momentum for the people involved. Using the concepts discussed in Chapter 7, please answer the following questions:

A. Do a majority of people in your organization derive a sense of meaning and momentum from what they do? Explain:
B. Is your organization populated more with free agents or team players? Explain:
C. Does the recognition and rewards system in your organization encourage free agents or team players? How?

D. In what ways does or might you or your organization encourage heroism?

E. How can leaders in your organization do a better job of giving to strengthen stakeholder relationships?

F. To what extent do people in your organization:	
1.	Understand the common purpose (explain):
2.	Plan to achieve the common purpose (explain):
3.	Use the common purpose to mitigate individualism (explain):

4.	Acknowledge their interdependence as they pursue the common purpose (explain):

G. What can you or your organization do to create conditions for more people to experience peak performance or "flow" in their work (focus or purpose, resolution, harmony)?

Chapter 8

Complete the Expected Exchange

People affiliate with groups for a number of reasons, but with every affiliation there are expectations. Initially the kind of group a person associates with may matter a great deal, but eventually it matters far less than what that person experiences as a result of that association. It might be volunteers supporting a nonprofit organization, fans following a team or employees working for a company; they all want their associations to be meaningful and rewarding. In a large part this is really why people affiliate in the first place. They want to belong; they want to contribute in ways that make a difference; and they want to be appreciated for their contributions. It is part of the reciprocity expected in a covenant.

Often there is great promise and excitement associated with new affiliations. Consider, for example, the attitudes and anticipation of recently recruited volunteers at a children's shelter. They are expecting to use their "time, talents and treasures" in meaningful ways to improve the plight of abused and neglected children. In exchange, they also expect to derive a certain amount of meaning and appreciation. Imagine what it would do to the commitment of these folks to have their expectations met by seeing how their work is changing the lives of young people for the better. Conversely, imagine their frustration if they rarely see or hear about the children and if the only way they are allowed to contribute is monetarily. Their enthusiasm and emotional enjoyment would quickly deteriorate.

The same dynamics exist in business. New employees come to companies wanting to use their gifts, talents and experiences to contribute to the success of their respective enterprises. In exchange for their efforts and their contributions, they expect to receive certain rewards. Those rewards are not just monetary. They also include being trusted and valued and having a continuing opportunity to contribute in meaningful ways and to receive appreciation and recognition for doing so. Regardless of whether it's in a non-profit organization or a business, the degree to which the expectations of employees are met through such exchanges, is the degree to which they continue to remain emotionally engaged and vested in the organization and its mission.

Providing Hope - What is really happening in these affiliations is a transaction that involves a promise of an exchange of gifts among the people involved. It is an exchange that is anticipated and even expected in a way that provides hope. In *Principle Centered Leadership*, Stephen Covey argues that any *"expectation is a human hope, the embodiment of a person's desires – what he or she wants out of a situation such as a marriage, a family or a business relationship."*[1] What leaders do in relationships with followers is to provide hope by creating an expectation of an exchange and then delivering on that expectation.

This does not mean that every exchange provides hope and therefore constitutes a covenant, but traditionally exchanges have been involved when people establish covenants. They symbolize the strong and committed bond between the partners. For example, according to anthropologist, Dr. David Lewis, on the Island of Sumba in eastern Indonesia, marrying a spouse without elaborate exchanges is unthinkable. The exchanges are complicated and costly and often they require a young man to have the strong support of his kinsman to be able to afford them. Dr. Lewis noted that the animals and treasures exchanged at marriage are so vast and the social ties forged are so extensive that divorce is extremely rare because returning and dividing all the possessions would be far too complex.[2] It is interesting to note that the more community interest (and less self-interest) involved in the marriage the tighter the bond. The complex interactions and exchanges of a covenant seem to build into the relationship a form of societal accountability, as well as strong expectations and hope that the covenant will last.

Meeting Expectations - If it is true that at the very heart of most relationships and particularly covenants is this idea of giving through an exchange, then it would behoove leaders of organizations to examine whether or not the expected exchanges are actually occurring. Whether we realize it or not, most organizations in America are built on the assumption or expectation of an exchange. People join a company with the intent of exchanging their talent, experience, allegiance, free agency, labor and commitment for pay, appreciation, a certain amount of security and an opportunity to contribute in a meaningful way. Minus the pay, volunteers and donors affiliate with non profit organizations with many of the same intentions.

In a covenant the job of each person is to create conditions for the promised exchange to occur and for expectations of covenant partners to be reasonably met. It requires the people of the covenant to recognize their responsibility to give to the other partners as well as receive from them. Organizationally applied, it means that leaders must give back value and serve their employees and customers, rather than just take from them. For example, with escalating player salaries, rising ticket costs and more complex negotiations; it is increasingly more difficult for some professional sports teams to generate a profit. This is particularly true in smaller markets where teams may not have broad television exposure or strong fan support. In this kind of environment a team owner or general manager might be expected to focus more on making a profit than on serving and giving back value.

Nevertheless, applying this principle of covenant can prosper a business even in the competitive world of professional sports. Consider the case of the Utah Jazz. It is far smaller than franchises in Los Angeles, Chicago, New York and other cities, but it enjoys excellent community support. In the 1980s and 1990s, The Jazz became one of the most financially successful NBA teams in the league by meeting and exceeding the expectations of fans. Former Jazz head coach and President, Frank Layden, explained the kind of exchange that he believes has made them successful:

> *"When I first came to Salt Lake City, I had to evaluate where we were there. I had to look at the compensation. We were competing for the entertainment dollar in the community. And so I said if we want to stay here, I have to make these people believe in our organization. I have to give something back to the community. The one thing I can't promise them is a winning team. But I can promise them that we are going to give a tremendous effort to be the best team that we can possibly be. And also to entertain but not only for our own reasons.... We live there and we buy. We provide jobs and we try very hard to be active in the community."*[3]

Mr. Layden went on to explain how he tried to set the tone and meet the expectations, not only of customers but also of employees. Using language like "team concept" to explain his methods might appear to overstate the obvious, but Mr. Layden made it clear to me that there was much more to their success than the players and coach. He explained,

> *"It is a team effort. To put us on the floor, it takes almost 900 people. We want all of them - the people that work in our front office, our interns, to feel very much a part of the Jazz team. In fact, I don't know if anybody else does this, but we take a team picture of the whole organization. We have a party at Christmas time that is just for employees and the players. I try to touch every employee every day. I can't do it obviously, but it might be a little thing to go in and say to one of the people in the stock room what do you think? 'What did you think of the game last night? Geez, coach, we should have done this or we should have done that. Good, that's not bad.' Let them feel that they have some input and don't be afraid to take criticism. Have a dialogue with all your people so that they can go home and sit around at their table and say, 'You know, I was talking to Frank Layden today and he said we might make a trade.'*

*And make them feel like they are a part of the organization
and not just a number."*[4]

Completing the Transaction -   In the field of sociology, exchange
theorists postulate that people enter into relationships with the
intent to maximize their benefits and minimize their costs. Similarly,
exchange theories of leadership hold that most leader-follower
interactions are exchanges in which rewards or punishments are given
for performance in pursuit of related purposes. James MacGregor
Burns referred to this as "transactional leadership," a relationship in
which leaders approach followers with the intent to exchange one
thing of perceived value for another. Burns notes that, *"The exchange
could be economic or political or psychological in nature: a swap of
goods or of one good for money; a trading of votes between candidate
and citizen or between legislators; hospitality to another person in
exchange for willingness to listen to one's troubles."*[5]

As leaders complete their exchanges and meet follower expectations,
they also deliver on their end of transactions and thereby gain
credibility with followers. Transactional credibility also builds trust
and strengthens relationships, which frees people to give more readily
to a purpose other than their own without fear of being burned.
As Burns explains, the credibility that comes from completing
transactions, fuses related purposes of leaders and followers into a
common purpose and links the power bases of each in support of
that same common purpose.

Aspiring leaders as well as their organizations often run into
trouble because they never complete the anticipated exchanges that
are expected in transactions. For example, in the organizational
development work we do many of our internal surveys and interviews
reveal employees who are disappointed because they receive only pay
and are expected to contribute only labor. What I find interesting
is the fact that most of these people clearly want and even expect
to give and receive more, yet they are not given the opportunity to
do so. Predictably, because workers are discouraged from giving
their full gifts and talents, they don't feel appreciated, they become
insecure and they lack meaning in their work. Also, because

appreciation, security and meaning are missing or limited in their work relationships, needs go unmet and the full exchange is never completed. Consequently, the organization suffers because it does not receive the full benefit of a person's talent and commitment.

Though these conditions are easily prevented, their presence inside organizations appears to be more the rule than the exception. This helps explain why a Gallup study of employees in 66 countries revealed that on average 80% of workers say that they are not allowed to do their best at work each day.[6] What they are really saying is that the expected exchange is not being completed because they are not being allowed to give their respective employers the full benefit of their talent, experience and commitment.

Exchanging gifts in this manner is an important part of meeting the needs of followers and establishing covenants with them. It represents a large part of the expectations in leader-follower transactions. Therefore, for leaders to establish and maintain covenants, requires that they initiate a process to ensure that the full exchange does occur and, as a result, value is added both to the relationship and to the organization. For example, when corporate leaders follow through on their end of transactions, employees tend to reciprocate by contributing in ways that add value to customers and produce loyalty and profit for the company. The same principle is true in charities, teams, communities and just about any kind of group, but the impetus for achieving this is on the leader. It requires trusting and giving and sometimes following on the part of a leader, by trusting and even abandoning oneself to the talent and good will of others.

Leading by Following - In some cultures it is a sign of bad manners and even an insult, not to accept a gift from someone who offers it. That's because a gift is considered to be an extension of a person. In rejecting a gift you are in essence rejecting the individual who tried to give it. As offensive as this seems, organizational power wielders regularly reject the gifts of their employees and thereby frustrate and insult them by seeking only labor from them and giving only pay. Allowing employees to contribute their gifts and talents is a daunting task for power wielders because it requires them to give up a degree of power or control and in some ways follow. Yet, that's exactly what leaders do. They receive the gifts and talents of their employees or covenant partners by allowing them to contribute. But again, sometimes that requires leaders to become followers. Former Goodyear Chairman and CEO Stan Gault explained it this way:

> *"I believe all of us are followers in some ways and at some time. And that goes back to the point that we will not always have all the bright ideas, we won't have all the attributes (necessary for success) on our own. And when someone has an idea, we certainly shouldn't be reluctant to honor that. I am not the slightest bit embarrassed to say that I am a follower. I think when you are following you also have an opportunity, perhaps even an obligation to ask how do you do that better than the one who originally initiated it."[7]*

Whether it is in a personal relationship or a complex organization, facilitating this kind of an exchange strengthens the bond among the people involved. It is doubtful that a covenant can be established at any level apart from such an exchange. Leading by following is really about trusting, trusting in the gifts and talents of the people being led and trusting in their integrity. As illustrated in the previous chapter, that's exactly what the leaders did at Martin Marietta and UPS and as a result their people pulled off incredible feats.

Giving Well ... Building Alliances - The concept of an expected exchange of gifts associated with the establishment of covenants is by no means modern nor is it uniquely American. On the contrary, throughout the history of man, covenants have been present in just about every culture and country imaginable. Virtually all of these covenant traditions have some form of giving or exchange associated with them. That's because both giving and receiving gifts are important parts of building alliances. For example, in his book, *Millennium: Tribal Wisdom and the Modern World*, David Lewis described a whole system of tribal exchanges in New Guinea called the Kula. First described by anthropologist Bronislaw Malinowski in the 1920s and 1930s, the Kula involves fleets of canoes carrying as many as 500 men with gifts. They travel for days to bring gifts and make exchanges with people in other villages. Lewis notes that men exchange gifts in order to build alliances and develop extensive networks of partners who in turn exchange the gifts given to them with other partners. The more paths a man's gifts travel, the wider the network he develops and the more famous and powerful he becomes. Thus, wealth and prestige come to men as a result of giving well and creating covenants with people who trust and are obligated to them.[8]

Lewis explains further that anthropologists have determined that throughout history, giving of gifts has been a primary way people have built alliances and established trust in relating to one another. He notes that giving something to someone in most cultures creates a sense of obligation and compels the recipient to reciprocate in some way.[9] In contrast, when people sense that they are not receiving from a relationship, their sense of obligation to give and persist often diminishes.

Strengthening Connections - As a kid growing up in the inner city of Chicago, I learned early in life the importance of being "connected" with others. Still today, who you know in the city is every bit as important and sometimes more important than what you know. I can remember many times when our family "connections" brought certain advantages but one in particular sticks out in my mind. Although it would probably not be too politically correct today, it gives you a glimpse of how leaders in political parties operated 40 years ago. Chicago Mayor, Richard J. Daley or as famed Sun Times columnist Mike Royko called him, "Boss" was known as a tough big city mayor. However, among the people in the city neighborhoods he was also beloved and well known for "taking care of his own".

My old neighborhood is a place called Canaryville, which was located on the south side of the city in Chicago's famed 11th Ward. One evening my father informed me that he wanted to introduce me to someone at the Ward headquarters who might be able to help me with funds for college. As it turned out, this night was what I called one of the "favor nights" at the headquarters. It was a time when precinct captains brought a constituent to ask for help or a favor from higher ups in the party. This night my father had me in tow. He had worked it out to have me nominated for a state legislative scholarship.

We sat and waited in a smoke-filled room, amidst a sea of people so dense, that they had spilled out the door and onto the sidewalk. Above the roar of conversation that grew louder by the minute, we heard, "Moisan". Just as I looked in the direction of the sound, my father leaned over and said to me, "Let's go." We walked through a heavy oak gate that separated the crowd from staffers who were diligently working on who knows what. Our guide greeted us and asked my father, "Is this Leonard?" My dad nodded in the affirmative and our guide led us through the waist high oak gate and then beyond the gate through a door and into an office. It was surprisingly quiet inside, considering all the noise that was just outside the door.

Our guide wasted little time. "Senator Nihil," he said, "I want you to meet Art Moisan's son Leonard." After handshakes and a brief exchange of pleasantries with my dad, the senator got right to the point. "I understand from your dad that you would like to go to college. Is that correct?" I replied, "Yes, Senator." He went on, "Well Leonard, we've nominated you and you've been selected to receive an Illinois State Legislative Scholarship. I want you to go to school, study hard, have fun and remember who helped you."

After I thanked the Senator, we left. The entire encounter took less than five minutes. Even though the funding only lasted a year or two and the total amount was about $2,000, it meant a great deal to us because we didn't have much. The experience also taught me a great deal about the importance of connections and the power of completing an exchange.

No doubt, there were lots of worthy students who could have been nominated. They surely had academic achievements equal to mine, but I received the nomination and eventually the scholarship on the strength of my father's relationships with the party leaders. True, my father had worked hard in our precinct to help people and get them out to vote and this was in part a reward for that. But they, as leaders, were also being attentive to my father's needs. As a result of their efforts to help meet those needs and complete this leader-follower exchange, it strengthened my dad's allegiance to Mayor Daley and to the rest of the leaders in the Democratic party who helped us. Being "connected" made me eligible to participate in this exchange, but completing the exchange and meeting or exceeding expectations as my father and these leaders both did, strengthened the connections between them.

Leaders in any environment who create conditions for such exchanges to be completed and the expectations of followers to be met, can also expect to strengthen their bonds with those followers. It is a concept that is as old as mankind and prevalent even in the most primitive of cultures. In *The Gift* French scholar and sociologist Marcel Maus documented his late 19th Century studies of societies in Polynesia, Melanesia and Northwest America. He noted that covenants in these societies involved more than exchanges of goods, wealth or produce, and they included groups as well as individuals in ways that were not simply confined to marriage. For example, according to Maus, in Samoa exchanges were present in childbirth, circumcision, sickness, children coming of age, funeral ceremonies and more. They could involve just about anything deemed valuable including food, possessions, charms, land, labor, services, religious offices and even women and children. As these things are given it strengthens the spiritual bonds among people. Maus explained further that the gifts represent spiritual matter that in turn represents an extension of the person doing the giving. In these societies, matter passes and re-passes perpetually between individuals, clans, ranks, sexes and generations. Thus, when a gift is rejected it is actually a rejection of that person. Maus observed, *"The pattern of symmetrical and reciprocal gifts is not difficult to understand if we realize that it is first and foremost a pattern of spiritual bonds between things which are to some extent part of persons."*[10]

Similarly, when people receive and are allowed to give as part of the exchange that is expected in organizations, it creates and/or strengthens connections among people in ways that heighten teamwork and increase productivity. The converse is also true. When people work or even volunteer in an organization and they are not allowed to give their talent, their experience or even their opinions and the exchange is not completed, it represents a form of rejection that can break bonds and create hostility. Whether it's in a business, a church or any other kind of organization, achieving an environment where such exchanges can be completed requires leaders who are willing to extend themselves to others and thereby strengthen their connections. In a covenant, to extend oneself as a leader, means to give to the other persons of the covenant. But it also means to trust and allow others to give as well, by receiving their gifts in an appropriate manner.

[1] Covey, Stephen; *Principle Centered Leadership* (Simon & Schuster; Summit Books; New York, NY; 1990, 1991) p. 204.

[2] Lewis, David M.; *Millennium: Tribal Wisdom and the Modern* World (Viking Penguin; New York; 1992) p. 68-69.

[3] Layden, Frank; Interview with Leonard J. Moisan, November 7, 1996.

[4] Ibid.

[5] Burns, J. MacGregor. *Leadership*; (New York, Harper and Row, 1978).

[6] Coffman, Curt and Gonzales-Molina Gabriel, Ph.D. *Follow this Path: How the World's Greatest Organizations Drive Growth by Unleashing Human Potential* (New York, NY: Warner Books, 2002) pp. 32-33.

[7] Gault, Stanley, Interview with Leonard J. Moisan, August 6, 1996.

[8] Lewis, David M. *Millennium: Tribal Wisdom and the Modern World* (New York; Viking Penguin; 1992).

[9] Ibid.

[10] Maus, Marcel. *The Gift: Forums and Functions of Exchange in Archaic Societies*; Translated by Ian Cunnison; (Glencoe, Illinois; The Free Press; 1954).

Chapter 8
Leadership Evaluation and Action
Discovery (LEAD)

The idea of an expected exchange between partners is an important part of a covenant and is present in most case where people affiliate with organizations. For example, in businesses employees come to the organization intending to use their gifts, talents and/or experiences to contribute to the organization's success. In exchange, they expect rewards that include not only pay but also the opportunity to be trusted, to contribute in a meaningful way and to receive recognition and appreciation for doing so. Using the concepts in this chapter, please answer the following questions:

A. What are the expected exchanges between leaders and employees of your organization?
B. To what extent are expectations met and hope about the future sustained? (Explain)
C. How can leaders in your organization better meet expectations, complete the transaction and lead by following?

Chapter 9

Recognize and Value People Appropriately

In his 1988 speech at Moscow State University in the USSR, President Ronald Reagan described freedom as *"... the recognition that no single person, no single authority of government has a monopoly on the truth, but that every individual life is infinitely precious, that everyone of us put on this world has been put there for a reason and has something to offer."*[1] In his comments the late President Reagan was clearly recognizing the value and importance of every person. He spoke with moral clarity because he believed in the transcendent truth that every life matters. His words represented a value system that stood in sharp contrast to the one prevalent in the Soviet Union where scholars estimate some 75 million people had relatives either slain or imprisoned by the totalitarian state terror machine. This repressive, power-driven "evil empire," as President Reagan called it, systematically eliminated freedoms of press and speech and executed some 35 million people in 70 years. Because the Soviet Union intimidated and exploited its people and failed to recognize their value apart from their power or their dramatic contributions to the system, it lost its ability to motivate them. This led to declines in both productivity and hope, and the government eventually toppled.

The Soviet example remains as a powerful reminder that even in an organization as large as a country, success is found in the dynamics of the relationships within its borders. Whether it's in a nation, a company, a team or a marriage, how people relate to one another matters. One simply cannot expect an association of any kind to be successful if the people within it do not experience the dignity and respect that come from being valued. That's why the manner in which we recognize others and demonstrate that we value them, influences greatly both our ability and, in some cases, our inability to motivate people and establish covenants with them.

Most Americans would agree that state sanctioned killings and political assassinations of the kind that occurred throughout the history of the Soviet Union are horrific. Yet CEOs in many of our companies and organizations quite regularly kill the spirits and assassinate the careers of innocent people with apparent impunity. This is particularly true of power wielders who treat many of their employees as commodities. They recognize, respect and value individuals only to the extent that they can facilitate the power wielder's agenda.

Respecting Others and Making Positive Assumptions About Them - Our recognition of others is driven by the degree of respect we have for people and the assumptions we make about them. For example, if I assume that our organizational success depends primarily on the talent, experience and effort of the individuals I supervise, then I will respect them more and recognize them differently than if I assume that our success depends primarily on me. In the former case, I am more likely to recognize the importance of these people, make an effort to communicate with them and express appreciation for their individual contributions. I am also better able to understand their needs, and as a result, I will know how to support them more effectively. At a minimum this means that leaders who assume that they are dependent upon followers for their success must work to enable those followers to be successful. They do this by removing barriers, empowering them with appropriate levels of decision-making authority and giving followers what they need to contribute to the collective success of the organization. That really was the vision of the Reagan presidency in the 1980's: to remove barriers installed by big government and allow the initiative and entrepreneurial spirit of capable Americans in the private sector to repair our economy and put our people back to work. It assumed and relied on the initiative and talent of the American people, not the power and/or bureaucracy of the American government. President Reagan's strategy worked because it demonstrated respect for Americans, and as a leader that respect endeared him to many people.

The opposite of this is an environment of power wielding, control and exploitation that is driven by attitudes of inflated self importance and blatant disregard for others. This happens when people in power assume that success is dependent primarily on them as leaders (or, as in the former USSR, if they're fearful of a loss of power due to the personal initiative of others), and there is very little accountability for their actions. As a result, the power holders tend to overemphasize their own importance and assume there is a need to control people instead of empower them. This tendency to control others is usually justified by the power wielder's assumptions of incompetence or ill will regarding the people around them. While this type of disrespect represents the norm in power-wielding hierarchical organizations, it does not build strong and committed relationships of the kind that are necessary to sustain long-term success. Covenants simply cannot be established and leadership cannot flourish without recognizing the importance and value of other people. Human beings are just not built to trust someone who does not respect and value them. Instead of strengthening relationships, disrespect weakens them.

Attracting, Rewarding and Keeping the Right People - Experts in the human resources field estimate that costs from employee attrition range from 50 percent to as high as 150 percent or more of a person's annual salary. Not only does it pay to recruit the best people, it also pays to keep them. Any CEO or manager who demonstrates that he does depend on other individuals who are allowed to use their talents and experiences to help, takes an important step in both the recruitment and retention process. It is also an important step both in establishing a covenant and becoming a leader. In fact, as Jim Collins found in his research on "Good to Great" companies, leadership is less about aggrandizing self and more about attracting and retaining the right kind of talented people and then serving and influencing them to secure their help in achieving a shared vision. It requires that we first take deliberate action to respect people and recognize both their potential and their contributions by rewarding them appropriately.

For example, in 2004 *Fortune* ranked the J. M. Smucker Company number one among America's best companies for which to work. Among its many benefits and rewards, the company provides healthcare for retirees and their spouses, as well as paid time off for employees to volunteer. In addition, supervisors celebrate and reward successes by hosting barbeques and lunches, and providing gift certificates to thank and recognize employees for their contributions. The Smucker leadership demonstrates respect in other ways as well. According to one employee, managers regularly demonstrate their willingness to listen to workers, address problems they raise and use their suggestions. With the high levels of worker appreciation and support that exist at Smuckers, it's not surprising that teamwork pervades the culture.[2]

When leaders in companies demonstrate that they respect and value their people and they are willing to reward them, their reputation as a "good place to work" grows. In the final analysis, it is not so much the brilliance of an individual leader that moves an organization to greatness. Rather, it is the quality of the mission and vision combined with the quality of the people a leader is able to attract and retain that allow greatness to be achieved. True, talent doesn't automatically produce. It requires leadership to mold people into a team, create conditions for success and use talent appropriately; but the stronger the talent level in an organization, the greater its capacity is. Simply stated, having the right people makes achievement more likely and recognition much easier. When I interviewed Coach Wooden he told me that one of the most important moves he made as a coach was to recruit talented players.

However, attracting the right people is only part of the equation. If leaders hope to sustain success long term, they must employ strategies to retain those talented people. Talented people regularly leave organizations because they believe their talent is either wasted or not appreciated. That's why, primary among the retention strategies employed by leaders should be to provide opportunities for people to engage fully and use their talents (completing the expected exchange) and to receive timely recognition of their contributions. Also, if the recognition is to be effective it will be customized to fit both the individuals and the achievements being recognized. Again, appropriate recognition includes respecting, valuing, serving and rewarding others. It is essential in authentic leader-follower relationships in much the same way it is in covenants. In *Good to Great*, Jim Collins explains it this way,

> *"Those who build great companies understand that the ultimate throttle on growth for any company is not markets, or technology, or competition, or products. It is one thing above all others: the ability to get and keep enough of the right people."*[3]

Of course, this is not to suggest that leaders who serve their people in ways that demonstrate that they respect and value them, need to compromise the quality of work or the commitment to mission. On the contrary, it is an understanding on the part of the leader that when I go the extra mile to give recognition and rewards to my workers, their commitment to success and their motivation to work diligently in achieving the mission will be enhanced.

Embracing Humility - In order to recruit, retain, reward and motivate the "right people," leaders must first recognize, in tangible ways, the worth of these individuals and the gifts and abilities they bring to the organization. Beyond that, leaders must use power to influence people so they willingly contribute their gifts and abilities in the work of achieving the mission. Most of the time, that means leaders must understand and serve simultaneously the mission of the organization and the needs of the people who work there. That's why a blend of humility and commitment to mission are central to Collins' "level 5" leaders. His research demonstrates that effective leaders must recognize that what happens in an organization is not always about them. No doubt, serving the needs of others and recognizing them in positive ways always requires a certain amount of humility. That humility in leaders is manifest in recognizing and accommodating the value and contributions of others and in putting the mission and the needs of others (including the need to contribute and be recognized for that contribution) ahead of his or her own needs. When that happens people are drawn to the leader. In *True Success:*

A New Philosophy of Excellence author Tom Morris explains it this way:

> "*The humble person can be extremely confident and can have the highest degree of proper self-esteem attainable. But the humble individual seeks to serve not just himself, but others as well. Because he opens himself to others, the person displaying proper humility draws the attention and efforts and goodwill of other people to himself and his projects in the best possible way. One of the happy ironies of life is that presumptuous self-centeredness is self destructive, whereas humility and altruism are self-fulfilling. Threatening, manipulative attempts at leadership are in the long run self-defeating.*"[4]

By contrast, power wielders have difficulty acknowledging the value of the abilities and experiences of others. They seldom trust their associates or people they supervise and exhibit a compelling need of almost Soviet proportions to control everything and everyone around them. In so doing, power wielders seldom move to empower other people to achieve. Instead, a great deal of a power wielder's energy is directed at accumulating power for his or her own benefit rather than giving it away for the benefit of the organization. It is behavior that stands in sharp contrast to the humility author Jim Collins found in "level 5" leaders, because it comes from a combination of a lack of trust in the ability of others to complete tasks effectively and an over-inflated opinion of the importance of self.

> The late management guru, Peter Drucker, gave his perspective on why effective leaders empower others and power wielders or 'misleaders' don't:

> "*... indeed, effective leaders are painfully aware that they are not in control of the universe. (Only misleaders – the Stalins, Hitlers, Maos – suffer from that delusion.)*"[5]

For a leader, sometimes recognizing and valuing people appropriately means relying on them to help us solve problems. Clearly, it is difficult to admit that we don't have all of the answers. If we're wrong about something or we might even be failing in a certain area of life or work, it is somewhat humbling to admit it. Yet, that kind of humility is exactly what is needed both to search for solutions to problems and to strengthen our relationships, relationships through which we are likely to find those solutions. The point is that very few problems get fixed without first admitting that there is a problem and then without getting help from others. People simply don't want to be led by or even associated with individuals who are never willing to admit mistakes, never consider that they are wrong and never ask for help. That kind of pride creates difficult working conditions and impossible relationships because, rather than unite people, it drives them apart.

One of the manifestations of humility that Jim Collins found in leaders of successful companies was their ability to consistently *"confront the brutal facts, yet never lose faith."*[6] Confronting brutal facts assumes a level of humility on the part of leaders that charismatic CEOs with strong personalities have a hard time achieving. According to Collins, *"the moment a leader allows himself to become the primary reality people worry about, rather than reality being the primary reality, you have a recipe for mediocrity or worse."*[7] That's because when the focus is on the leader and his vision, any information that doesn't align with that vision is often ignored or missed. Not surprisingly, when the truth about one's condition is not heard and the brutal facts are not confronted, relationships tend to become less functional and the long-term health of the organization is jeopardized. Sustained results demand at least some humility on the part of leaders.

Consider the case of Frank Lorenzo. In the early 1980s he headed Texas Air Corporation, which at the time was one of the largest airline conglomerates in the world. Financed with junk bonds, the corporation combined Eastern Airlines along with Continental, Frontier and People's Express. Lorenzo developed a system for dealing with unions at Continental that represented the antithesis of humility. Despite having a significant amount of cash, he filed for Chapter 11, which had a loophole that allowed him to abrogate union contracts. Congress eventually closed that loophole, but at Texas Air, even after the Congressional action, Lorenzo still refused to deal with the unions. He chose again to file bankruptcy which set up a massive picketing demonstration by pilots, flight attendants and ground personnel. Mr. Lorenzo refused to confront the facts that the people who worked for him were part of the solution and not the problem, and that his approach was an outdated strategy.

In addition to his adversarial dealings with the unions, Mr. Lorenzo's reputation as a tough boss intimidated employees in such a way that few of his managers were willing to bring him bad news. A former colleague spoke of how Lorenzo's presence would change both the chemistry and outcomes of meetings, *"Once people saw which way he was going, they would hop on it, and the train was rolling."*[8] Unfortunately, this kind of ego-driven environment perpetuates poor decision making, because the information a power-wielding CEO receives is filtered with a bias towards pleasing him. It is clearly no basis upon which to build effective working relationships. As Jim Collins noted, conditions like these become a recipe for disaster because the CEO becomes the primary reality employees worry about instead of the actual reality. In the case of Eastern Airlines, Mr. Lorenzo's style proved Mr. Collins' point, as thousands of people lost their jobs and the assets were finally liquidated in 1991. His power wielding and refusal to build effective relationships and seek appropriate answers in cooperation with the professionals on whom his success depended, eventually led to his demise.

The former head of ITT, Harold Geneen, also had the reputation of being a power wielder. After leaving the company, he freely admitted that "egotism" is probably the worst disease that can afflict a CEO. In fact, Geneen noted that the narcissism that flows from an ego-driven CEO can impair his judgment every bit as much as the alcoholic is impaired by martinis.[9]

In the case of Mr. Lorenzo, confronting the brutal facts of his and the company's condition required a level of humility that he simply did not appear to have. Because of his stubbornness, or pride or whatever else blinded him to the truth, he failed. He lacked the humility both to seek answers to his problems and to confront the brutal facts of his condition. What I find interesting is the fact that

Lorenzo intimidated and fought with the very people who needed to be recognized, valued and involved in helping find a solution.

The kind of humility required of leaders is not so much a behavior as it is an attitude that must be embraced personally by individuals. In their book, *Credibility*, authors and business consultants, James Kouzes and Barry Posner, speak to this point about the importance of leaders embracing an attitude of humility:

> *"The antidote to vanity is humility. Leaders need to be aware of their own and their organization's shortcomings and be willing to admit to them. They need to encourage and support others in admitting they are wrong without fear of punishment or refusal."*[10]

What Kouzes and Posner discuss here is exactly the kind of humility that Jim Collins found in level five leaders of "Good to Great" companies. They are leaders who are humble enough to recognize their own weaknesses and secure enough not to let those weaknesses get in the way of achieving the mission of the organization.[11] When they are able to embrace such an attitude in their daily work, leaders are better able to engage followers in ways that result not only in productivity but also in strong, enduring and dynamic relationships.

Allowing People to Contribute - The late W. Edwards Deming, a famed international consultant, transformed Japanese business and helped them become an economic giant. Among his 14 point system were the exhortations for leaders to drive fear out of the workplace and remove barriers that rob people of their right to the pride of workmanship.[12] A fundamental method of providing positive recognition is allowing people to use their talent and experience in the first place to contribute to the success of the team and/or the organization. It is what Deming meant when he talked about the "pride of workmanship." But Deming also knew that people are not likely to freely contribute or to experience pride of workmanship if they are driven by fear and intimidation.

Also, when people do contribute, it's important to recognize them for doing so. Not only does this help meet their needs for achievement and recognition, it also expands the capacity of the organization. It is at the heart of the "Expected Exchange" principle discussed in the previous chapter. I see frequent examples of the power of recognizing contributions in the leadership training sessions our company facilitates, I often take participants through a series of 20 questions early in the day. The questions are designed to identify people in the group who have had unique experiences and have developed a variety of talents and skills. Typically, I find among the participants that their experiences are broad and their talent is impressive. The sessions are interactive and lively as people enthusiastically share about themselves. This particular exercise is used to illustrate some important assumptions underlying covenant leadership:

1. In any group there is a wide range of experience and talent.
2. That experience and talent represents a major resource for the relationship … the team … the organization.
3. People come into relationships, teams and organizations with a desire to give others the benefit of their experience and talent.
4. If one wants the relationship, team or the organization to be successful … allow the people to contribute their experience and talent by:
    a. removing barriers,
    b. encouraging initiative, and
    c. empowering them to take risks and make decisions.
5. When they do contribute, recognize them.

To demonstrate further the power of these principles, I ask members of the group to recall specific instances when they scored a basket, got a hit or made a play to win a game. As volunteers share their experiences, it never ceases to amaze me how much detail people remember about specific events that occurred 20, 30 and even 40 years earlier. Typically individuals become animated as they relate the particulars of how they made the play or how they contributed and how they were recognized. Many of them experienced what

Professor Csikszentmihalyi described as "flow", a time when everything came together. They will own that moment in time forever because they were allowed and even depended upon by their coach to use their talents to contribute to the success of the team, and they were recognized and valued for their contributions. The exercise clearly shows the power of recognition, and that kind of recognition and the affirmation it represents are central to covenant leadership.

Creating Positive Self-fulfilling Results - Douglas McGregor pointed out in Theory X and Theory Y,[13] that the assumptions I make about people influence both my attitudes and behaviors toward them. Those same assumptions also affect the kind of recognition I give them. For example, if I assume the people I supervise are unmotivated, inexperienced, lazy, can't be trusted and need to be controlled, and I act on those assumptions, then any recognition I give them is likely to be negative. Likewise, those same assumptions are likely to influence their behavior and attitudes toward me. In a self-fulfilling way my negative assumptions have created angry, frustrated, unproductive, unmotivated and even vengeful employees. Yet, it is also true that if I make positive assumptions and take positive actions towards someone, it will usually create positive results.

As silly as the negative approach seems, many managers operate in just this manner. However, instead of trying to control others, these managers or "would be" leaders might benefit from taking a covenant approach by making positive rather than negative assumptions about people. In fact, a fundamental assumption of a covenant is that the whole of the relationship and the value of the people working together towards a common purpose are much greater than any single effort or individual part. Many people instinctively know and would agree with this approach. However, as authors and Stanford University professors, Jeffrey Pfeffer and Robert Sutton, note in their work, *The Knowing-Doing Gap: How Smart Companies Turn Knowledge Into Action: "The gap between learning and doing is much greater than the gap between ignorance and knowledge."*[14] In other words, it's much easier to know that it is right to align behavior with core values, to make positive assumptions about people and to allow them to contribute than it is to do it. As these authors conclude, closing the "knowing-doing gap" begins by turning the knowledge about leadership into action first by valuing, trusting and empowering individuals to contribute to the success of the organization and then by recognizing them when they do so.

---

[1] Rogers, Jay; *President Reagan's Speech;* Moscow State University, USSR – May 31, 1988 (Media House International; PO Box 362173, Melbourne, Florida 32936-2173) www.forerunner.com/forerunner/X0692_Reagans_Speech_in_mo.html_14k_.

[2] Smucker, J. M.; *"100 Best Companies to Work For."* (*Fortune;* January 12, 2004).

[3] Collins, Jim, *Good to Great;* (Harper Business; New York, NY, 2001) p. 54.

[4] Morris, Tom Ph.D., *True Success* (Berkley Books, New York, New York, 1995) p. 247.

[5] Drucker, Peter F. *The Essential Drucker* (Harper Business, New York 2001) p. 270.

[6] Collins, Jim, *Good to Great* (Harper Business; New York, NY; 2001) p. 72.

[7] Ibid.

[8] Business Week, *CEO Disease* (Best of Business Quarterly; 1991) p. 47.

[9] Ibid.

[10] Kouzes, James, and Posner, Barry. *Credibility* (Jossey-Bass, Inc.; San Francisco, California; 1963) p. 267.

[11] Collins, Jim, *Good to Great* (Harper Business; New York, NY; 2001) p. 54.

[12] Deming, W. Edwards, The W. Edwards Deming Institute, "Teachings," on www.deming.org/theman/teachingsoz.html.

[13] McGregor, Douglas; *The Human Side of Enterprise* (McGraw-Hill, New York 1960).

[14] Pfeffer, Jeffrey; Sutton, Robert. *The Knowing-Doing Gap: How Smart Companies Turn Knowledge into Action.* (Berrett-Koehler Publications, San Francisco 2000).

Chapter 9
Leadership Evaluation and Action
Discovery (LEAD)

If the stakeholders of any kind of organization do not experience dignity and respect as a result of their association, then it's not likely that the organization will be successful. Simply stated, people want to be recognized and valued as individuals, and the way we do that influences our ability to motivate people and establish covenants with them. Using the information in Chapter 9, please answer the following questions:

A. How and to what extent do leaders in your organization respect stakeholders and make positive assumptions about them (their abilities, work ethic, trustworthiness, value, etc.)?
B. Would people in your organization say enthusiastically that it is a "good place to work"? Why or why not?

C. In what ways can leaders in your organization demonstrate higher levels of humility and allow people to contribute more fully (i.e., removing barriers, encouraging initiative, empowering and recognizing contributions)?

Chapter 10
Embrace Self-Imposed Accountability

Most CEOs will acknowledge the importance of accountability. In fact, they even appoint a person called a "controller" to help ensure that their people are accountable for how financial resources are used. While controllers are important, to assume they have sole responsibility for accountability, represents a limited view of the concept. Structured appropriately, accountability extends well beyond the "controller" and involves more than just financial resources. Actually the most effective form of accountability is not the kind that is forced or controlled under a cloud of suspicion; instead, it is willingly embraced and owned by everyone. It is a self-imposed form of accountability where individuals assume responsibility for the purposes, people and prosperity of the organization. It relies on the integrity, transparency, and open and honest communication of the people involved, the kind of accountability that people expect in a covenant. True, from time to time covenant partners can hold each other accountable, but for the covenant to be sustained long term requires that accountability be primarily self-imposed. Of course, understanding the principles of covenant is a lot easier than living by them. But if people in a relationship aren't willing to be accountable for their responsibilities and actions, then the relationship is not likely to prosper.

Knowing What to Expect – To assume accountability for a job of any kind, employees must first understand the parameters and expectations of the job. At first glance that might appear to overstate the obvious, but it is not unusual for us to work with organizations where an employee's version of a job is quite different than his or her supervisor's version of the same job. For a system of accountability to work employees and supervisors alike must have the same understanding of both the job responsibilities and the expectations. Also, responsibilities and expectations can't be a moving target that changes without warning. Of course, this implies effective communication of the responsibilities and expectations by leaders inside the company. The point is that if accountability is ever to be self-imposed, this kind of mutual understanding must precede it. Simply stated, if a leader wants people to buy in to the mission, they must have an idea of what will be expected of them. Beyond that, leaders who are successful in building a self-imposed system of accountability will also make it clear what followers can expect from them and from the culture they have created.

Stepping Up - Self-imposed accountability, if it is to be embraced widely throughout the organization, must start at the top. Why? The fact is that people at the top are usually the ones who create the culture of the organization. They set the pace and they create behavioral expectations. For example, control oriented power wielders are not likely to create an environment of self-imposed accountability because they don't trust people enough to allow them to assume ownership and responsibility for their jobs. They also can not become trusting, covenant keeping leaders without a change of assumptions, behaviors and core values because these are the basics that help form the culture in the first place. The point is that self-imposed accountability doesn't just happen automatically. It requires leaders who are willing to step up, take actions and if necessary transform the culture of power and control into a culture of trust, commitment and transparency. It means that beyond being willing to clearly communicate job expectations and hold others accountable for aligning their behavior with the purposes, responsibilities and core values of the covenant, leaders must be willing both to hold themselves accountable and to be held accountable by others for the same kind of alignment.

It is not unusual for leaders to hold themselves and other people accountable. In most cases it is expected. But for leaders to expect that people will hold themselves accountable is quite a different matter. In a covenant that's exactly what happens because the covenant partners actually create conditions for a self-imposed form of accountability to flourish. Organizational covenants presuppose that leaders will assume their people to be responsible, capable, honest and willing to contribute. But that presupposition also involves those same leaders stepping up and acting on their assumptions. How do they accomplish this? They do it by trusting and empowering others to act in good faith on the goals and purposes of the organization.

No doubt, the presuppositions and assumptions we make about people as well as the behaviors that follow, flow from our core values. And the values that are consistent with covenants put a high emphasis on the importance of and commitment to each individual involved. The point is that when leaders truly value people and are willing to step up and act on that value, it supports an environment that allows accountability to thrive, not as a threat but as a natural part of keeping a rewarding relationship alive. It follows then that individuals who experience leadership in this manner are also likely to be more willing to share information, perpetuate a culture of mutual respect and trust and support both the objectives of the organization and the people who lead it.

When our Covenant Group associates see this kind of leadership, where strong covenants exist between leaders and followers, they know it's not by chance. Those relationships are deliberately cultivated by leaders who believe that, given the opportunity, followers can and will contribute their talents, assume ownership for the organization and share accountability for success or failure. The leader's alignment of his or her behavior with these same beliefs is crucial because it models what is expected of everybody and it helps build credibility for the leader. That credibility is both facilitated and maintained through a system where leaders and their covenant partners hold themselves accountable for living the values and achieving the goals of the organization. As covenant leadership becomes more evident through the consistent application of covenant principles, credibility and mutual accountability grow among followers. That tends to foster trust and constructive internal cooperation instead of destructive internal competition. But it all starts with the leader.

Our experience has taught us that creating a system, which is really a culture of mutual accountability, takes time and patience. It is a proactive process that requires a deliberate and continuing effort on the part of the leader to give trust, develop rewards and incentives, create partnerships, encourage ownership and provide dignity, responsibility and hope. And, despite the culture, there are likely to be people who will choose to operate contrary to it. However, that too requires leaders who are willing to step up and hold those individuals accountable for aligning their behavior with the expectations of the job and the values and culture of the organization.

Giving Trust - Whenever I present the covenant model of leadership, I inevitably get comments like this one: *"That's good in theory, but what about accountability?"* My answer is simple. Consider the case of a direct marketing giant, Land's End. Though they were purchased by Sears in 2002, this company has long been known for trusting employees in this covenant leadership model at their Dodgeville, Wisconsin headquarters. Several years ago, prior to their acquisition by Sears, I had the opportunity to talk with the director of customer service, Joan Conlin. Despite the fact that there were millions of dollars worth of merchandise in their warehouse, at the time I spoke with Joan there were no gates or guards at the employee entrance. There were also no timecards for employees. She enthusiastically described the covenant approach to leadership and the trust that pervaded the culture at Land's End:

> *"Land's End does a terrific job of taking care of the employee.... We have the tools to do our job. The front line operator has all kinds of information that they can provide to the customer. They have a lot of control of what they can do for the customer; they make the decisions ... if they think the customer should get the product free because we made a mistake, that's their decision and they make that.... You have to trust your employees to do the best job that they can for the customer. And they know that we trust them. And when they make a decision, we don't*

go back and question. Sometimes we'll have suggestions on maybe a better way to handle it, but you don't ever say it was a bad decision, because they tried to service the customer the best they can.... I've never worked for a company like Land's End, and I've been here for 13 years, so I haven't worked a lot of places. I mean, I love my job, I love the company, it's a fun place to work. They empower people to do what needs to be done. Nobody's ever criticized if you make a mistake. You can take a chance. It's just a very good environment. And that's probably the best thing about Land's End.[1]

This does not suggest that covenant leadership means a lack of accountability. On the contrary, accountability is central to a covenant, but it comes from trusting and being trusted. True, the levels of trust and authority for new employees are different from those of 13 year veterans like Joan. But by giving appropriate levels of trust to Joan and other workers, the leaders at Land's End created a form of self-imposed accountability. Giving our trust also does not mean that people will always respond in a like manner. Most of us work with people who have a variety of needs, motives and experiences. As I noted earlier, in that mix we are likely to find individuals who either don't understand or choose to operate contrary to the common culture of a covenant and the common purposes of the group. When that happens, it demands that we serve our common interests by holding them accountable for their actions.

Further, what is great about a covenant is the fact that the culture allows people at all levels of the organization to hold each other accountable. That means workers also have the freedom to hold leaders accountable when their actions are contrary to those same common purposes. While that requires honesty and a certain amount of humility on the part of leaders, it also engenders credibility, trust, and eventually an even higher level of accountability. In such an environment, the potential for cooperation is greatly enhanced because there are no double standards and people don't have to look over their shoulders constantly as they work. They are trusted and therefore free to make decisions and take risks without fear of reprisal.

Developing Rewards and Incentives - The culture of an organization develops, based in part on what is rewarded within that organization. Therefore, if accountability is to be embraced and become self-imposed, it must also be rewarded. The most obvious forms of rewards are raises, bonuses and promotions, but they are not the only forms. Actually, while financial rewards are important to individuals, management specialist, Bob Nelson, argues that "What tends to motivate them to perform – and to perform at high levels – is the thoughtful, personal kind of recognition that signifies true appreciation for a job well done."[2]

Nelson acknowledges that different people and achievements need different kinds of rewards and he provides three simple guidelines for effectively rewarding and recognizing employees. These include:

1. Matching the reward to the person;
2. Matching the reward to the achievement, and
3. Being timely and specific with the reward.[3]

Accordingly, if I reward the "performance" of self-imposed accountability, it is likely to be embraced and become part of the culture. In the case of Joan Conlin, some of her rewards included the trust and empowerment she was given at Lands End. While those rewards didn't cost the company leaders any more money, they served as a major incentive for Joan and others to embrace their work and become more engaged in helping make the company successful.

Creating Partnerships - In the 1980s and 1990s there weren't too many CEOs who were more successful than Stan Gault. His great performance at Rubbermaid was followed by an impressive turnaround at Goodyear. Mr. Gault discussed the condition of the company when he took over in June of 1991:

"I became chairman of an $11 billion organization fighting to rebuild itself in a fiercely competitive global market. The company's financial performance and market position had seriously deteriorated . . . resulting in Goodyear's first loss in 58 years (1990) . . . . Goodyear's stock had fallen from $76

to below $13 . . . . Interest costs were over a million dollars a day."[4]

In his first 45 days Mr. Gault and his associates developed and began implementing a plan with 12 simple objectives that sought, among other things, to reduce debt, increase financial performance and maximize employee capability. The plan worked and within 18 months, half of the $4 billion in company debt was gone. By the time he retired in June of 1996, sales growth had achieved its highest level in the company's history, earnings per share quadrupled and Goodyear made more money in one year than the rest of the industry combined worldwide. In commenting about the Goodyear turnaround and subsequent success, Mr. Gault noted the importance of creating what he called "partnerships" both inside and outside of the company that enabled people to work together productively toward a common purpose.

> *"Partnerships at all levels begin with one word . . . trust. It is the development of an attitude that says, 'Let's work together, exchange information, develop new approaches, look at our mutual problems and opportunities, and create ideas to make our relationship more productive.' True partnerships break down the ego barriers and antagonism that often exist between companies, between countries, and between individuals."*[5]

Leaders who create an environment where such partnerships or covenants can flourish, also heighten accountability for outcomes and actions because "partners" usually do not want to disappoint their fellow partners. Essentially, partners assume ownership and hold themselves accountable for the success of the enterprise.

Encouraging Ownership - The concept of self-imposed accountability is probably best illustrated through the idea of ownership. When a person purchases something, accountability for its condition rests primarily with that new owner. Accountability is not a question with ownership; it's an assumption and a self-imposed obligation. Conversely, the absence of ownership tends to accommodate less accountability. For example, when my wife and I were first married, we rented a house. Though we worked to keep that place clean and the grass mowed, we were nowhere near as vigilant about upkeep and maintenance as we were when we actually bought our first home. That's because we were tenants occupying a temporary space and doing a minimal job of upkeep on a property that was owned by someone else. We were waiting until our circumstances changed and we could find a home of our own before we put our full effort into improving the property. As tenants, we did not feel a heightened sense of accountability or stewardship for the property entrusted to us. Any work we did on the house was done purely for selfish reasons, related to our desire to have a clean and comfortable place to live.

A lot of organizations have employees who act in a manner and with attitudes that are similar to mine as a tenant. They occupy space temporarily, putting forth a minimal amount of effort for purely selfish reasons. They do only what they have to do, with little sense of accountability for stewardship of the job they do or the organization they serve. Many of them are waiting for an opportunity to come along and for their circumstances to change. What they are looking for is a home for their talents, a place where they can both receive and assume more ownership for what they do and how they do it.

Therefore, one of the ways leaders heighten accountability is by encouraging followers to assume more ownership of their jobs and how they do them. What does it mean to make people owners? It means giving them power to make meaningful decisions; allowing them to use their talents to allocate and grow resources; trusting them to eliminate waste and increase productivity and sharing with them the financial fruits of their efforts. In some cases it also means allowing them not only to share in the profits but also to earn stock ownership.

Certainly the path to ownership is something to be earned and not everyone in an organization assumes or is even allowed the same degree of ownership. Yet, people are willing to work quite hard when the opportunity for ownership exists at some level. By contrast, when the top end of the hierarchy controls all the power, makes most of the decisions, allocates all of the resources and keeps all of the profits; there is not much opportunity or incentive for people to assume ownership and embrace accountability. Covenants encourage partners to assume ownership for the outcomes and condition of the relationship because they benefit so much from it. In the same way, the covenant partners of a marriage assume ownership for nurturing and growing their relationship and for improving its condition; so too do covenant partners in an organization do the same.

Providing Dignity, Responsibility and Hope - While self-imposed accountability is both implied and enhanced by a covenant, giving trust, creating partnerships and encouraging ownership are not the only things that leaders do to create conditions for that kind of accountability to flourish. People are more likely to hold themselves accountable for achieving the purposes and goals of an organization if they know that leaders treat them with dignity and provide for their general well-being. That happens by ensuring that followers are respected, provided with opportunities to assume and/or earn responsibility and given reasons or conditions for hope. Consider the case of Humaita prison in Brazil, a country with a prison system that is known for overcrowded and brutal conditions. One could hardly expect any kind of self-imposed accountability to be prevalent among the prisoners. As Prison Fellowship Founder Chuck Colson tells the story, conditions were so bad at Humaita that the judge assigned to its district considered closing it. A lawyer and a psychologist convinced the judge that Humaita could be operated humanely and securely if those operations were based on Christian principles. The judge conceded and allowed them to take over a portion of the prison. So successful was the experiment that they were asked to take over the entire prison.[6] Eventually the program was instrumental in changing the entire Brazilian penal code toward more humane treatment of prisoners. The organization, which became known as The Association for the Protection and Assistance of the Convicted (APAC), began working in other prisons with similar results.[7]

Colson recounted his conversation with one of the founders of this concept, *"When a prisoner comes to Humaita,"* he said, *"the first thing we do is tell him that he is important to us as an individual and that he will have the opportunity to earn our trust. Restoring his human dignity, giving him hope for the future is our first priority."* [8]

At Humaita (and now other APAC facilities) people worked hard and accepted responsibility for every aspect of the prison operations including security, and Colson noted that escapes are rare.[9] There is both ownership for the condition of the prison and self-imposed accountability for achieving the goals and perpetuating the culture, because the prisoners are treated with dignity and are able to earn trust. And according to outcome studies, the results have been incredible. While about 86 percent of the total population of Brazilian prisoners are re-offenders after release, less than 5 percent of the APAC prisoners are re-offenders.[10]

As the experiment in Brazil demonstrated, accepting responsibility and embracing a self-imposed accountability for a job or a lifestyle do not occur as a result of fear, intimidation and a lack of trust. On the contrary, these prisoners were transformed by being treated with dignity, trusted with responsibility and given hope. If it works in a prison system, it can certainly work in any kind of organization, regardless of how large or small it is.

---

[1] Conlin, Joan, Land's End executive (1996). Personal interview by Leonard J. Moisan, Ph.D.

[2] Nelson, Bob; *1001 Ways to Reward Employees* (Workman Publishing; New York; 1994) p. xv.

[3] Ibid.

[4] Gault, Stanley; Interview with Leonard Moisan; September 20, 1996.

[5] Ibid.

[6] Colson, Chuck, and Eckerd, Jack; *Why America Doesn't Work* (Word Publishing; Dallas; 1991).

[7] Creighton, Agnes; *A Report on Humaita Prison*; November, 1998; www.pficjr. org/programs/apac/reports/humaita.

[8] Colson, Chuck, and Eckerd, Jack; *Why America Doesn't Work* (Word Publishing; Dallas; 1991) p. 181.

[9] Ibid.

[10] Ibid.

Chapter 10
Leadership Evaluation and Action
Discovery (LEAD)

Most organizational leaders will acknowledge the importance of accountability. They even appoint people like a "controller" to enforce it. Yet, the very best kind of accountability in an organization is not one that is forced, but instead it is the kind that is willingly embraced and owned by everyone in the organization. Using the information in Chapter 10, please answer the following questions:

A. To what extent have you been willing to hold yourself accountable and allow others to hold you accountable for achieving the purposes and aligning your practices with the values of the organization?
B. In what ways and to what extent are people in your organization trusted and how might they be trusted more in the future?

C. How are people rewarded or how can they better be rewarded for assuming accountability for their jobs and/ or the success of the organization?

D. In what ways can leaders in your organization create partnerships and encourage ownership?

E. In what ways do leaders in your organization uphold the dignity of every individual and how can they improve?

Chapter 11

Commit in a Way that Inspires

One of the most inspirational people I've ever met is Ron Clark. This incredibly committed and gifted teacher is the winner of the 2000, Disney Teacher of the Year Award. He was tabbed as Oprah Winfrey's first, "Phenomenal Man" and has been called "America's Educator." Recognized for his work worldwide, Ron has been invited to the White House on three separate occasions. In addition to his appearance on the Oprah Winfrey show, Ron has appeared on the Today Show and numerous nationally syndicated radio and television programs. He has been invited to speak about his educational philosophy all over America and is also the subject of the critically acclaimed 2006 television movie, "The Ron Clark Story" starring Matthew Perry in the lead role.

I have had the great pleasure of hearing Ron tell his story at two separate events and after one of those events I got to know Ron and developed a friendship with him. Besides his incredible energy and enthusiasm for teaching, what is inspiring about Ron is his unwavering commitment to children. After viewing a television program in the mid 1990s about schools in Harlem that couldn't attract good teachers, Ron packed up his car and left his rural North Carolina home for New York City. Ron landed a job at P.S. 83 and took over as teacher for a 5th grade class of children that the school officials had pretty much given up on. He fought through racial barriers and cynicism from educators, parents and the children themselves. He dealt with being spit on, laughed at and much more during his time in New York. Ron eventually broke through all of those barriers by demonstrating that he cared about the students, that he was excited about what he was teaching them and that he would continue to believe in their capacity to learn. Certainly Ron's approach was structured and his expectations were high, but everything he did was driven by his love and respect for the children.

As a result of his commitment, not only did his students pass their subjects and earn the highest test scores of any class in the school, they achieved so well that several of them were admitted to one of the most exclusive junior high schools in Manhattan. [1] Ron has developed creative techniques and 55 rules that have helped this high energy educator become highly successful, but what is inspiring about Ron is his unwavering commitment to kids. That commitment led him to start The Ron Clark Academy in Atlanta for underperforming children who wouldn't normally be able to afford a private school. He explained to me that teaching children is his calling and his primary work in life. Clearly Ron's is an inspirational covenant commitment to his students and his profession. It has inspired a group of underprivileged children to achieve at the highest levels and inspired me and many others who heard his story to help him in his mission of educating children.

Covenants can not occur apart from this kind of deep and abiding commitment on the part of all the covenant partners to the relationship and to each other. In an organizational setting that means that leaders not only choose to make a commitment to the purposes and people of the covenant, they choose to evoke or inspire that same kind of commitment in others. The concept of choice as it relates to inspiring commitment from followers is more fully developed in the next chapter. However, as it was in Ron Clark's case, the leader's choice to commit to, assume responsibility for and take action on the covenant must come first.

Because organizations vary by type, purpose and industry, it is sometimes easy to assume that these relational principles of covenant don't always apply to them, particularly in environments that are heavily contract-driven. Regardless of the venue, an erosion of commitment to the common purpose and people of a relationship can be costly. In fact, research clearly demonstrates that customer and employee attrition costs untold millions each year in lost productivity as well as increased marketing, recruitment and acquisition expenses. And what is attrition? It is a manifestation of a lack of commitment.

At the heart of most attrition is a relational problem of some kind. For example, a boss is too controlling or doesn't appreciate a worker, so she leaves and finds a job elsewhere. A customer service representative is rude, so the customer buys from a competitor. A teacher ridicules a student publicly, so he shuts down and quits. The only time a donor hears from the school is through the mail when they need money. Sometimes they even forget to send a thank you letter, so after 10 years of faithful support she stops giving. Relational breaches like these occur daily and they can be devastating for individuals and organizations. Not only are such relational problems costly, but they are also difficult to repair.

Professional baseball learned this lesson the hard way when the players and owners tried to negotiate all of the intricacies and contingencies of complex human relationships into a contract. The free agency of players was pit against the sovereignty of the owners and everyone lost. And it wasn't just relationships between players and owners that were damaged; it was also their relationship with the fans. In the aftermath of the 1994 strike in order to repair the breach, the owners and players had to put aside some of their self-interest and cooperate. They came together and scrambled to restore the trust of fans who had stopped coming to the ball parks en masse. The attitude of many of the fans was that the players were not committed to baseball beyond the money they were receiving and therefore the game had lost its perceived value. Fortunately, the leadership demonstrated in the unselfish play, commitment and sportsmanship of individual players like Cal Ripken; inspired fans, restored trust, added value to the game and filled the stadiums. Like it did in Mr. Ripken's case, the kind of commitment that inspires others is almost always one that involves an individual giving in some form.

Choosing Responsibility Over Rights - A closer look at Mr. Ripken's actions, as he set a record for playing in 2632 consecutive games, reveals some interesting points about what and how he gave. Certainly Cal Ripken had the right to miss a game once in a while. As the Baltimore Orioles short stop, he was playing one of the most demanding positions in baseball, but he also had a higher, more compelling purpose for which he assumed a strong sense of responsibility. Mr. Ripken realized that he was part of something bigger than he was. In pursuit of this larger purpose, he chose to give up some of his immediate individual rights and make a longer-term commitment to what he considered to be a greater return for everyone involved.

Mr. Ripken's choice was to commit and give himself to a larger purpose and then assume responsibility for achieving that purpose. That commitment required uncommon degrees of selflessness and maturity, but those qualities are exactly what allowed Cal Ripken to forego some of his immediate short-term rights for future long-term greatness. His body of work and his inspiring commitment were recognized and established permanently as a part of baseball folklore, when on January 9, 2007 he was elected into the Baseball Hall of Fame on the first ballot.

Leaders recognize that while they may have the legal right to do many things, what they actually do should be driven in a large part by their responsibility to and for the organizations and the people they serve. When leaders violate this concept and choose instead to serve themselves at the expense of others, they miss the opportunity to lead, to enjoy the benefits of a covenant and to establish reciprocal cultures of trust and benevolence that are so crucial to success. This is not to suggest that Mr. Ripken or other would-be leaders need always to be selfless. Nevertheless, because he did commit with a strong sense of responsibility to the game, Mr. Ripken led by example and enjoyed the benefits of his covenants with his teammates, the fans and the game. As a result of his commitment, many people were engaged and inspired, and he established a legacy that will be admired for many years to come.

Performing Beyond Expectations ... Creating and Adding Value - In the mid to late 1980s when Frederick Reichheld and several of his colleagues at the Boston based consulting giant, Bain & Company, were trying to explain growth and profit disparities among companies in the insurance industry, they found something they didn't anticipate. First, they realized that traditional competitive strategy models did not apply in industries where knowledge and intellectual capital were primary assets. Then, they searched further and learned that when companies were able to earn superior levels of customer loyalty and retention, they grew faster and earned profits that were consistently higher. They also learned that customer loyalty is closely linked to employee loyalty and that loyalty is earned by creating and delivering superior customer value. Reichheld and his colleagues tested the findings in other industries and discovered that they applied there as well. He explained, *"... creating value for customers is the foundation of every successful business system. Creating value for customers builds loyalty, and loyalty in turn builds growth, profit and more value.... Profit is indispensable, of course, but it is nevertheless a consequence of value creation...."*[2] Essentially what Reichheld and his colleagues found is that when a company's leaders commit to performing beyond expectations and they give to customers in ways that add value, it inspires loyalty and increases profitability.

Again the Cal Ripken story provides a good illustration of this point. In 1995 when Mr. Ripken broke Lou Gehrig's record of 2,130 consecutive games, he certainly performed well beyond any contractual expectations people may have had for him and thereby created value. From a market perspective, going to see a game in which Mr. Ripken played was perceived to be well worth the price of admission. There was value, not only in seeing a game but also in watching an outstanding performer make history in an incredibly graceful and benevolent way. For example, he did not bask in the glory of his accomplishment, as might have been expected. Instead, he took advantage of the opportunity to call attention to the dreaded disease (ALS) that claimed Lou Gehrig's life. Cal Ripken set up the Cal Ripken, Jr. / Lou Gehrig ALS Research Fund at Johns Hopkins to help find a cure. His unselfish commitment was demonstrated in his good sportsmanship and the way he gave back more than was expected to the game of baseball. It inspired fans and brought them out to the parks in great numbers.

In an environment of free agency and mistrust, this kind of commitment to a higher purpose is unusual but still very much admired. That's why the leadership manifest in what Cal Ripken did and how he competed became so inspiring. He has clearly added value to the game and created a legacy that will not soon be forgotten. Regardless of the industry in which they operate or whether they do it for customers or employees or fans, when leaders perform beyond expectations as Ron Clark, Cal Ripken and others have done, they not only lead by example, they also add value to their organizations and relationships in ways that inspire other people to follow them. As that happens, leaders also strengthen the covenant they share with those followers.

Extending Grace, Provoking Gratitude and Inspiring High Performance - Leaders who initiate actions like these and operate in other-centered rather than self-centered ways, also become role models who set an example that people around them tend to follow. Simply stated, benevolence on the part of a leader usually breeds benevolence in the form of gratitude and high performance on the part of others. That was truly the case in the 2004 summer Olympics in Athens. In one of the most exciting swimming races of the entire meet, teammates and rivals Ian Crocker and Michael Phelps faced off in the 100 meter butterfly. Crocker, who had been sick during the meet, led much of the race but he was out-touched at the wall by Phelps. Though it was close, Michael Phelps had won his fifth gold medal by .04 of a second. In so doing, he had also won the right to swim butterfly in the 400 medley relay the next day, even though by his own admission Crocker had better relay starts and would likely do better than Phelps in the relay.

Michael Phelps swam on the relay team in the prelims, and their performance qualified the U.S. to swim for gold in the medal heat. However, Phelps shocked the world with what was arguably one of the most gracious and benevolent gestures ever in sports. He stepped aside and gave his teammate, Ian Crocker, the opportunity to take his place in the finals. Though he admitted it was a tough decision, the 19-year-old Phelps also noted that Ian Crocker was one of the best relay swimmers on the U.S. team. Said Phelps, *"This is a decision that I chose ... I will be in the stands, and I will be cheering as hard as I can for the U.S. team ... we came as a team, and we're going to be leaving as a team."*[3]

When Crocker was first told of Phelps' decision he said, *"I'm kind of speechless ... I feel like it was a decision that only Michael could make ... I feel like it's a huge gift that is difficult to accept but makes me want to go out and tear up the pool ... I couldn't be more proud ... I'm going to do everything I can to make it feel like it was the right choice."*[4]

Not only did Michael Phelps demonstrate leadership in putting the team and a fellow teammate ahead of his own self-interest, the benevolence and grace he extended to his teammate inspired gratitude and an outstanding performance on the part of Ian Crocker and the rest of the relay team. The American team won the gold medal in world record time and with a margin of nearly three seconds. Also, as promised, Crocker really did "tear up the pool," finishing the butterfly leg of the relay nearly a full second faster than Phelps' gold medal winning time from the previous day. By all rights, Phelps deserved to swim in the relay final. He had worked for four to six hours a day for years and he beat the best in the world to earn that right. Measured against any standard, his commitment to excellence was unquestionable. However, Michael Phelps' leadership was demonstrated not so much by his world-class performances in the pool but by the grace manifest in his selfless commitment to teammates, a commitment that moved and inspired them.

Showing Mercy – For leaders, to make a covenant commitment of the kind that inspires followers, sometimes requires that they give by showing those followers mercy. Shakespeare's *Merchant of Venice* provides a good illustration of this point. Shylock is a Jewish money lender and the play's chief antagonist. He is angered by the poor treatment and disrespect he experiences from Venice's Christian community, and in particular Antonio, a wealthy merchant. After guaranteeing a loan from Shylock to his friend Bassanio, Antonio has a business set back and he can not repay the loan. He becomes indebted to Shylock, and the money lender decides to seek justice by demanding the full penalty for not paying the debt, which is a pound of Antonio's flesh.

Portia, the heiress of Belmont and friend of the debtor, appeals for Shylock to reconsider. She disguises herself as a man, confronts Shylock and in one of Shakespeare's most well known and quoted passages Portia says, *"The quality of mercy is not strained. It droppeth as a gentle rain from heaven upon the place beneath. It is twice blest: it blesseth him that gives, and him that takes..."*[5]

Like Shylock, all too often today power wielders inside organizations refuse to give even a slight amount of tolerance for error. They rule with fear and are more ready to collect their "pound of flesh" for mistakes, than they are to show mercy by forgiving. The problem is that if mercy does, as Shakespeare noted, create a double blessing that accrues both to its giver and receiver; then it follows that the lack of mercy creates a double hardship.

As Shylock insists legalistically on extracting his pound of flesh, Portia clearly sees the injustice of his demand and uses deception and the law to turn the tables on Shylock. The law might allow him to extract his pound of flesh from Antonio, but it would clearly not allow Shylock to draw blood or to kill him. As a result of his persistence and lack of mercy, Shylock was met with resistance that threatened his estate, his livelihood and his very life. Eventually his unreasonable actions put him at the mercy of the very person he sought to destroy.

As is frequently the case, power wielders like Shylock who lack mercy and treat people unjustly, eventually meet with resistance they can't overcome. When heads of organization choose to operate this way, they put their organizations, their people and their careers in peril. The point is that leaders who are merciful in their dealings with followers, also demonstrate commitment in ways that bless those followers and inspire loyalty from them.

Mother Theresa is a good example of a leader who inspired others by her selfless commitment to the poor and dying. Her commitment was manifest in the mercy she extended to the people she served. Mother Theresa gained credibility as a leader, not because she demanded justice and retribution for mistakes or poor choices the people in need may have made. Instead it was her selfless acts of mercy driven by her faith commitment that won admirers throughout the world. She simply respected, served and loved people in ways that not only blessed them but also inspired others to commit to her cause.

Earning Loyalty - Commitment is both inspired and demonstrated by loyalty. As I thought about this statement, I was reminded of the attractive and endearing nature of stories about loyalty. Consider the immensely popular 1994 movie, *Forrest Gump*. It's a fictional story in which the title character (played by Tom Hanks) takes us through a narrative history of his own life from the 1950s to the 1980s. We see Forrest as a part of most of the major historical events and interacting with most of the major characters of that period. Through the eyes of this simple Alabama man with a sub-normal IQ, viewers are treated to a nostalgic ride through some tumultuous times by this endearing character. The movie deals with many themes and introduces us to several characters, but one of the constants is Forrest's strong character and enduring commitment to people. This is evidenced in his loyalty to his lifelong love Jenny, his army pal Bubba and his commander in Vietnam, double amputee Lieutenant Dan. Despite Jenny's wayward path and promiscuous behavior, Bubba's death and Lieutenant Dan's anger and disability; Forrest maintains his commitment to all of them. Forrest never loses faith in people. He assumes the best and over time and through his persistence he earns their admiration. Though the story is a fictional one, Forrest also won the hearts of movie goers as the film grossed over $300 million and was nominated for 13 Academy Awards.

It is difficult to pinpoint any one thing that made this movie such an overwhelming success. However, beyond the nostalgia I believe it uncovered a deep yearning that people have, a yearning to be believed in and committed to in the same way that Forrest believed in and committed to his friends.

Yet, commitment and loyalty rarely come to leaders in an unconditional manner. In fact, it is usually quite to the contrary. Commitment and loyalty more often than not have to be earned, and where the leader-follower relationship is involved there are several principles that apply. First, while loyalty and commitment are not exactly synonymous, loyalty is both a form and an outgrowth of commitment. I can be loyal and also earn loyalty by being committed to others and acting in their best interest. At the same time, one of the ways I demonstrate commitment to friends and family members is by being loyal to them. Clearly, in relationships the two terms are interdependent. Forrest's commitment to his friends was demonstrated by his loyalty to them. He believed in his friends, acted in their best interest and kept his promises to them. He acted in a manner that considered their interests ahead of his own and as a result he earned their friendship and their loyalty.

Second, from a leader's perspective, loyalty should be a natural outgrowth of the commitment the leader makes to followers. But what "should be" is not always what "is". Certainly leaders want their commitments to inspire loyalty on the part of followers, but loyalty must be earned through hard work as much as it is inspired. And in the leader-follower relationship, it is the leader who must initiate action that demonstrates commitment to the followers. Despite his sub-par IQ, we find in Forrest a good example of what leaders do to earn loyalty and inspire commitment of others. Based on the core values Forrest learned mainly from his mother, he made positive assumptions about people, he made and kept commitments to them, he gave generously to them, he took action on their behalf, he performed well beyond their expectations, he delivered on his promises to them, and he demonstrated grace and showed them mercy.

Third, as leaders do take steps to demonstrate in their own actions and inspire in the actions of others, the kind of commitment that brings loyalty both inside and outside of the organization, it clearly pays. Of course, the converse of this is also true. When commitment and loyalty among customers (internal and external) diminishes, it can be quite costly. In *The Loyalty Effect*, author and consultant

Frederick Reichheld notes that on average major companies replace 50 percent of their customers every five years and about half of their employees every four years. On the investor side the attrition rate is even more rapid. A typical company loses an average of half of its investors in just one year. The author cites studies demonstrating that an increase in customer retention rates of just 5 percent can increase profits in companies from 25 percent to as much as 100 percent.[6]

Beyond the benefits of customer retention, improving employee retention by earning loyalty also has economic advantages. Study after study confirms that the hidden expenses of high employee turnover, expenses that include recruitment and training costs as well as lost productivity, can reach as much as 150 percent or more of a person's annual salary. In addition, companies spend on average about 36 percent of revenue on human resources expenses according to a Mercer/CEO Magazine Study. Therefore, a company with $100 million in revenues spends about $36 million on payroll and other expenses. That means that at 100 percent replacement cost, a 25 percent turnover rate costs the company an additional $9 million per year. In this case, (assuming a 10 percent profit margin with the turnover) reducing the turnover rate to 10 percent (slightly below the national average) would increase profit by 54 percent. A real live example of this is found in the fast-food industry where management turnover rates average about 35 – 40 percent. By working to keep store operator turnover rates at 5 percent, Chick-fil-A enhances its profit margins so significantly that the company can allow its operators to earn as much as two to three times industry averages.[7]

No doubt, declining employee loyalty can be costly. But a lack of loyalty on the part of employees is found not only in turnover. It can also be evident in things like low productivity and employee theft. Consider the February 2005 case of an ex Time Warner employee who pleaded guilty to federal charges that he conspired to steal and sell 92 million names and passwords from their user database. In May of the same year, eight former employees of major banks were arrested for selling account information illegally from some 500,000 customer accounts for $10 per record or $5,000,000.[8]

While these and other examples demonstrate that loyalty pays, leaders must know how to earn it. In *Loyalty Rules*, Mr. Reichheld discusses principles for earning loyalty that according to him, "... encompass standards of excellence, simplicity, honesty, fairness, respect and responsibility."[9] It should be noted that, he summarizes those principles and his philosophy by explaining that earning loyalty is really about building and maintaining partnerships, and he qualifies this by describing the dynamics of these partnerships and distinguishing them from *"self serving alliances."* He notes,

> *"True partnerships must be driven by mutual caring, respect, responsibility, accountability and growth. In a true partnership, each individual must willingly put the success of the relationship ahead of short-term personal gain. And, of course, for each partner to prosper in the long-term, the entire system of relationships with employees, dealers, vendors, and investors must successfully create value for the ultimate customer. Each individual must be willing not only to put the partner's interest ahead of his or her own, but also to make the interests of the final consumer the highest priority."*[10]

What Mr. Reichheld is really describing here is a system of covenants and covenants clearly are based on and also build loyalty. If loyalty pays and we have demonstrated that it does, the question for a leader is, *"How do I facilitate loyalty?"* The simple answer is to create and build a culture of covenants through teaching and modeling the principles.

Teaching and Facilitating Loyalty - Covenants imply commitment, and the kind of commitment that is inspired and nurtured by a leader in a covenant also evokes loyalty. However, that comes full circle because the loyalty that comes in a covenant also evokes and strengthens commitment on the part of the covenant partners. In fact, when Reichheld found in his research that loyalty comes from true partnerships that are driven by a culture of mutual caring, respect, responsibility and accountability; he uncovered the truth about covenants. But simply knowing the truth does not automatically create a culture where covenants can flourish. That process is much more time consuming and deliberate.

Modeling loyalty daily and teaching it deliberately are among the primary methods leaders use to create cultures where covenants flourish and loyalty results. For example, the covenant my wife and I have shared for over 30 years has been expanded to include our three children, our son-in-law and grandson and several other relatives and friends. As parents we have worked hard to cultivate in our children a strong, caring commitment to each other and to our family. My wife in particular has been quite consistent in that endeavor. Through her teaching and her consistent example, she has created culture for our family, and particularly our children, where they are expected to be kind to and respectful of each other. We have also told the children that it is important for them to "stick up" for (be loyal to) each other, particularly if someone is unkind to one of them. As they were growing up, certainly that expectation was tested from time to time, but for the most part they were loyal to each other.

While all of the kids understood our family expectations and acted on them over the years, when it came to commitment and loyalty, our daughter, Sarah, went above and beyond our expectations. In fact, she demonstrated an intense loyalty toward her brothers that was unusual for her age. A good example of this loyalty is found in a school bus incident when our daughter was about eight and our son, Dan, was eleven. As boys often do with each other, a neighbor and one of our son's friends named Andrew was teasing and pestering Dan. The longer Sarah sat on the bus and listened to it, the angrier she became. Finally, the bus stopped and Andrew got off with our son and daughter. By this time Sarah was beside herself and she could contain it no longer. As Andrew walked toward his house in front of Sarah, she slammed her book bag down and called his name loudly, *"Andrew!"* When she did this, she also ran full speed toward Andrew. As he was turning around toward Sarah, she leapt on him, dress and all, and knocked him to the ground. Sarah then commenced to whale on him and yell at him to leave her brother alone. Eventually Andrew extricated himself from his assailant, but he didn't mess with our son again, at least not in front of his sister.

We certainly talked to Sarah about the inappropriateness of attacking Andrew, but we also told her we were proud of her for sticking up for her brother and for caring about him. The point is that Sarah understood well her covenant commitment and responsibility to her brother, so well that she was even willing to put herself at risk to fight for and support her brother. In fact, she didn't even consider herself or her safety when she took action, since Andrew was also older and bigger than she was. Even though our son and daughter continued to disagree and argue from time to time, their acts of commitment and loyalty towards each other have brought them closer together. While we laugh today about the incident, the covenant between Sarah and her brothers deepens every year and now it has been expanded to include Sarah's husband and son.

Leaders who teach and create a culture of covenant, also encourage commitment of the partners to each other and to the organization. Moreover, when leaders demonstrate commitment and loyalty by considering followers above themselves, it greatly enhances the commitment and loyalty of those followers and creates a bond among them that lasts. In the final analysis, loyalty breeds commitment in much the same way as commitment breeds loyalty. In *Credibility*, authors James Kouzes and Barry Posner argue that a leader cannot demand loyalty; it must be earned. It comes as the leader meets the needs of people. They note, *"There is greater connection between leadership and customer service than there is between leadership and traditional management. We further assert that there is much more to be learned about leadership from reading the customer service and quality literature than from reading most management texts."*[11]

True leaders are keenly attuned to the concept of customer service both inside and outside of their organization. As a result they are able to facilitate the growth of commitment and loyalty because both qualities are taught and modeled in the leader-follower relationship. Not surprisingly, those same qualities are essential to and products of the covenants leaders create.

Engaging People Emotionally - Making and keeping a commitment in ways that inspire others, involves more than just the logic of whether or not that commitment adds up; it also involves the emotions of whether or not it feels right. Simply stated, to be human is to have and express emotions, and our emotions influence heavily the commitments we make. In fact, we choose friends, marry spouses, donate to charities and vote for politicians much less on logic and much more on emotion. How we feel about people and how we connect with them on an emotional level determines a great deal about how we relate to them. Therefore, to be committed to other human beings or their organizations, also means feeling good about them and being connected and engaged with them emotionally.

In *Follow This Path* Curt Coffman and Gabriel Gonzalez-Molina discuss their work as researchers with the Gallup organization. Their book highlights the power of what they call an "emotion driven economy," where companies prosper because their employees and customers are emotionally engaged with them. Specifically, Coffman and Gonzalez-Molina were using the Gallup data to try and determine the distinguishing characteristics of the strongest and the most vibrant, productive and profitable workplaces. After analyzing Gallup data from 10 million customers, 3 million employees and 200,000 managers from all major industries, they found that one of the leading predictors of organizational success is the level of emotional engagement that exists among both employees and customers.[12]

Commenting on their findings, Coffman and Gonzalez-Molina note that, *"Emotional engagement is the fuel that drives the most productive employees and the most profitable customers."*[13] Ron Clark, for example, is highly productive because he is emotionally engaged in what he is doing. It makes sense then, that improving emotional engagement will also improve both productivity and profitability. Alarmingly, the authors also found that there is a great deal of room for improvement in most companies. The findings revealed that in a majority of companies (more than 60 percent), only about 20 – 30 percent of the employees are engaged emotionally in their work. That's because in a typical workplace, the conditions necessary for engaging the workforce are missing.

Of course, leaders are the ones who create conditions for workers to be engaged emotionally in the first place. For example, Michael Phelps created the conditions that heightened the emotional engagement and the productivity of Ian Crocker. Likewise, the leaders at Chick-fil-A created conditions for their managers to be far more engaged and profitable than their peers at other companies.

The conditions Coffman and Gonzalez-Molina cite in their book are similar to those that exist in covenants. They include a culture where leaders attract talented people and determine their strengths, equip and allow them to do what they do best, care about them as individuals and listen to them, provide them with a clear purpose and challenging goals, build supportive relationships with workers and allow them to do the same, recognize the importance of individuals and their contributions and allow them to grow.[14]

While this is not an exhaustive listing of the conditions presented by the authors, it does capture the essence of what it takes to engage someone emotionally. What is immediately apparent is that those conditions are predominantly relational. Building stronger, more fulfilling relationships (covenants) is clearly the key to strengthening commitment, enhancing emotional engagement and increasing productivity but, as the research demonstrates and these authors point out, most organizations are lacking in this area.

Satisfying Customers Profitably - Closely related to emotional engagement is employee satisfaction. Simply stated, employees who are engaged emotionally are more likely to be satisfied. In fact, there is a substantial amount of empirical data demonstrating a direct correlation between employee satisfaction and customer satisfaction and therefore profitability. Simply stated, if leaders commit to a common purpose and the people who share that purpose, they are likely to inspire loyalty, engage employees emotionally sand satisfy them in ways that enhance profitability.

For example, a study of the relationship between employee satisfaction, employer engagement and business outcomes revealed nationwide that those business units with above average employee satisfaction outperformed those units with below average employee satisfaction by 103 percent.[15]

Similarly, a major study at Sears, Roebuck & Co. revealed that a four percent increase in employee satisfaction improved customer satisfaction by an identical four percent and led to a $200 million increase in revenues.[16] Around the time of that study I had the opportunity to talk with one of the authors, Steve Kirn, who was then the Vice President for Education and Human Resource Development at Sears. Steve talked about the importance of building loyalty and a sense of personal connection with the company:

> *"There are some who are saying that loyalty is not a relevant variable, but Sears got to where it is through lots of loyalty over an extended period of time. A lot of that loyalty was built by building a sense of personal connection with the business. What I think we're trying to balance now is a long tradition and a set of expectations and a way of building the sense of real oneness with the company which is the kind of thing that makes you do extraordinary things even when times are tough."*[17]

People who are satisfied in relationships tend to stay in those relationships and grow in their commitment to them. Whether its customers or employees in a business, members of a church or partners in a marriage; the more emotionally engaged and satisfied people are, the more committed and productive they become.

Making a Decision Courageously – Taking the First Step - It is important to realize that inspiring commitment on the part of others requires the deliberate and decisive action of a leader. Assuming responsibility for achieving a purpose, engaging people emotionally and all the other activities that work together to evoke commitment do not naturally occur in most organizations. In fact, the natural tendency is to act first on one's own self-interest, unless there is both a visible example and a strong incentive to do otherwise. For that to change requires someone (a leader) to make a decision and take the first step courageously to perform at a higher level than expected or to extend benevolence to someone else. Beyond that, the leader must proceed in a manner that builds commitment in others, sometimes in spite of the prevailing atmosphere or culture.

During the latter part of the 18th century, William Wilberforce made a commitment to the cause of abolishing slavery and courageously took action that eventually inspired the entire world to follow his lead. He added value to the world in ways that continue to benefit mankind today. Achieving what he did wasn't easy, but he knew it was right. His commitment, vision and persistence eventually inspired commitment in others, but to get there he had to take the first step.

Born of a wealthy English family, he was a well respected and popular member of the London Society and eventually he obtained a seat in the British House of Commons in 1780. While his first few years of service demonstrated that Wilberforce was a talented and capable debater, there was very little that distinguished him from his peers. At that time it would have been hard to believe that this same fun-loving and admirable man would eventually transform the thinking, not only of the English people but also of most of the people in the free world regarding the issue of slavery. No doubt, Wilberforce could have remained quite comfortable, continuing to live and serve in the way he had been accustomed. Yet a life-changing spiritual encounter in 1785 caused him to reconsider his own life and values and compelled him to action. Wilberforce struggled with what he found, noting in his diary, *"I must awake to my dangerous state, and never be at rest till I have made my peace with God."*[18]

In the midst of his struggle, he lost his taste for politics, but after a candid talk with a friend about Christian duty, Wilberforce returned to the House of Commons and eventually took the lead in the fight to abolish slavery. He was driven by a covenant commitment to Christian principles of justice, respect, responsibility, grace, mercy and the dignity of human beings. Though he received death threats and was subjected to unfounded rumors about his morals, neither the threats, nor the loss of popularity deterred him from continuing to take action and persevere patiently in his unselfish public service. Finally, after many years of struggle and calculated action, slave trade in England was abolished and declared unlawful in 1807 and slavery itself was outlawed in 1833. Eventually, many other countries would follow Britain's lead and make slave trade illegal.

It is an understatement to say that Wilberforce was a committed and inspiring leader. Yet, had he not made the decision to get involved and then taken action on that decision, he would have missed the opportunity to lead. What Wilberforce was really demonstrating in his action was his covenant commitment to the country, people and God he served. Maybe that's why, though people honored Wilberforce for these inspiring victories, he never changed his modest, unassuming and benevolent ways. He chose responsibility to others over his right to certain comforts. Wilberforce denied himself the luxuries of wealth, donating 25 percent of his income to charity. He "gave back" to society in order to better serve mankind. Through his denial of self in favor of service to others, Wilberforce performed and served well beyond expectations, and as a result he clearly became an inspiring and transforming leader.[19]

Not every leader has the opportunity to act so selflessly on such an important issue; but the absence of some degree of selfless, committed and inspiring leadership in an organization leads people to pursue self-interest more aggressively. The eventual result of an atmosphere driven by self-interest is a rise in conflict due to the inevitable clash of competing interests that is bound to occur. Though some conflict can be healthy in an organization, when managers must spend an inordinate amount of time mitigating it, resources are often wasted and organizational effectiveness is compromised. By contrast, in an environment where committed and inspiring leadership, heightened performance and widespread benevolence are prevalent, teamwork is enhanced because people are less likely to feel the need to protect themselves and more likely to help one another.

Even in the most hostile of environments, hard work earns respect and benevolence tends to break down conflict, but these things require a leader to step out and choose first to model them. That means working to deliver beyond expectations, taking actions that benefit others and then holding people accountable for doing the same. The actions can come in a variety of forms that include listening, respecting, helping, providing necessary resources or support, recognizing contributions, accommodating a need or interest or style, and even forgiving; but whatever the actions are, they are always initiated by a leader. True, that leader can operate at any level of the organization and may not necessarily have a formal "leadership" position; but for high performance, benevolence, teamwork or anything else to permeate a culture, requires a leader to make a decision and take the first step to initiate them.

But in the final analysis what inspires us about the leadership of Ron Clark, Cal Ripken, Michael Phelps, Mother Theresa, William Wilberforce and many others, is not simply that they stepped up to lead or that they achieved great things. It certainly is all of that, but it is also the fact that stepping up to lead, to commit in the ways that they did, to operate contrary to the status quo, cost them all something personally. In fact, they knew that it would, but they chose to act anyway. That has given them credibility as leaders, and it has inspired countless others to follow their example.

---

[1] Clark, Ron; The Essential 55; (Hyperion, New York, New York; 2003) also see www.ronclarkacademy.com.

[2] Reichheld, Frederick, F.; The Loyalty Effect; (Harvard Business School Press; 1996) p. 3.

[3] Ruane, Michael E. Phelps Is Golden, Gracious (The Washington Post; August 21, 2001) p. A01 or www.washingtonpost.com, pp. 1-3.

[4] Ibid; p. 2.

[5] Shakespeare, William; The Merchant of Venice The Oxford Shakespeare second edition, Stanley Wells and Gary Taylor general editors, (Clarendon Press, Oxford; 2005) p. 473.

[6] Reichheld, Frederick F.; The Loyalty Effect (Harvard Business School Press; 1996).

[7] Ibid.

[8] Yuan, Li; Companies Face Data Breaches From Inside, Too; (Wall Street Journal; Marketplace; June 1, 2005) p. B1, B4.

[9] Reicheld, Frederick F.; Loyalty Rules (Harvard Business School Press, Boston, Massachusetts; 2001).

[10] Ibid, p. 16.

[11] Kouzes, James M. & Posner, Barry Z.; *Credibility* (Jossey-Bass; San Francisco, California; 1993) pp. 9-10.

[12] Coffman, Curt and Gonzalez-Molina, Gabriel, Ph.D. *Follow This Path: How the World's Greatest Organizations Drive Growth by Unleashing Human Potential* (New York, NY Warner Books; 2002.)

[13] Ibid.

[14] Ibid.

[15] Harter, James K.; Schmidt, Frank L.; Hayes, Theodore L.; Business-Unit-Level Relationship Between Employee Satisfaction, Employee Engagement and Business Outcomes: A Meta-Analysis; "Journal of Applied Psychology"; 2002; pp. 268-279.

[16] Rucci, A.J.; Kirn, S.P.; Quinn, R.T.; The Employee-Customer-Profit Chain at Sears; "Harvard Business Review"; January-February, 1998; pp. 82-97.

[17] Kirn, Steve; Interview with Leonard J. Moisan, Ph.D.; January 4, 1996.

[18] Martin, Hugh, ed.; Christian Social Reformers Of The Nineteenth Century; "William Wilberforce" (1759-1833); by R. Coupland; Freeport, New York: Books For Libraries Press; p. 55.

[19] Ibid.

Chapter 11
Leadership Evaluation and Action
Discovery (LEAD)

Covenants imply commitment on the part of all covenant partners. A leader's choice to commit to, assume responsibility for and take action on the covenant must come first. Using the information in Chapter 11, please answer the following questions:

A. People in our organization tend to ...		YES	NO
1.	Choose work responsibility over individual preferences.	❏	❏
2.	Perform beyond expectations.	❏	❏
3.	Create and add value for customers.	❏	❏
4.	Receive grace and extend grace to others.	❏	❏
5.	Be grateful and inspired.	❏	❏
6.	Be loyal.	❏	❏
7.	Earn the loyalty of customers.	❏	❏
8.	Learn how to be loyal through example of leaders.	❏	❏
9.	Be engaged emotionally in their work.	❏	❏
10.	Be satisfied in their work.	❏	❏
11.	Satisfy customers.	❏	❏
12.	Make decisions about their work.	❏	❏

B. Give examples of how leaders in your organization have chosen to serve stakeholders (employees, customers, suppliers) over their own self-interest. How can they improve?

C. In what ways do your organization's leaders perform beyond expectations and create or add value for your stakeholders? How can they improve?

D. What role does or can the concept of grace play in your organization (i.e., allowing others to take risks and make mistakes)?

E. In what ways do your leaders earn and/or facilitate loyalty among the stakeholders of your organization?

F. Emotional engagement is directly related to productivity and profitability, yet in a typical company only about 20 – 30 percent of employees are actively and emotionally engaged in their work. What steps can you and other leaders in your organization take to enhance emotional engagement?

Chapter 12

Communicate...Communicate...Communicate

I debated whether or not to have a separate chapter on communication because communication is implied in everything we've discussed thus far. Yet, communication is such a central part of sustaining relationships and in particular, applying the principles of covenant, that I thought it would be important to spend some time discussing it separately. For example, it's difficult to establish and maintain any sense of common purpose or any kind of a relationship apart from effective communication. You don't build trust, align values, create partnerships or recognize others appropriately without communicating. In fact, no matter how large or small the organization is, when relationships lose sight of their common purposes and begin to break down it's usually because of a communication problem. Because we live in a fast-paced society, we see gaps in relational communication all around us in our marriages, our families, our businesses and more. Inside any of these relationships, filling those gaps and making communication and the relationships themselves more effective, requires leaders to create channels for communication, to employ those channels in ways that engage people in pursuit of the common purposes and then to keep those channels open.

Being Open, Honest and Credible- How do leaders achieve all of this? It begins as they start speaking honestly and sharing information openly. Beyond that, effective communication also includes leaders asking questions, listening to the answers and then taking action that is consistent with what they have heard. Actually it is the action leaders take that demonstrates whether or not they are listening in the first place. And taking appropriate action also works to keep the channels of communication open because it contributes to the leader's credibility. Credibility is very important in maintaining communication between leaders and followers because people are just not likely to talk openly and honestly with someone they can't trust.

Being Interested - Vice Admiral John Scott Redd is the Director of the U.S. National Counterterrorism Center. At the time I interviewed him he was Commander of the U.S. Naval Forces, Central Command headquartered in Bahrain in the Persian Gulf. Geographically, the Central Command territory ranges from Egypt down to Kenya and from Iraq and Iran to Pakistan. He has also been Commander of the U. S. Fifth Fleet. In addition to making crucial strategic decisions on a daily basis, Admiral Redd was responsible for serving (as he described it) 10,000 - 15,000 Marines and sailors who were under his command in the Middle East. As a leader, he believes communicating effectively and having appropriate information in a timely manner are essential to the kind of effective decision making that best serves the people under his command and the interests of the United States. The way to accommodate good information flow, according to Admiral Redd, is to be interested, accessible and approachable and also to remember that the leader does not always have all of the answers. Securing crucial information sometimes requires, as the Admiral has described, putting the transmitter on hold and using receivers to listen to advice and counsel from others. He explained,

> *"The key point is to make sure that people are comfortable bringing you bad news as well as good news. I mean, bad things are going to happen -- it's not a question of 'if,' but 'when.' In the first eleven months of my tour we conducted six real-world operations, including the evacuation of United Nations Forces from Somalia and deterring an unrepentant Iraqi leader in the wake of the Gulf War. There are bad things going on and that means that we have to deal with some pretty unpleasant issues on a routine basis... If people are afraid you are going to shoot the messenger, there's a natural tendency to avoid being the bearer of bad tidings. Bad news doesn't go away and problems*

have to be dealt with. So what you want is to get the bad news as soon as you can, in as objective a way as you can, so that you can deal with it."[1]

The Admiral related some practical advice to me on how leaders can demonstrate interest in followers, build loyalty and trust among them and keep the communication flowing:

"Now the practical way of doing that is convincing people, first by saying it but most importantly, by doing it, that if they bring bad news or good news or whatever news, the information will be dealt with on its merits...if there's one personal attribute which I would encourage a leader to incorporate it's the concept of service for those that work for you. That, more than anything else, builds the bonds of trust and credibility between senior and subordinate which are the basis of success. Followers need to believe and understand that their leader is someone who is not self-serving but who genuinely cares about them and their well being. The leader who is preoccupied with his or her own career or selfish interest will not inspire loyalty or respect, no matter how individually competent. Conversely, the leader who genuinely cares for and acts on the well being of his subordinates has built a solid foundation of teamwork which will overcome many shortfalls in other areas."[2]

Unfortunately, both empirical data and our consulting experience tell us that not all CEOs are, or even want to be, effective communicators. Some CEOs simply get too busy in their work and don't take enough time to communicate, while others take employees for granted and don't believe communicating with them will be fruitful. Whatever the reason is, it certainly doesn't make communication any less important. That's exactly the point that Robert Crandall made. As Chairman of AMR Corporation, he was the head of a holding company that provided scheduled passenger and airfreight services to customers around the world through its American Airlines subsidiary. The company employed some 92,000 workers. According to Mr. Crandall, leading that many employees to achieve a common purpose in an effective manner requires that executives listen to those employees on a regular basis.

Providing a Forum for Expression-To ensure the continuous flow of what he considered to be vital information from employees, Mr. Crandall annually presided over dozens of forums at a variety of company locations. Some of these sessions would last up to five hours and, when he appeared before them, Mr. Crandall would be accompanied only by his assistant (for note taking) to encourage their candid remarks. The purpose, of course, was to accommodate open and honest communication without the fear of reprisal, so he could learn and adapt and make more effective decisions. Though Mr. Crandall found this communication to be quite important to his decision making, he also observed that most executives aren't really interested in hearing from their employees or continuing discussions about how to achieve the common purposes. He believes this is due to the fact that most CEOs don't believe their employees have any relevant information to offer or they don't have the energy or discipline to act on the information they receive.[3]

In order to achieve a common and ethical purpose, leaders must communicate effectively with followers in much the same way that covenant partners must communicate with each other. That requires interest and attention as well as a forum for expression. The forum for expression can be open meetings like Mr. Crandall held, employee surveys or even suggestion boxes. But effective communication demands that it exist in some form. Regardless of whether it's in a business relationship, a political alliance or a marriage, communication in a covenant is a proactive process that takes a deliberate effort on the part of the covenant partners to take time to listen and share information openly and honestly. This kind of communication is really what helps bind people together as they pursue a common purpose.

It follows logically that in the absence of such communication, where leaders fail to provide opportunities for expression and demonstrate a lack of interest, it weakens relationships in ways that contribute to organzational waste, dysfunction and uncertainty among its people.

For example, when a husband and wife are either not speaking to one another or communicating poorly, the marriage is less functional than it could be. If this condition persists, the children are likely to become unsettled and insecure about the future, which could impede their success. The same thing can happen in any environment where there is ineffective communication among leaders or between leaders and followers.

Listening Aggressively - Effective communication includes more than simply sharing information; it requires as much listening as it does talking. In its best organizational form, it is an aggressive attempt to bring understanding between leaders and followers as they work together to achieve common purposes. Leaders simply will not build covenants with followers if they aren't willing to listen and understand them. In Stephen Covey's *Seven Habits of Highly Effective People,* he makes the case that effective communication comes from seeking first to understand and then to be understood. Covey notes that typically our first inclination in the communication process is to be understood instead of achieving understanding.[4] But effective leaders go to great lengths to listen aggressively and thereby understand. For example, at Federal Express executives take on personal responsibility to improve proactively in at least one defined area of company performance each year. To accommodate this improvement, company executives must work hard to stay in touch with the operations. It requires a deliberate and aggressive process of communication in which everyone on the executive team, from President and CEO Fred Smith on down, meets with workers on the job and listens. In an aggressive way these executives seek to learn what factors might be bottlenecking performance or operational success. In order for them to meet the company expectations for leaders to be champions of change, to improve operations and to enhance employee well-being, Mr. Smith and his executive team must proactively listen and communicate effectively.[5] By the mere fact that they extend themselves to do this, demonstrates respect for employees and acknowledges their importance.

In commenting on the importance of creating a shared vision and communicating with employees, Fred Smith said, *"The way I see it, leadership does not begin with power, but rather with a compelling vision or goal of excellence. One becomes a leader when he or she is able to communicate that vision in such a way that others feel empowered to achieve excellence. We must create organizations with a shared vision of excellence.*"⁶ To ensure that the vision is indeed a shared one and that communication flows both ways, the Federal Express leadership team has created a communication system that includes a grievance procedure, an open door policy and regular employee surveys. This is in addition to the sit-down listening sessions that Fred Smith and the rest of the executive team conduct regularly.⁷ All of these efforts are for the purpose of ensuring that the common purpose is still "common" and that the common purpose is achieved. That just doesn't happen apart from leaders, followers and/or covenant partners communicating effectively. It is crucial for leaders to realize that communication, as demonstrated by Fred Smith, is not just about speaking and distributing information; it's also about asking, listening and then taking action in proactive and aggressive ways that demonstrate that you've heard. That's really at the heart of the give and take necessary for effective communication as well as living and leading in the context of a covenant.

Leading and Not Managing, Manipulating or Controlling People
- In the same way that there are plenty of different ways people try to live and relate to one another, there are also plenty of different ways people try to lead. Some would-be leaders try to manage people while others try to manipulate and control them like they would inventories. It's not surprising the frequency with which all of these methods eventually lead to breakdowns in communication and eventually relationships. People don't want to be managed, manipulated or controlled by power wielders; they want to be understood, appreciated and led. As individuals are led, they want reliable information and some of the normal 'give and take' that comes from effective communication. Author and consultant to hundreds of CEOs, the late Peter Drucker, explained that restricting the flow of information to followers is what misleaders sometimes do to manage people. But as he also said, *"The task is to lead people. And the goal is to make productive the specific strengths and knowledge of each individual."*⁸ In his comments Mr. Drucker implies that these

leaders have taken the time to communicate effectively and thereby understand the specific strengths and knowledge of the individuals they are leading.

Often the reason power wielders or misleaders try to manipulate or control others without giving them much information or input, is that they are either insecure about their own position or ability or they are, as Drucker says, *"convinced of their own infallibility."* Either way they are not leading and cannot expect to be effective long-term. People are smart and when they sense someone is trying to use them, it makes them defensive and hinders communication.

Peter Drucker explains further the difference between leaders who communicate with and involve associates and misleaders who try to manipulate them: *"Because an effective leader knows that he, and no one else, is ultimately responsible, he is not afraid of strength in associates and subordinates. Misleaders are; they always go in for purges. But an effective leader wants strong associates; he encourages them, pushes them, indeed glories in them...He also knows that the gravest indictment of a leader is for the organization to collapse as soon as he leaves or dies, as happens...all too often in companies. An effective leader knows that the ultimate task of leadership is to create human energies and human vision."*[9]

A leader's ability to create human energies and human vision does not come from managing people; it comes from leading them. That works best in relationships where leaders are able to engage followers emotionally. No doubt, the kind of relationships that hold the greatest potential for creating what Drucker has suggested are covenants. But again, building and maintaining covenants both require much conscious effort over time. Living, leading or operating in a covenant involves people making an effort to communicate effectively and to lead and not manage people. Through the processes of communicating and leading, leaders must also make conscious choices and give conscious choices that bond people together and demonstrate that the leader in particular is listening and cares. Though that can require a certain amount of selflessness and even sacrifice, the benefits are clear.

Making Conscious Choices - The values of a leader influence both the choices and decisions that leader makes. To this point business ethicist Al Gini wrote, "*Whether they are right or wrong, good or bad, values, both consciously and unconsciously, mobilize and guide how we make decisions and the kinds of decisions we make.*"[10]

To lead or live according to the principles of a covenant is a choice a person must make about how to relate to others, and that choice is greatly influenced by one's values. The choices an individual makes and actions he or she takes communicate a great deal about a person. But beyond the initial choices leaders make about the value of the people they lead and the kind of relationships they will build with them, there are many other choices that come as leaders seek to engage those people. For example, if I choose to lead according to the principles of covenant, then I must also choose to trust the people I lead by relying on their talent, good intentions, commitment and integrity. That means that I must also choose to communicate effectively with them by understanding who they are, what they can do, how they can contribute and what I as the leader need to do to maximize their potential. As I act on the choices I have made, it communicates something about me and my values as a leader.

Again, one of the primary choices leaders must make is how and to what extent they will communicate with followers. Certainly volumes have been written about the "how tos" of effective communication. But again, the choices leaders make are driven by what they believe about people. If I as a leader value and trust people, then I am more likely to share information and communicate openly and honestly. By contrast, if I don't trust people or value their opinions, then I am more likely to hoard information and limit communication.

Ultimately, the choices about how to deal with followers and how to communicate with them belong to leaders who base those choices on what they believe about people. Those choices matter because, as I noted earlier, the actions that follow them communicate something about the leader. For example, poor communication can be the result of a conscious choice to withhold information or limit communication because the leader mistrusts people. It can also be the result of an introverted person who chooses not to communicate or an extroverted person who chooses to speak whatever comes to mind without much regard for the people who are listening. Either way, people formulate opinions about leaders based on the actions leaders take and the things they say. And people do pay attention to what leaders communicate. Consider the experience of a friend of mine who has built two successful companies. He told me about learning early in his career that as a leader he had to make conscious choices about what he said and how he said it. It seems that one of his innocent, off-the-cuff comments about the company was taken very seriously by employees who heard it and it nearly created a company wide crisis of confidence as a result.

Covenant leaders make the choices to be interested, to listen aggressively and to trust followers in communicating with them. They understand that rigid rules designed to control people at some point fail. Living in fear of others taking advantage of you, is a far greater tyranny than getting burned a few times by trusting them. To this point, former trial lawyer and author Philip Howard notes, *"Freedom depends at least as much on deciding how to do things as on deciding what to do. Thousands of rigid rules are not needed...."*[11]

Understanding that point alone is a major step in turning control-oriented managers into covenant-keeping leaders. At its best, approaching leadership as a covenant can change and revitalize the entire ethos of the organization and greatly heighten the fulfillment and productivity of its people.

In the final analysis, the risk of wasting talent by making the choice to demand sovereign, contractual control of people is far greater and far more stressful than making the choice to value and trust followers, to communicate openly and understand them and then to empower them so they can contribute. Covenant keeping leaders model the latter, recognizing also that the choice of living, working and leading by the principles of a covenant does not change with the circumstances. Again, effective leaders understand almost instinctively that how one relates to others and how one communicates are first and foremost conscious choices over which they have control.

Giving Others Choices - Committing to a specific purpose and then assuming ownership for that purpose is not only a choice that leaders make, it's also a choice leaders give to followers. Allowing followers to use their talent and experience to make choices in their work communicates clearly that their leaders trust and value them. Without the give-and-take of choice in a relationship, then communication quickly breaks down. In fact, if people are not given any choice and are forced or even manipulated into pursuing a particular purpose in a particular way, then they are not likely to commit fully to that purpose anyway. James Kouzes and Barry Posner argue that getting and keeping people committed to the pursuit of a common purpose is the leader's primary challenge. They note that people are more likely to become committed when leaders communicate effectively with them and when at least three conditions (all related to giving choices) are present in the leader-follower relationship. These conditions include:

1. *Giving People a Sense of Choice* - This means listening to people, understanding and trusting them and finally communicating that trust by allowing them to take real responsibility, make real decisions and take real actions on their own. According to Kouzes and Posner, "Choice is the cement that binds one's actions to the person, motivating individuals to accept the implications of their acts."[12] Individuals are less likely to "accept the implications of their acts," if they are consistently micromanaged both in what they say and what they do.

2. *Making Choices Visible to Others* - If my choices are publicly visible through public statements or actions, continuing commitment is more likely. I'm more likely to follow through on a choice that I've communicated to others because I am, in a sense, inviting people to hold me accountable. For example, beyond the ceremony, a marriage is a public statement of my choice to commit to a covenant partner and my intention to keep the vows I have made to that partner. As they hear those vows and witness those events, friends and family members also serve as a form of an accountability group that is intended to support and encourage my commitment. In business, leaders do this by putting pictures and notices of promotions, special

assignments or achievements in the newspaper. They also make company-wide presentations; they select people to represent the company at an event; and they take any one of a number of actions that allow people to make a public commitment to a specific choice.

3. *Creating Choices That are Hard to Revoke* - When my oldest son graduated from college, he went through a series of very competitive interviews in attempt to secure a position as an investment banker on Wall Street. There were telephone interviews as well as on-site interviews and, when he was finally selected for the position, he was put into a twelve hour per day, six day per week, twelve week training program. Technically, all the trainees were on probationary status and during the training program they participated in interviews with various departments in the bank. He had communicated publicly to family and friends that he was going to Wall Street to work for J. P. Morgan, so from the time he was hired into the training program, he was committed to succeeding with that company. This was a choice that he believed mattered a great deal. Despite the long hours and sometimes intense work, my son had made an important choice that he made public and there was no turning back.

Leaders accomplish this same kind of commitment in part not only by allowing people to have some choice in making decisions but also by giving them choice in decisions that matter and then allowing them to make their choices public. It makes sense that when the choices I make and communicate publicly have implications for me and for the organization, then my commitment to making them work is much more intense.

In places where people lack opportunities to have a voice, to use their own gifts and talents and to make and communicate choices like these, relationships are weakened and commitments lack staying power. It is a clear sign that people are being controlled rather than led and empowered and that internal communication and understanding are less than desirable. By contrast, I find it refreshing to be able to talk to a customer service representative who can actually make decisions to help me right on the spot, without having to send my request up the chain of command several levels. When leaders demonstrate respect for employees and their opinions, when they communicate effectively, when they choose followers for specific purposes or tasks and then empower them to make decisions and communicate their choices on how best to achieve those purposes; it strengthens the bonds of those leader-follower relationships. Under such circumstances, the commitment and resolve of the individuals involved to do whatever they can to be successful, can't help but improve because they know that the leaders value who they are and what they contribute. The late Henri Nouwen put it this way, *"When I know that I am chosen, I know that I have been seen as a special person. Someone has noticed me in my uniqueness...."*[13] In a sense, that's what covenant leadership is about, choosing to notice and respect the uniqueness and the value of the people being led. But it is also about choosing to act on that value by giving them the opportunity to make choices that make a difference.

Sacrificing in a Selfless Manner-A Lesson from 9/11 - The idea that leaders communicate not only by the words they speak, but also by the choices they make and the actions they take is certainly not an obscure concept. In fact, most people can point out individuals who have distinguished themselves as leaders through their actions. A good example of leaders communicating a covenant commitment through their choices and actions is found in the inspiring, heroic leadership we witnessed in the wake of the World Trade Center attacks. We saw great strength and character manifest in the many gracious and selfless acts of some incredible human beings. Based on their positions, many of the heroes of the New York City attack on the World Trade Center would not have been considered leaders by most Americans prior to September 11. Yet, it's difficult to deny that the firemen, construction workers, police officers, clergy and volunteers who chose to sacrifice in such a selfless manner by taking the bold and decisive action that they did, were very much leaders. They communicated their commitment and their leadership not through the words they spoke, but through the choices they made and the actions they took. And, no one ever doubted their motives.

In the final analysis, it was those same choices and the sacrificial actions that followed and not their positions in a hierarchy that distinguished them as leaders. Therein lies the irony of leadership. Though we ascribe the title of leader to most heads of organizations, leadership is rarely defined by position. Instead, it is demonstrated (and thereby communicated) by action that is motivated by values. In the case of New York City, we saw leaders who made choices and took actions that were motivated not by a contractual responsibility or a sense of personal gain, but by a love of humanity and a higher sense of purpose. The noble purpose of these selfless individuals led them to labor tirelessly, to give from the depth of their souls and to sacrifice even their lives for the sake of their fellow citizens and the covenant they shared.

Promoting a Way of Life by Walking the Talk - If people are led instead of manipulated or controlled, then their leaders will communicate in ways that advocate and model certain core values. Those values are really promoting a way of life both inside and outside of the organization. In a parents' orientation meeting I attended on the campus of the University of Notre Dame just prior to the World Trade Center attacks, I had the good fortune of hearing the women's basketball coach of the 2001 national champions, Muffet McGraw, give this advice to entering freshmen: *"When you were born you cried and people rejoiced. Live so that when you die people cry and you rejoice."*[14] Though I'm not sure that saying is original with her, in those few words, Coach McGraw was promoting a way of life that captures the essence and the bigger picture of covenant leadership. Leadership is about choices ... how to live, how to lead and how to leave a legacy. Coach McGraw's comments remind us that the choices we make influence the legacy we leave. Leaders who are able to engage others, build a strong coalition of support and leave a lasting legacy are also those who choose to serve a purpose that is larger than their own. The way they operate in pursuit of that purpose communicates by example what is important to them and what they believe. It is communicating by "walk" which is more effective than "talk".

Again, this does not suggest that the leader's self-interest is never served. That would require a level of altruism that is admirable but unrealistic. However, for a person truly to demonstrate leadership (as Burns defines the term), the choices that leader makes and the life he or she leads must also serve a larger common purpose. In fact, the degree to which leaders choose to act on common and ethical purposes that serve the interests of others is often the degree to which they are able to create powerful and enduring legacies. Our country was founded by leaders who made exactly these kind of selfless and sacrificial choices. They were people who, in the midst of crisis, covenanted together and pledged their lives, their fortunes and their sacred honor to work for a common purpose and promote a way of life. Because of the strength of their covenant, they were able to cast a powerful vision that has endured and led our country for many generations. Of course, that's one of the basic truths about leaders and followers. The strength of their covenant will always determine the power and achievement of their vision.

Creating an Inspiring Legacy...Preaching What You Practice - Making the choice to live and lead in accordance with the principles of a covenant involves thinking about the kind of legacy one hopes to create. In the *Seven Habits of Highly Effective People*, author Stephen Covey calls this process *"beginning with the end in mind."* [15]

Almost prophetically, Coach McGraw described the state of many Americans as they mourned both the victims and the heroes who died as a result of the World Trade Center attacks. Although we mourned their deaths, we also celebrated their lives and their noble passing. Also, beyond the mourning, as we heard the stories of bravery and benevolence, we were also encouraged to see that the same American spirit of bravery and the same kind of covenant leadership that gave birth to our country were still alive and on display in New York City. Like our founders did in the 18th century, in the midst of crisis these modern day leaders stepped forward in powerful and inspirational ways and showed us all how to lead. But then again, that is exactly what we expect from real leaders, an unconditional and exemplary covenant commitment to a higher purpose. The communication of that commitment was found not in words but in these incredible acts of bravery, acts that both communicated and created a powerful and inspiring legacy that will not soon be forgotten.

In that sense, leadership truly is a covenant that inspires others and reminds us how to live, work and relate to one another. What those leaders of 9/11 really did is what all leaders should do; they preached a powerful sermon on what to do and how to do it. To this point, author and Bain & Company consultant, Frederick Reichheld, argues that the most effective kind of leading is in part a form of preaching, where leaders *"preach what they practice."*[16] However, preaching and leading alike demand advance thought and preparation about the "end" or the desired legacy the preacher hopes to create. Reichheld explains, *"If you aspire to preach with great impact, you must realize that the greatest sermons have one thing in common. They remind us that we are going to die."*[17]

Reichheld affirms that while most people try to deny the fact of death, the best way to deal with it is to confront it and thereby gain understanding of, *"... the full impact of living a life committed to the right principles and to building relationships worthy of loyalty."*[18] For Reichheld, the best preachers and the best sermons also communicate lessons about life because they *"help us think more clearly about how we want our stories to end and, therefore, what we must do today and tomorrow to achieve our ultimate goals."*[19] A good example of what Reichheld is talking about is the collective season of prayer and reflection and the subsequent career and lifestyle changes that occurred across America in the wake of the events of 9/11.

Like preachers, Covenant leaders are concerned about what and how they communicate and how that communication influences the big picture. They think about the overall outcomes and the legacy their leadership will create in the lives of both the organizations and the people they lead. To these points Reichheld notes that, *"... the job of business leadership is not simply to exhort our partners to tend to the list of actions that must be taken on Monday morning; it is also to help ensure that when there are no more Mondays, those partners will have made the most of their lives."*[20]

Certainly the crisis in America on 9/11 was dramatic, but these kind of crisis conditions always seem to provide opportunities for leaders to emerge, and emerge they did. But, leadership doesn't require a crisis; it requires a choice. Whether we do it actively or passively, consciously or subconsciously, we all make choices about how we will live; where, when and to what extent we will lead; and what we will leave as a legacy. Throughout history we have had many great examples of leadership, but in each of these cases an individual made a choice about how to lead. The success any leader has in motivating and inspiring people is not a function of his or her ability to wield power over them or to make things happen. On the contrary, what inspires and motivates people are leaders who choose to *"preach what they practice"* and use or even give away power to influence and motivate others in achieving a common and ethical purpose. Those choices communicate powerful and even inspirational messages about the leader.

Ultimately, contractual obligations enforced by power don't inspire us, but covenant commitments from leaders who care do. Maybe that's why Americans were so inspired to volunteer thousands of hours in a very short time period and to give more than $1.5 billion to the relief efforts in New York City. We were moved to give and to follow the brave and benevolent examples of police officers, firemen, construction workers and ordinary people who cared. It is a spirit of caring and benevolence that has continued through both the tsunami and Hurricane Katrina relief efforts. In their brave and exemplary actions these city workers and volunteers demonstrated leadership as well as a covenant commitment to each other, to the people they served and to a larger ideal. The bravery of these men and women serves as a strong testimony (or sermon) to the fact that they were motivated by a purpose higher than their own individual safety or interests. That higher purpose compelled them to act and give in ways that went well beyond their contractual obligations. Without using words they communicated a powerful message. And, in the final analysis, whether it's in the workplace or at ground zero, we all become better people when we are inspired by that kind of covenant driven leadership.

[1] Redd, Vice Admiral John Scott; Interview with Len Moisan ; July 27, 1995.

[2] Ibid.

[3] Hymowitz, Carol; *Like Rumsfeld, CEOs Who Seek Questions May Not Like Them*; (The Wall Street Journal; Tuesday, December 14, 2004) p. B1.

[4] Covey, Stephen; *The Seven Habits of Highly Effective People*; (Simon & Schuster; New York, New York; 1989) pp. 235-260

[5] Stankard, Martin Productivity Development Group; *Best Practice Examples from High Performance Companies*; www.martinstankard.com/index.html.

[6] Smith, Frederick W.; *"Creating an Empowering Environment for All Employees"* in *The Book of Leadership Wisdom* (Peter Krass, Editor; John Wiley & Sons, Inc.; New York; 1998) p. 223.

[7] Ibid, pp. 216-217.

[8] Drucker, Peter; *The Essential Drucker* (Harper Business; New York, New York; 2001) p. 81.

[9] Ibid, pp. 270.271.

[10] Gini, Al; *Moral Leadership and Business Ethics*, in *Ethics: The Heart of Leadership*, (Edited by Joanne B. Ciulla, , Praeger Publishers, Westport, CT, 1998) p. 36

[11] Howard, Philip; *Death of Common Sense* (Warner Books; New York, New York; 1994) p. 173.

[12] Kouzes, James and Posner, Barry; *The Leadership Challenge* (Jossey-Bass Publishers; San Francisco, CA; 1987) p. 227.

[13] Nouwen, Henri. *Life of The Beloved* (The Crossroad Publishing Company; New York, 1992) p.45

[14] McGraw, M. (August 26, 2001). Quote from her freshman orientation address at University of Notre Dame.

[15] Covey, Stephen; *The Seven Habits of Highly Effective People*; (Simon & Schuster; New York, New York; 1989) pp. 235-260.

[16] Reichheld, Frederick F.; *Loyalty Rules* (Harvard Business School Press; Boston, Massachusetts; 2001).

[17] Ibid., p. 186.

[18] Ibid., p. 186.

[19] Ibid., p. 186.

[20] Ibid., p. 186.

Chapter 12
Leadership Evaluation and Action
Discovery (LEAD)

People don't want to be managed or manipulated or controlled by power wielders ... they want to be led. Also, as people are led they want some 'give and take' and choice in the relationship. Using the information in Chapter 12, please answer the following questions:

A. In what ways can I communicate with stakeholders and ensure the continuous flow of information from them?
Speaking
Listening
Reinforcing

B. Why and in what ways would it or would it not be advantageous for you to make the choice to lead according to the principles of a covenant?

C. To what extent do people in your organization have the
    opportunity and freedom to make choices about their work
    and then commit to those choices?

D. What choices can you make about communicating with
    stakeholders and acting in a selfless manner on a covenant
    commitment to them?

Conclusion

Knowing the definition and principles of covenant is obviously not the same thing as applying them. It takes a commitment of time, energy and leadership to develop covenants, and it takes the same to maintain them. Leadership, whether it is in one's personal or professional life, is crucial both for covenant initiating and covenant keeping because, despite the will to do so, a covenant won't happen apart from a leader taking action to develop one. Covenants also assume that the partners will be active participants both in aligning their behavior with the core values of the covenant and assuming responsibility for the outcomes. In other words, for covenants to work requires a certain amount of leadership on the part of everyone involved.

No doubt, in an organizational setting not everyone will immediately be aligned with the core values of the enterprise, nor will they always assume responsibility for its outcomes. Nevertheless, by building a foundation of trust, aligning behavior with a set of reasoned and ethical core values and pursuing a common purpose in an environment where the worth and contributions of individuals are recognized; leaders can develop those traits in followers. This kind of dynamic interaction between leaders and followers is precisely what James McGregor Burns described as transformational leadership, a relationship in which followers become (or are transformed into) leaders and leaders become mentors and moral agents.

One of the wisdom books of the Bible is Proverbs and one of my favorite Proverbs insightfully notes, *"As iron sharpens iron, so does one person sharpen another."* That Proverb really captures the spirit of a covenant. As a result of the relationship, the covenant partners and the organization they represent all become better than they would on their own; they are all "sharpened" by the association.

While covenants are designed to benefit everyone involved in the relationship, they do not naturally occur. They require a conscious decision and a commitment to embrace and align one's behavior with the purpose and core values of the covenant. Again, all of that takes the kind of time and effort that are not in abundance in our fast-paced, short-term profit and immediate gratification society. The norm in most organizations, particularly when its leaders are seeking solutions to problems, is to find a quick prescription. That's why some of the most popular books on the market are those that promise quick steps or secrets to success. But covenants are complex relationships that do not lend themselves to applying a simple formula. Even where there is spontaneous bonding in a relationship, there is still a process that must occur in order for covenants to develop and endure. Though broad, in one form or another, that process demands that individuals and eventually organizations incorporate the following four steps:

Seek and Learn - Covenants develop usually as a result of people seeking more meaningful and productive relationships in their lives. Whether it's in a person's personal or organizational life, what usually motivates that "seeking" is an awareness that something is lacking. That awareness may be manifest in a sense of imbalance, emptiness, underachievement or even pain, but it often works its way out in relation to other people. That's why even though what a person lacks may come from a condition or a concern, it usually boils down to something lacking in a relationship. At its core, seeking in the context of a covenant is seeking ways to improve my condition or the condition of my organization by creating more effective, productive and fulfilling relationships. It is a process through which individuals search for answers to questions, solutions to problems or better ways of doing things; believing that those improvements will come through people.

Believe and Commit - As individuals seek and learn, their purpose is not simply to accumulate information. Certainly it involves that, but an honest and thorough process of inquiry eventually leads to the seeker formulating beliefs. Because the realm and motivation of seeking can vary with the individual, so too can the beliefs that develop. As a result, people formulate beliefs on just about anything related to living, dying, working or relating to others. Nevertheless, while the beliefs may vary the process of developing them is quite similar. It usually begins with the accumulation of information that helps generate alternatives. But, for a leader to come to a point where he or she actually believes a specific alternative is true or right also demands a certain amount of due diligence and testing. While the testing can come from personal experience or the experience of others, apart from the kind of validation in which beliefs are tested and proven reliable, individuals and organizations alike wind up bouncing from one person, idea or program to the next. This is particularly true in developing covenants. In order for covenants to form and then to work, leaders must believe in and then commit to the principles and the people of a covenant.

Poet and author, T. S. Elliott once said, *"We know too much and are convinced of too little."* If seeking and learning are to be effective we must listen and make observations, formulate and test hypothesis and become convinced that both our condition and our proposed solution are true and right for us. Accordingly, beyond seeking and learning, developing covenants requires being convinced (believing through a process of due diligence) that this kind of relationship or alliance of relationships is right for me because it:

a. Represents the most effective, rewarding or fulfilling way of relating to and engaging the person or persons with whom I'm involved;

b. Promises that what we as covenant partners will achieve in this relationship is far greater than what we would be able to achieve by ourselves;

c. Will create and support an organization where common purposes are pursued, people are respected and valued, the organization prospers and mankind is served;

    d. Is desirable and beneficial for me, my organization, and my partners;

    e. Will be well worth the personal commitments I must make or service to another I must provide in order to make the relationship work; and

    f. Has been proven reliable to me through my own experience or the experience of others.

Whether it's in personal or professional life, unless seekers believe these things about covenants and the people involved, they are not likely to initiate or sustain them. However, regardless of how strong one's beliefs are, by themselves they will not produce a covenant. Beliefs come to life as a person chooses to commit and take action that is consistent with them.

For example, there is a scene in *Fiddler on the Roof* that illustrates this point. Tevye asks his wife, Golde, if she loves him. Her response is not a simple yes or no. Initially, as Tevye asks Golde, *"Do you love me?"* Golde is surprised and responds, *"Do I what?"* Tevye asks again and Golde tells him to go inside and lie down because he might be having indigestion, but Tevye is persistent and asks again if she loves him. Golde then responds, *"Do I love you? For 25 years I've washed your clothes, cooked your meals, cleaned your house, given you children and milked the cow...."*

Tevye then reacts and says, *"I know ... but do you love me?"* At this, Golde answers, *"For 25 years I've lived with him, fought him and starved with him. Twenty-five years my bed is his. If that's not love, what is?"*[1]

What Golde is conveying to Tevye is the fact that evidence of her love is manifest in her actions. Those actions clearly demonstrate her long-term (25 year) commitment to and belief in Tevye and the covenant they share.

It is quite common today to hear CEOs refer to their employees as "family". Our company has worked with several entrepreneurs who have used this language. In some cases we have found leaders who demonstrate through their actions that they have a deep regard and respect for their people. Employee surveys reflect good will and loyalty towards these leaders, many of whom have gone to great lengths to help and provide for workers both professionally and personally. Conversely, I have also worked with ineffective CEOs who use the language of "family" to describe their relationships with employees. But unless their notion of family is one of dysfunction, they clearly have not taken any actions that would indicate a strong commitment to having such an atmosphere.

Regardless of what CEOs say, if they fail to make commitments and take actions consistent with their stated beliefs, then these "beliefs" are simply rhetoric. If leaders hope to build covenants with other people, then like Golde, they must take action that demonstrates their covenant commitment. That action is the alignment of behavior with the principles of covenant.

Trust and Give - A person's belief in and commitment to the concept of covenant comes to life as he or she takes action that is consistent with those beliefs. Apart from deliberate action that demonstrates commitment both to the purpose and to the person/s of a covenant, this kind of relationship simply will not occur. Additionally, for a true covenant to exist, commitment must be reciprocal among the covenant partners in ways that create a culture of continuing commitment. But reciprocity assumes a level of trust among the covenant partners that allows them both to give and to expect that at some point their partner/s will give back to them. Often, when relationships fail, it's because one person can not get to the point of commitment by trusting another person. Of course, a reluctance to commit might be the result of a lack of interest, but it might also come from a fear of being hurt.

That is exactly the point of the movie, *Runaway Bride*. Actress Julia Roberts plays Maggie Carpenter, a woman who has been engaged to be married several times. Each time Maggie gets to the altar she simply can't bring herself to make the commitment necessary to initiate a covenant, so at the last minute she runs. Because Maggie can't follow through on her verbal commitments with action, the townspeople become somewhat cynical and begin to poke fun at her. Her dilemma is resolved when she meets New York newspaper writer, Ike Graham (Richard Gere) and does finally commit to a relationship. For Maggie, getting to the point of actual commitment required that she first recognize the inherent unhappiness and futility of her dilemma and then bring herself to trust and give herself to someone else.

In establishing a relationship usually one person takes the lead in initiating positive action towards another by giving attention, respect or consideration of some kind. As that giving is reciprocated in some way by the other person, the relationship begins to grow and the bonds between the people are tightened. The converse of that is also true. At some point if reciprocity begins to diminish, then the bonds between people are loosened and the future of the relationship is put in jeopardy. Maggie continued to put her relationships in jeopardy because she could not reciprocate with commitment to trust and give of herself to others.

The same dynamics are true in larger organizations with one exception. It is primarily the leader's responsibility to create a culture of commitment, a culture that is evident in high levels of trusting and giving that permeate the organization. True, followers can be held accountable for operating within the context of the culture. But leaders are the ones who initiate the action of trusting and giving that creates the culture in the first place. How do leaders achieve this? They do it by creating a norm of reciprocity, by giving meaningful work, by acknowledging contributions, by sharing information, by becoming vulnerable, by forgiving and admitting mistakes, by embracing an attitude of grace, and by all of the other actions we discussed that help leaders build trust.

Change and Grow -The Greek philosopher Heroclitus postulated more than two millennia ago that the only constant in the universe is change. Though I don't agree fully with his observation, I certainly understand the sentiment it conveys. Anyone who has lived through the past couple of decades should certainly be able to relate to what Heroclitus said. The issue people must deal with in their lives is not the possibility of change but the reality of change. No doubt, change is inevitable and those organizations whose leaders understand that fact will be able to adapt effectively to change, and even grow through and direct it.

Change influences both how organizations relate to their customers and how individuals inside those organizations relate to each other. The same kind of adaptability to customer needs that is important in making organizations successful is crucial in making relationships work. Sometimes we just have to do what is necessary to change and adjust our wants and desires to accommodate other people. A company that refuses to change to accommodate customer needs can soon find itself bankrupt. The same is true of individuals. Show me a person who has changed or grown very little over a 20-year period, and I'll show you someone who has very weak, shallow, and emotionally bankrupt relationships. Covenants simply cannot develop without willingness on the part of the covenant partners to adapt and change to accommodate both the priorities and the people of the covenant. When that occurs it strengthens the bond among the covenant partners and it induces growth on the part of the ones doing the accommodating.

It follows then that the key to maintaining covenants is committing to an attitude and process of continuing change and improvement. While this concept of continuous change and growth sounds logical, it doesn't always come easy. Continuing to change and grow requires much more than self-discipline and willpower. It requires deep and abiding regard for the people with whom we share the covenant and the organizations that we serve.

The movie, *Billy Elliot*[2], provides a clear illustration of this point. It is a story about a young man growing up in a northern England mining town. The movie is set in the Margaret Thatcher era during a coal strike in which Billy's father and brother are both participating. As the plot progresses, the eleven year old Billy becomes intrigued by the ballet class that meets after his boxing club. He joins in on some of the class activities and soon discovers that he has an incredible talent for ballet. Of course, this causes problems in the family (the organization) because his macho father and brother want nothing to do with his dancing.

They are essentially stuck in a rut of personal bias, and they stubbornly reuse to change. A pivotal incident occurs when Billy's father, who is angrily coming after Billy to catch him dancing, actually sees Billy dance for the first time. As Billy performs his very best, his father is moved and changed instantaneously. He knows he was wrong about Billy and his dancing. In fact, so moved is Billy's father that he decides to cross a picket line during the coal workers strike. Of course, Billy's father wanted to work and cross the line so he could earn enough money to send Billy to the ballet academy. Prior to his confrontation with the truth about Billy's talent, Billy's father had stubbornly refused to see him perform. Still, in order for the father to change in such a dramatically repentant manner required humility. The father had to first have his eyes opened and learn of his son's talent and then humbly acknowledge the truth and admit that he was wrong. Second, he had to believe that going to the academy was in Billy's best interest and commit to send him. Third, he had to trust that this was the right course of action, and give something of himself to make that action occur. Finally, he had to be willing to change and through this process of change he grew.

That's really what seeking is intended to do; it can open our eyes to the truth, the truth about our condition and the truth about what we can do to improve it. The truth here is that Billy Elliot's father was, in the language of *Good to Great*, confronted with the "brutal facts" of his own stubbornness and error as well as his son's exceptional talent. As a result, he realized that his attitudes and actions were driving a wedge between Billy and him. After being exposed to the truth, Billy's father believed that his relationship with his son was more important than his own pride and that the ballet academy was right for Billy. Therefore, he committed to go back to work. Billy's father then trusted his instincts, and he acted and gave in ways that cost him personally. As a result of all this, Mr. Elliot changed and grew and his relationship with Billy was strengthened as was his family (the organization). The story leaves us with an important and sometimes obscured truth about leadership. None of this would have happened apart from Mr. Elliot's deep and abiding regard and love for his son, Billy. Similarly, leaders change and grow more out of love for the work they do and the people they serve, than they do out of self- discipline and a desire to win.

St. Augustine made this point well when he observed that it's not in the acts of the will that change occurs but in the loves of the heart. Ultimately, covenants are about love, love of yourself, love of other people and love of the organizations we serve. When leaders, or for that matter any other individuals, are willing to seek and learn, believe and commit, trust and give and change and grow, not only will they be able to build covenants, but also they will be able to demonstrate love of the kind that will motivate others to join them in their quests.

---

[1] *Fiddler on the Roof*, official soundtrack, 1971; www.demos.com/lyrics/ fiddlerontheroof.htm#10.

[2] *Billy Elliot*, Universal Studios, 2000 .

Index

D

Daley, Richard J. 156
Dalla Costa, John 102, 112
Death 51, 64, 111, 117, 126, 131, 132,
    144, 195, 204, 224, 225, 227
Death of Common Sense 111, 117,
    126, 227
Deming, W. Edwards 169, 172
Democracy In America 8, 20, 125, 126
Denial of Death 131, 144
DePree, Max 124, 126, 135, 137, 145
desire xiv, xv, 14, 15, 48, 74, 83, 120,
    134, 139, 150, 170, 182, 237, 239
DiBello, Tom 79
Dickens, Charles 36, 41
dignity 26, 28, 161, 173, 178, 183, 184,
    186, 204
donors 55, 80, 151, 189
Drucker, Peter xi, 65, 67, 166, 172,
    216, 217, 227
Duke University 75
Dyer, Jeffery 93, 112
Dynamic Orthotics 79
dysfunction 25, 35, 235

E

Eastern Airlines 167, 168
Elliot, T.S. 238, 239
Ellis, Joseph 74, 88, 112
emotional engagement 201, 202, 210
employee xii, xiv, 7, 8, 21, 22, 31, 32,
    33, 34, 55, 57, 68, 75, 80, 83, 96,
    97, 98, 101, 102, 103, 104, 106,
    113, 114, 119, 120, 123, 137,
    149, 150, 151, 152, 153, 154,
    155, 160, 162, 163, 164, 168,
    171, 175, 176, 178, 179, 180,
    181, 182, 184, 189, 191, 192,
    197, 198, 201, 202, 203, 207,
    209, 210, 213, 214, 215, 216,
    219, 222, 227, 234, 235
employee attrition / retention 7, 163,
    189, 197
employee satisfaction 202, 203

empowerment 140, 180
engagement 25, 35, 144, 201, 202, 207,
    210
Enron 86, 100, 120, 121, 123, 126, 127
exchange ix, 19, 29, 149, 150, 151, 152,
    153, 154, 155, 156, 157, 158,
    159, 160, 164, 170, 181
expectations xi, 15, 17, 18, 28, 31, 62,
    87, 92, 121, 122, 143, 149, 150,
    151, 152, 153, 154, 158, 160,
    175, 176, 178, 188, 191, 192,
    196, 199, 203, 205, 208, 209, 215
experience x, xv, 15, 28, 30, 37, 39, 50,
    53, 63, 64, 65, 66, 73, 77, 79, 98,
    99, 100, 116, 129, 136, 138, 139,
    140, 141, 142, 143, 144, 148,
    149, 150, 151, 154, 157, 159,
    160, 161, 162, 163, 166, 169,
    170, 173, 177, 178, 179, 193,
    213, 219, 220, 233, 234

F

faith 16, 17, 49, 51, 58, 66, 119, 167,
    177, 195
family v, xiii, xv, 7, 10, 12, 25, 26, 30,
    35, 36, 52, 53, 60, 92, 93, 100,
    101, 108, 132, 133, 134, 150,
    156, 196, 199, 204, 211, 221,
    234, 235, 237, 238
fear 31, 35, 85, 98, 103, 106, 117, 118,
    119, 131, 153, 169, 179, 184,
    194, 214, 219, 235
Federal Express 215, 216
Fever Pitch 133
Fiddler on The Roof 234, 239
Flow 138, 145
following 11, 21, 22, 23, 39, 42, 43, 68,
    69, 89, 107, 113, 127, 146, 149,
    154, 155, 160, 173, 185, 208,
    228, 232
Follow This Path 159, 201, 207
Ford, Henry 63, 67
Forrest Gump 195
Founding Brothers 74, 88, 112

Printed in the United States
88692LV00003B/1-111/A